Introduction

▨ WHAT IS THIS BOOK TRYING TO SAY?

How true are management theories?
How useful are they?
These are the key questions this book is intended to address. The central theme is that management research in general has a misplaced emphasis on validity.

This is not to say that management research is not valid at all. But *how much* validity attaches to the outcomes of management research, and (more importantly) what can we usefully do with these outcomes? The answer to the first of these is mainly sceptical. Management research does not characteristically yield valid results in the way that other sciences (be they social or natural) do. But this does not lead to a sceptical conclusion for the second question: management research is not useless – and it does not mean that research is only useful when it is valid. There are many ways in which management ideas and management writing can be valuable to professionals and scholars alike, even when its truth cannot be established. Ultimately, though, the key conclusion of this discussion is that 'management', as a subject of study, should abandon its academic pretensions and celebrate its practical value.

Some of the points we shall encounter along the way:

- management research is not *designed* to generate validity
- management *ideas* have a value which does not depend on how true they are
- knowledge in management is basically local, and not normally generalisable
- management knowledge is at least partially understood in terms of the purposes of individuals
- managers can themselves be theoreticians
- the hard vs. soft distinction applied to management research is misplaced

- management is complex and based on practice; theories of management in general do not reflect this complexity
- methodologies are generally uni-dimensional, when what is required is a multi-dimensional approach to research

The underlying challenge, then, is whether or not 'management' can maintain its growing manifestation as a subject of study, or should it be reinvented as a field drawing on a range of subjects, but itself best thought of as a practice.

WHY WAS THIS BOOK WRITTEN?

There is a growing split in management studies. As the subject acquires more of an academic air, a scholastic sub-field has developed, one which follows all the classical canons of academia – progress is measured in terms of development of theory and established results, activity measured by research papers and books, and quality judged by the opinions of the academic peer group.

At the same time, however, there is no slowing down in the rate of publication of books and journals aimed at practising managers. Progress for this practitioner oriented area is measured in terms of dissemination and applicability. Quality is judged by publishing success more than by the nature of the content.

One worry about this split is that neither side really measures its success by organisational performance (though both sides affect to do so). On top of this, there is a difficulty about knowing how the academic side takes account of the interests and needs of professionals, and how academics manage to influence actual practices of businesses. All too often managers work with ideas acquired years ago on a course, or on flashy immediacies publicised through the media – a virtuoso conference performance, the latest snappy book, or on the soundbite from TV or radio news (one can hear the breakfast TV announcer – 'And now here's a story – researchers have proved that stress is all in the mind').

This book attempts to deal with part of this issue. It does not depict all management research as narrowly practical, still less does it argue that all managers should become more academic (although I shall suggest that effective managers are subtly rather more academic than they themselves recognise). It is rather trying to evaluate management research as an academic field. Coming from the academic end, in the first instance, at least, the book asks if management research establishes anything at all – what can we really say we learn from all these research papers, articles, and books? As the book progresses, the answer comes again and again in different ways – management research

Management Knowledge

A Critical View

Paul Griseri

palgrave
macmillan

To Becci, Dan and Fleur

First published 2002 by
PALGRAVE
Houndmills, Basingstoke, Hampshire RG21 6XS and
175 Fifth Avenue, New York, N. Y. 10010
Companies and representatives throughout the world

PALGRAVE is the new global academic imprint of
St. Martin's Press LLC Scholarly and Reference Division and
Palgrave Publishers Ltd (formerly Macmillan Press Ltd).

ISBN 0–333–77093–5 hardback
ISBN 0–333–77094–3 paperback

This book is printed on paper suitable for recycling and
made from fully managed and sustained forest sources.

A catalogue record for this book is available
from the British Library.

Library of Congress Cataloging-in-Publication Data

Griseri, Paul.
   Management knowledge : a critical view / Paul Griseri.
      p.   cm.
Includes bibliographical references and Index.
ISBN 0–333–77093–5
   1. Management—Research.   2. Knowledge management.   I. Title.

HD30.4 .G75 2001
658.4′038—dc21

                                          2001036527

Printed and bound in Great Britain by
Antony Rowe Ltd, Chippenham and Eastbourne

Contents

Acknowledgements

Unlike my previous book, this one had a relatively short gestation period, and was influenced mainly by those around me at the time of writing. Chief amongst these are Tony Emerson and Jon Groucutt, who both shed light on many aspects, and to whom I am very grateful. More recently, I have benefited from the support of Nigel Laurie and Chris Cherry. Penultimate but by no means least, many postgraduate management students have in different ways contributed to my understanding of this subject matter.

Last and best, I am continually grateful for the support from my wife, Lyn, who is not afraid either to praise or challenge my ideas.

is generally not sound in formal terms. As an academic study, it has little truth; such value as it possesses comes from practical application and is measured in practical terms.

This does not mean, though, that every worthwhile piece of management research should be a narrowly 'practical' technique or list of 'golden rules' or the like: rather that all management ideas, whether technical or reflective or highly abstract, ultimately refer to actual practices of managers (in fact this is actually what managers tend to do with management ideas). 'Management' has no future as an academic study. In the final chapters of the book we shall try to outline how management research can preserve its usefulness despite rarely being able to prove anything.

A key argument is that the different approaches to management research methodology are NONE of them correct in their pure forms. Four characteristic approaches will be discussed, each of which is normally proposed as a 'grand' theory of research in social contexts. What we will see is that they all have serious weaknesses. But nevertheless each of them has significant *merits as well*. The resolution of this is that management research should incorporate elements from each approach – hence most current forms of management research are essentially incomplete (and so do not represent knowledge about management at all, or at best do so only incompletely).

Since this is a sceptical work, it may be thought that it is intentionally destructive. Not so. The intention is to *critique* management research, to gain an idea of the *limits* to what we can prove. It is not an attempt to try to stop people researching. The argument is intended to help people understand what management research *can* achieve. One thing we shall see is that proof and validity are not the only aspects of management thinking and writing which are valuable – other aspects are at least, if not more, important.

WHO IS THIS BOOK INTENDED FOR?

There are two main groups for whom this book is intended. The first is the growing body of individuals who undertake management courses – undergraduate degrees, post-experience and/or postgraduate courses, such as the Master of Business Administration (MBA) or other specialised Masters courses in related subjects, such as Human Resources, or Marketing. Many people following such courses are required to write a dissertation, identifying an issue (often focused on one organisation), reviewing existing literature, and carrying out a small scale field investigation. It is important to map out the limits of what such investigations can achieve.

One crucial aspect of this is central to the validity of any study, be it MBA dissertation or academic research paper: research design, and the underlying approach to validity which the design embodies. There are many options open to the researcher when designing a study. These options often reflect the range of alternative methodologies, each of which has a claim to soundness, which its adherents often press to the exclusion of other methodologies.

One paradigm holds that something is not 'really' true unless there is a clear quantifiable element. For example, if someone with this view undertook a thesis relating to a particular marketing strategy, they would tend to develop material expressed in percentages, proportions, correlations, and so on. Anything less would seem for them too vague to be of value. On the other hand, an alternative paradigm holds that production of hard facts of that kind is too specific, and too impersonal. For that kind of researcher, what matters is understanding the range and depth of people's feelings. A researcher following this paradigm would produce a thesis on marketing which focused on, for example, how individuals felt about a certain strategy.

One common misunderstanding is that just *one* of these methodologies represents the optimum (or maybe sole) way of getting to the truth about management. Another extreme (and equally misleading) which the literature does not satisfactorily counter, is that these different research designs represent a *choice*, almost as if methodology were just a matter of taste. Many people completing dissertations as part of a management course may come to regard different methodologies as alternatives, each of which they could validly take. At a more sophisticated level, someone may recognise that they almost instinctively find one kind more convincing, more 'real', than another.

This is an aspect of the process of management research which is intrinsically variable. Because individuals have different underlying philosophical assumptions, researchers producing papers and reports approach their task differently, and their output reflects this fundamental difference. Similarly, reviews and reactions of readers reflect their own responses as much to the *approach* as to the content and results of the research.

But there is a deeper problem. The sheer fact that some people find one kind of research more convincing than another raises the question: which approach is the most valid? Are they equally so? Or equally *invalid*? This issue dogs all applied social research, and therefore should feature as a leading element of any dissertation – is it saying *anything true* about its subject matter?

This issue is highly controversial, but has not surfaced in sufficient depth at the level of the material accessed by management students, for it to have had an impact on, for example, the typical MBA dissertation.

But without this understanding, people do not really know whether their research reflects what is really there in their organisations, or is it just their story, their 'take' on the phenomena studied?

So this book is intended to help management students develop a view on what would count as validity, and therefore how valid their own researches may be, and perhaps most importantly how much the issue of validity matters for their dissertation.

People completing dissertations do need to understand the practical pitfalls of conducting organisational research – the best methods of data collection, the most appropriate ways of answering a particular research question and so on. Many books are available which can help with these – to an extent. There are practical texts, many of which deal very effectively, in technical terms, with specific data collection methods, such as interviewing. There are also texts which present an overview of management research. But none of these presents a *critique* of research, which is precisely the gap this book is intended to fill. We shall see later that this element of critique is essential to understand fully what a research programme can achieve.

So for this group of readers the main function of this book is to take them through a range of arguments which will give them a more critically informed attitude towards the research material they read *and* the research which they conduct. It is not intended as a substitute for texts dealing with the practical issues of social research. But it will put those texts into context, as presenting methods which *contribute* to management knowledge, rather than *creating* it. This ambiguity between *contribution to* and *creation of* knowledge, will underlie the whole of the book.

The second audience for whom this book is intended is the community of academic management researchers. Again the same degree of variation in approach to validity may be found – a pluralism of approaches, styles, and underlying philosophical assumptions. The prime difference between this group and post-experience graduate students is that it is *this* group which sets the rules.

What counts as appropriate research is, basically, determined by what editorial panels of prestigious journals are prepared to accept.[1] These panels are generally composed of leading academics in the field. The uncertainty about what can be validly inferred from the results of research activity in the management field (that is, the uncertainty as to what counts as management knowledge), is a feature of the subject which this academic community as a whole has failed to resolve.

For this group, the purpose of this book is to present a definitive answer to the question 'How valid is management research?', one which is sceptical without being entirely dismissive. The answer (indicated earlier) is that most management research is not anywhere like as valid as might be supposed, or is claimed by its authors. However, this is not to dismiss its usefulness. Each of the four research paradigms referred to earlier has a valuable contribution to offer – the trick is to understand how these *jointly* contribute to the development of management knowledge. But this contribution is not to be found in academic scholarship. The most valuable material in this field is better understood as training material, rather than as a claim about what is real.

An academic audience will want to know where the argument of this book stands in relation to other theoretical approaches, such as positivism, relativism, hermeneutics, critical theory, phenomenology, etc. It owes most to the participant research paradigm and critical theory, without really being either. Overall I stress an eclectic approach to research methodologies. But this is not out of agnosticism. Rather my argument for saying that there is a value in considering a range of social research methodological paradigms is that they *all have something to say* – it's just that most methodologies have one of them saying too much and the others saying nothing at all.

Chapter 12 will adapt some of the ideas of Jurgen Habermas, but with a focus on the needs of practising managers as the central test of the value of any management research. The key issue is less what *is* management research, so much as what in day-to-day terms one can make of it. It should be more of a concern that so much research yields so little of concrete value, than whether it supports this or that theory of research.

WHAT IS THE MAIN CONTENTION OF THE BOOK?

I have already stated the main point: management research is not generally valid and is best not thought of in those terms. The central theme is that general problems of research methodology in social science apply with even greater acuteness to management research. In other fields of social enquiry, such as pure sociology, there is a consciousness of the questionable nature of research into human behaviour. It is recognised within that general academic consensus that there is a cluster of related problems which render such research highly controversial. There is far less such recognition in fields of applied social research – as management is. My intention is to bring these problems of methodology more centre stage in the discussion of management knowledge.

In much of the literature on management research there are two polarising approaches. Some writers present social research analogously with research in the natural world (some even suggest there is no essential difference at all). For them the real business of the social researcher is to measure and develop testable hypotheses about people's behaviour. Others point out that having *people* as the subject matter of the research process makes it extremely difficult, if not impossible, to have detached enquiry in the way that a chemist may be detached from the object of their study (for example, the behaviour of a certain silicone based compound). This pluralism of research methods and methodologies therefore raises this key question – are they all valid? Do they all describe aspects of management reality?

If management research *can* discover an independent reality, then different researchers working in the same field should come to the same conclusion – a test of reliability of results: if there is an underlying pattern in the events being researched, different methods of collecting data ought to converge to a similar or identical, result. This reflects an instrumental conception of methodology – methods of investigation are seen as a *device* to enable the researcher to get closer to the underlying reality. But if *different* researchers come to *different* conclusions, one naturally wonders whether *either* methodology has accessed that underlying reality.

Consider the analogy of the telescope. If the pope of the day had looked down Galileo's telescope and seen quite different sights from what Galileo had seen (say he looked down it and saw tiny angels dancing on pin heads) the telescope would not have been accepted as presenting a new and striking aspect of reality. It would not have been regarded as a way of revealing reality, but more like a kaleidoscope – just a way of seeing unusual images, with no implication about what exists in the world. The *consistency of results* which different viewers saw when they looked through telescopes was part of what convinced them that here was a valuable new instrument for research. One key issue in ascertaining consistency in management research is how results in this field could be sensibly compared. As it is, different paradigms lead to very different kinds of outcome: focus group outcomes look totally different from statistical analyses, so how can they be different ways of researching the same phenomenon?

On the other hand, some point out that research is not a mechanical process. People have to conceive of models, think up research questions, and interpret results. Crucial to social research, the researcher has to consider how to collect and interpret information about or *from other human beings*. The investigation is an *interaction*, and the result of research is a product of two elements – a subject, and an investigator who in some way or another makes an intervention, be it as little as privately observing and interpreting the behaviour of a group of workers or as much as conducting extended action research. This conception of methodology as creation emphasises how a researcher *evolves* their results. It depicts the process as a *relationship* between research and subject, as opposed to the previous approach which depicts the process as an attempt to mirror the world via a theory or repeatable result.

These two are not exhaustive of the variety of approaches to applied social research. A third crucial element in studies such as management is the fact that they are about *practices*.[2] This therefore creates two dimensions for mapping out methodologies: the first, a 'natural science – human interpretation' dimension; the second, 'researcher independence – researcher engagement in practice'.[3] As we shall see in the first two parts of the book, most approaches are in some way or another attempts to take these dimensions into account. I shall argue that the extensive – and often quite densely expressed – controversy about social research in general misses the point, for it tends to focus on the merits of particular approaches or the weaknesses of others. In fact they are ALL at best incomplete. I shall eventually propose an integrated approach, indicating how the development of management *knowledge* requires some contribution from a range of different *research* paradigms.

What this means, crudely, is that academic researchers are doing it wrong, and that the needs and interests of professional managers should be more directly taken into account. Further, maybe we would be better off leaving it to managers to organise themselves to research their problems and develop the solutions which they need.

An additional issue arises from the range of methods available. The method chosen to collect evidence in a research study represents a major influence on the *kind* of result which may be obtained. Ask people about their feelings, and you get answers about feelings, so you have a dissertation about feelings. Interrogate an economic database searching for information on strategic threats, and you get economic data, and you end up with a dissertation analysing the economic environment. You get what you look for – not specifically, but certainly in terms of the range of *possible* answers. Someone may be objective in collecting and analysing material about feelings of their respondents, and they may arrive at surprising results (always an indication of a degree of researcher independence). But the choice of research method has still affected what kind of answer they *could* have reached. Two different research methods inevitably arrive at different *kinds* of result. So how can both have a contact with a single unique reality? How far can a study based on so partial a determination of the subject matter claim to be the truth, or even part of the truth, about that subject?

We shall explore this and related issues in the main text of the book, but the reason for mentioning them here is to indicate that there *is* such a controversy, for many books on management research make the subject too straightforward.

Perhaps a symptom of this may be found by looking at the main academic journals in the management field. What the reader will find in current journals (such as the Harvard Business Review, the Academy of Management Review, the British Journal of Management, or the Journal of Management Inquiry) is a variety of types of research and types of presentation. In some cases, formal surveys are *de rigeur*, in others the emphasis is on explaining the substance of the writer's new concept, in still others there is emphasis on an interpretative approach. But the variety itself indicates that there is no simple consensus of what counts as valid research. It is as if all these publishers are living inside a controversy without being able to resolve it. Most worrying are journals which have a strong statement of their editorial philosophy – is this academic conviction or professional self defence?

THE STRUCTURE OF THE BOOK

The book is in three parts. In Part I we look at knowledge itself in management. The field is itself defined – this is not a book about all business research. It is about *management* research specifically. So we establish clear boundaries to the discussion. We then consider incompatible demands on management ideas which make it difficult to maintain both a level of truth and a degree of utility. We then look at factors such as ideology and national culture. The general message is that there are several factors which seriously undermine the claims of much management research to be genuine knowledge.

In Part II we look at methodologies in greater detail. We shall look at the approaches which provide a direct comparison with natural science (which embody what I have called the instrumental conception of methodology) as well as considering the more recent proliferation of approaches which argue that social research should not try to imitate methods of natural science (and which tend to embody the creation based approach mentioned earlier). Amongst these are the so-called postmodern tradition, participant inquiry (including action research), and related approaches of hermeneutics and phenomenology.

We shall find serious difficulties in maintaining any of these as an overall foundation for the validity of management research.

The first two parts of the book jointly suggest that truth is difficult to find in management research. The final part argues that this is less of a problem than it might at first sight appear. It is argued that the utility and value of ideas in management is *not dependent* on whether or not they are true. This discussion draws partially from the concept of *critical theory*, though in an adapted form. The springs for the four characteristic methodologies discussed in Part II (all found wanting to some degree or another) come from different features of the way we put ideas about practice together. Each of these can make a valuable contribution to management knowledge by interacting with other features.

THE STYLE OF THIS BOOK

The discussion will be focused on practical issues which arise for the researcher, whether student, practising professional manager or professor. Some writers have wishfully claimed that good theories are intrinsically practical. If what is meant is that the better the research approach the more useful the result, then this is too naive. The solution a researcher adopts to problems such as data insufficiency, or how to operationalise broad concepts, has a significant influence on the results obtained and thereby on their practicality. And 'practical' is anyway a pretty vague term. The line between theory and practice is not anywhere like as clear as the hope that 'good theories are intrinsically practical' portrays. The approach adopted in this book is to *acknowledge* the grey area between theory and practice, and make best use of it. This is not to dismiss the need to evaluate theories and ideas in practical terms, but to do so in a more critical way – acknowledging that the direction of fit is not often from good theory to practical application, but more likely from practical application to good theory. The real crime, however, would be to pretend that this polarisation is not there, or that since this is the best we can do we might as well ignore it.

Stylistically this book will be similar to my previous text, 'Managing Values': there will be concrete practical discussion, some more analytic material, and illustrative examples. There will be a significant level of fairly abstract discussion – unavoidable in this area. If readers find themselves wondering what the real issue is or where the whole discussion is going, they are advised to think in concrete terms about what the text is saying about actual research projects – this may not always work, but it helps. Every chapter has a summary of the main points – one way of reading the whole text could be to read through each of those summaries first and then go back through the body of each chapter.

Another stylistic aspect is that it is *polemical*. Not haranguing or expressing extreme criticism, but *persuasive*. The main outcome I hope for is to persuade people that the current state of management research methodology is unsatisfactory, and that therefore the whole research endeavour in this field needs to be rethought. If the reader comes away with a *doubt* about management research, then this book will have achieved its main job.

Where the argument is pulled in one way by the demands of clarity and in another by those of balance, more often the former takes priority. 'Balance' is anyway somewhat relative – there are hosts of descriptive books on how to do management research which are either shamelessly positivist or skate over these very difficult issues, so if someone wants 'balance' they could do no worse than comparing the comments made here with those in other texts on the subject.

The intention of this book is to look at the whole range of management ideas that are constructed and presented in the public domain. 'Management research' may suggest an academic model, organisational boffins, producing research papers and delivering results at formal conferences. This is a small part of the area I wish to discuss. At least as important is the plethora of material which is publicly available and which may come from less formal research sources. The academic might dismiss these as 'popularisations' at his or her peril. I shall argue that they have an important value which goes way beyond their lack of pretension.[4]

So we shall discuss management *research*, management *knowledge*, management *ideas*, and management *writing*, sometimes using the phrases interchangeably, sometimes referring just to one of these elements. This eclecticism is essential – the central driving force of the argument is that management research should contribute to management practice, and therefore all products of thinking and investigating management which might impact on practice are relevant, even though the central and most characteristic examples are of more academic format.

A final preliminary point: have I been faithful to the precise thoughts of the writers discussed here – especially in Part II? Not entirely. What is important is to get an *idea* about a *range* of approaches to management research and knowledge and to evaluate how that range can help us understand the processes we use to develop that knowledge. The specifics of particular approaches are less important than overall patterns. Therefore none of the discussions of the ideas of writers in this text are interpretatively exact. It is not the point if I have got it 'wrong' about, say Karl Popper, or Michel Foucault (which I almost certainly have, in the eyes of some Foucault experts[5]). The real point is how far does an idea *something like* Popper's or Foucault's have relevance to our understanding of the processes by which management knowledge is developed. The *kind* of idea is far more important than the precise form in which its originator expressed it. Yes, I may have distorted some ideas. All the same, it matters less what was said by this or that person as what is the relevance of the idea under discussion, wherever it came from.

As was mentioned earlier, this is only apparently a destructive argument. Only by getting clear what we are doing when we carry out research in the field of management can we have any idea of what reliance we can place on it. I hope it provides food for thought, but also that its thoughts may be food for your own practices and perceptions.

NOTES

1 A caricature of the pattern for developing a new academic field these days is to collect a number of like-minded academics together, run a few conferences or seminars on the field you want to establish, start your own journal, using your group of like minded academics as the editorial panel, and overnight you've got a new academic subject. An interesting hypothesis (an investigation of which I personally have not seen) is whether the sub-fields within management reflect individuals' career tracks. So that, a trainer who moves into management education may go into HRD, whilst an engineer will become a specialist in operations management, an accountant specialises in financial management, etc. So on this hypothesis the categorisation of management subjects is less determined by the nature of the subject and more by the educational and professional background of its exponents.

2 It is also expected that a researcher will contribute something original to the field. The impact of a piece of research is less to do with its actual truth as the degree to which it seems to answer some questions, suggest new ones or change the way people view the subject matter. Validity becomes less important than use.

3 This will be the basis on which existing methodological paradigms will be discussed in Part II.

4 As indeed have others. See especially the very interesting text on popular management writing – Furusten (1999).

5 Though this is not difficult – there are radically different schools of 'Foucauldian' interpretation.

Part I

The Idea of Management Knowledge

◼ INTRODUCTION

In the first part of this book we shall look at the intended outcome of management research – management knowledge. What do we mean by 'management' or by 'knowledge'? How far is this independent of social context, ideology and culture?

This is not a book about business research, but about *management* research specifically. The difference is important. Therefore we will first look briefly at the idea of management itself, and how far it may be defined, in order to bring more focus to the main argument.

In Chapter 2 the tension between truth and usefulness is explored in detail – for the first time (it crops up again). One aspect which affects the meaning and significance of management research is the environment within which the research is done. In effect the discussion resembles a PEST analysis of this environment, identifying key factors which influence both the results of research and the manner in which they impact on the business and academic community.

In Chapters 3 and 4 we look at two factors, ideology and culture. Management ideas need to be understood in terms of the national cultures within which they originate and also in terms of the political and social theory which provides the dominant backdrop to the process. Economic and political events are also relevant, though I shall dwell on these more briefly.

Basically this first part of the book is intended to demonstrate that many different factors affect whether or not a piece of management research represents knowledge. The main theme is that management is deeply complex. Because so many different factors are involved, it is in practice extremely difficult to establish the validity of a specific theory or concept of management.

Many of the ideas we encounter here will recur in Parts II and III, so do not expect that the key issues will be resolved in these early chapters – they will be raised here, and in some ways answers will come much later, whilst in others they may not be fully resolved at all in this book.

Chapter 1

What is Management?

Why *management* research? What is distinctive about management, as opposed to other areas of applied social science? Why management rather than business? In this chapter, I intend to draw the boundaries of the discussion: management research specifically, rather than the wider field of business as a whole. 'Business' includes a variety of subjects, some of which cross over each other, and most if not all of which in some way contribute to management. The study of management itself, however, contrasts with these other subject areas.

Inevitably, as there are so many different theories of management, we shall skip lightly over just a sample of these. The intention is to provide sufficient discussion here to establish what we need to develop the argument in later chapters.

1.1 IS MANAGEMENT A DISCIPLINE?

What kind of subject is management? Is it purely practical? Can it be an academic discipline? If so, is it a discipline of itself? Is it multi-disciplinary? Or does it not admit to the kind of public study which can be directly checked by others? Figure 1.1 suggests that it is primarily practice based, but can take a (quite limited) degree of academic study. It involves synthesis of material from a variety of different contributory disciplines, but is not an academic discipline in its own right. Because it combines material from other disciplines, there is a *personal* element in the conception of management which makes it partially resistant to the open challenge and debate which characterises

Interviewer: So what do you do as a manager?

A: Well, I take decisions, I manage budgets, people, deal with operational issues . . . things like that.

B: Yes, but don't you have to think about underlying issues, like motivation theory, or economics, or marketing theory. You must be using these even if you don't realise it.

A: I never went to business school, so I haven't got all the jargon. I just get on with the job.

B: I don't think you can without somehow taking account of the theories, even unconsciously.

Figure 1.1   Two contrasting views of the manager's task.

unified subject disciplines. Without being too misleading, one can say that the definition of the subject area has an element of, if not subjectivity, then at least *individuality*.

One preliminary issue we need to resolve is what is meant by the term *discipline*. 'Discipline' has associations with rules or conventions of behaviour or, in this case, of thinking. A discipline represents an arena for discussion, debate and shared investigation. To acquire expertise in a *discipline* suggests that one has learned *how to discipline* one's thinking relating to that subject, that one has *acquired the discipline* of approaching phenomena in a characteristic way defined within the canons of the subject. Hence there must be a shared understanding of the key issues and the key ways of investigating these. Though there may be controversy and disagreement about specifics, such as a range of theories or results, or even about certain methods of investigation, there is a general agreement about the overall range of subjects and methods of investigation. A common set of problems, presumptions, paradigms, or methodologies is character- istic of a subject discipline. Without these, it is difficult to see how a group of people could be regarded as having a debate at all.

If two people differed over a question of human behaviour, they could be talking from different starting points. 'That's a sociological question, not a psychological one' is a reasonable rejoinder to some- one if the discipline is psychology. But management is not a unified discipline in this sense. 'That's a sociological question, not a manage- ment one' is not an appropriate response. If something relates to the management of organisations, it is a management issue, whether it is formulated in sociological terms, or psychological, or economic, or whatever. Management is, in effect, an *inclusive* subject area.

As I shall argue below, there is a significant and substantial vari- ation in how people approach the subject. Management is not itself a discipline, though it draws upon material from several disciplines in the proper sense of the term, that is, unified areas of study with a shared view of the range of subjects and investigatory methods. How it draws upon these is a key aspect of the following discussion. For I shall argue that this occurs partially at an individual level. So management is a *multi-disciplinary* area of study (that is, it uses more than one discipline) but it is not *inter-disciplinary* (that is, there is no systematic way in which the material integrates).

So what is management? One key point is the *applied* nature of management research. The study of management *has* to involve some aspect of what managers and/or the managed choose to do. There is an intimate connection with practice which is not always there in, say, psychology, operational research, or economics. Though this is a point of *difference* from other business subjects, it represents a *similarity* with other practice-based areas of study such as education or health care. This connection with practice is the most important feature of management research. It means that there are subjective as well as objective elements to the idea of management. It also means that the key criteria by which we evaluate the outcomes of management research are not simply those of intellectual elegance, or methodological soundness. *Management research has to be in part judged by what impact it has on management practice.* However well evidenced a theory might be, if it has nothing to say to the practitioner then it must be, to that extent at least, defective.

As mentioned above, practice implies a multi-disciplinary aspect. The concrete world in which management takes place can be investigated from a wide range of different points of view. Each of these may be a discipline in its own right. For example, one can look at a business in terms of how the people who work in or around it interact. In taking this perspective one is looking at the organisation through the discipline of Organisational Behaviour (OB). Similarly, an organisation can be viewed from the end users' perspective – how customers' needs are identified and provided for, how the organisation makes this known to customers, etc. Marketing is thus also a discipline in its own right (albeit one which itself draws on other areas such as economics and psychology) – it has a shared arena for debate, shared presumptions, shared conceptions of what is a valid method of investigation, etc.

Management, however, involves the *total* perspective – that is, it necessarily pulls all of these disciplines together. A manager is responsible for achieving objectives, using the range of resources available to her/him. They may have to deal with any or all aspects of the resources they use, as well as with the different ways in which the environment impinges on the organisation's activities. They have to deal with finance, people, information, and resources, all within the multiple complexity of the market, legal framework, social context, etc. You cannot be an effective manager by systematically ignoring some aspect of the problems which surround you.[1] You have to take all aspects into account – at the very least, you are held to account if some key factor is *not* taken into account. So *all* theoretical perspectives which have some kind of reference to organisations are relevant to a manager's activity. Management is therefore best seen as a cluster of activities, roles and tasks, drawing on a wide range of disciplines each of which makes some contribution but none of which could be said to be sufficient in its own right to explain the whole cluster.

This holistic view of management underlies functional as well as empirical approaches to the analysis of the management role.[2] But it implies further that the range of ways in which people perceive the manager's role are not determined by a single group of academic disciplines. The subject has its own history.[3] At one time the key management disciplines were mainly related to engineering and finance. At others sociology and psychology. More recently areas such as ethics, anthropology and philosophy have become more accepted as having a relevance for managers.

Because of the link with practice, the contribution of these various feeder disciplines to the subject depends on the manner in which they are combined and synthesised. *Different people create their own version of the managerial role*, and different writers present different perspectives on the same cluster of phenomena. In both academic and practitioner spheres, some parts of that cluster are emphasised and highlighted as having greater priority than others. As argued above, management is not a discipline in the ordinary sense of the term, but operates with material emanating from various other subjects which could more properly be called disciplines: a *meta-subject*, which involves the reflection on, analysis of, and experiment with these various disciplines regarding how they combine and interact in managerial actions and how they contribute to theories about what managers do.

One surprising implication of part of the above is that practising managers are more theoretical than they or others would normally acknowledge. A standard image of the manager in an organisation, deriving from the influence of the empirical studies of the 1950s,[4] is of a highly pragmatic, action oriented individual, impatient with discussion and analysis, uninclined to reflect on their behaviour, but keen to get results. Though this may be factually true as a description of the surface of many managers' behaviour, it is, in my opinion, too superficial a picture. For one thing, a large part of any manager's role involves the use of communication skills to influence and persuade, which intrinsically involves taking a view on something and trying to gain understanding and support for this. The 'vision thing' is about changing how people see things – in other words, reconceptualising.

There is, though, a second and much more important aspect of why effective managers are essentially theorists (of a sort). Doubtless many managers simply do not have the time to sit and quietly reflect – timescales are short and the enhancement of performance is always a pressing concern. But in most manager's jobs there is a high discretionary element. In their day-to-day practice the patterns of choices managers make (for example, about which problems to address and which ones to leave) represent and reflect a particular way of conceiving the task they face. In other words, the theory is evident in their actions. To borrow a term, theory *emerges* from their behaviour, in the sense that what they do embodies a theoretical perspective.[5] Charles Handy talks of the manager as a GP.[6] One of the central skills of any doctor – diagnosis – is also conceptual, for it involves perceiving a range of phenomena, and then putting these together in a way which provides a clear bridge or link between the patient's observed condition and the doctor's repertoire of known ailments and their associated remedies.

This is a *personal* aspect of a manager's approach to their job. That is why I said earlier that different individuals have their own version of the managerial role. The cluster of activities, roles, tasks and responsibilities which managers face is unevenly distributed. How the manager's task is brought into focus depends on several things which fall outside of their imediate job description, such as:

- the structure, culture and operations of the organisation and/or industry
- the unconscious competences of the individual
- the individual's conscious self beliefs about their own competence
- unconscious and invisible ways in which the activity of others complements and supports the manager's role

Note that although this is personal, that does not mean that it is necessarily *individual*. Management action is action within a social context, and generally involves some element of collective behaviour. So the degree to which practising managers are theoretical includes an element of *inter*-subjectivity, of collective perception.

These factors are key influences on how an individual manager conceives their role. Someone starts with an idea of what it is to be a manager, derived from education or their experience of being managed, and so on. Their organisation may have a culture which requires a certain attention to some tasks and less to others. A role culture, for example, will naturally influence people to follow procedures. So a manager in such an organisation is likely to see the completion of documentation as being an important component task (though not, one hopes, an end in itself). Some power cultures or task cultures may find this less important. So managers in these organisations will have a correspondingly lower interest or concern with that aspect – it simply falls to a lower place in their idea of what it is to be a good manager.

As well, the organisation has systems and processes which interlink with what individual managers do or can expect. In some organisations, an account manager, for example, may be expected to do a lot of supporting administrative work. In others, this may be done by supporting staff. So in the former organisations, an account manager, when asked what their role is, would describe their professional responsibilities as well as some administrative elements, whilst someone in the latter kind would omit the administrative aspect. In the first figure we saw an example of how an individual's education might influence the way they conceive of the management task. But people's definitions of a manager's role can also vary because of how different organisations do the work. Figure 1.2 gives an example of this.

This is a resume of a discussion held in a postgraduate management course. Both individuals had a conception of their role as a manager which included a central core – achieving results. But each customised this to their own situation, in the light of the specific culture and practices of their organisations. In practice, it is possible that the two managers involved in the discussion may not have differed in what they did day-to-day as much as the discussion suggested, but the *direction* of their thinking is very different. A is oriented towards individual autonomy, whilst B thinks more in network terms, in line with the standards of practice in their own organisations. *Organisational practice* had contributed to their *understanding* of what their role is.

In addition to organisational culture and a manager's education and background, their own abilities affect their idea of the management role. Individuals will unconsciously solve some problems effortlessly. So those areas of the manager's role do not feature highly, if at all, in their idea of management – they may simply fail to recognise these as key tasks, because they are more than competent. Other aspects of the role are more difficult and they have to focus more directly on these. So they are strongly aware of those tasks as being part of their responsibility – they have to try harder, so they are more aware of them.

So someone's personal theoretical perspective on the managerial role becomes apparent through behaviour which is significantly conditioned by the above factors.

Tutor: A and B, you're both assistant store managers. What does the job involve?

A: At XYZ, a store manager is expected to do the lot – hire and fire, customer complaints, local advertising, doing the orders for our deliveries, even purchasing some of the perishable food on occasion, everything.

B: Oh it's quite different at UVW [a direct competitor]. Central deliveries send an allocation of products based on your sales – they've got a direct link to the tills, so they know what's being bought and what isn't – you only let them know what changes to make to the basic supply, for example if you want to do a promotion. Even then you have to get permission from marketing at head office. We're not allowed to do any of the recruitment – personnel do it all, same with dismissals, disciplinaries, everything like that. And we have standard letters for customer complaints, we just sign the appropriate one and send it off.

A: We have central services too, but they really are there to make sure we can get our job done. You must have to have some kind of local responsibility. Suppose a customer complaint doesn't fit into one of those standard letters?

B: Send it to the regional HQ.

A: But what if there was a crisis, like the building was found to be unsafe. You wouldn't wait to hear what your central office decided before doing something, would you?

B: Oh on, we would be expected to use our own discretion, but that would only be in unusual situations. Normally we follow the book.

Tutor: So, B, in a nutshell, what do you think a manager's job really is?

B: Creating the opportunity for each part of the business to fulfil its functuion. Co-ordinating with the different support services to get the job done.

Tutor: A, what do you think?

A: It's making sure everything gets done to meet the customer's needs. If central or regional don't do it, I have to make sure that it gets done in the store.

Figure 1.2   Comparisons of a manager's role
(based on actual classroom discussion).

I can hear someone thinking 'But someone's personal idea of what management is may be right or wrong. You cannot be saying that each manager makes their own definition, and that these are equally valid'.

I *am* saying that every manager makes their own definition, to an extent. The question of validity I leave for the moment. What is important is that, valid or not, the construction an individual manager places on the idea of what their role is plays a major role in how far or whether management knowledge impinges on their behaviour and practice.

There is even greater variability than this. For organisations 'create' conceptions of managerial practice not only in virtue of their structure and culture, but also in terms of the challenges which the business environment presents to them. Management theory is a response to the present circumstances which businesses face. New circumstances – new

large western companies	western state organisations
challenges:	*challenges:*
globalisation e-commerce rise of service orientation	convergence with private sector demand for increased value for money increased public concern over services
central view of management:	*central view of management:*
international vision and technological	operational efficiency and stakeholder sensitivity
companies in developing countries	**aid and charitable organisations**
challenges:	*challenges:*
growing industrialisation managing from low capital bases	reducing public donations increasing scope of needs focus on developing independence of recipients
central view of management:	*central view of management:*
operational efficiency and focus on enhancing quality of delivery	advocacy, funds management

Figure 1.3   Organisational challenges and their influence on the management task (a snapshot at the start of the millennium).

theories. And this too is an unevenly dispersed aspect. Some industries in some countries face certain challenges at a different time than others – economic trends, for example, do not happen all around the global economy simultaneously. They do not even proceed uniformly like a 'Mexican wave' in a football crowd. Technology transfer is another similar factor which moves irregularly through the global business world. So one nationally based company may not recognise a problem which a multi-national competitor is feeling keenly (and vice versa).

In Figure 1.3 we see a snapshot illustrating some of the challenges facing four sectors of the global economy in late 2000. Doubtless these will change, as technology changes, as markets demands change, and as the balance of different nations' competitiveness changes. But the point is that what is sought from management varies partially in the light of the overall challenges facing a sector.[7]

The very idea of management is strongly affected by this correlation between theory and socioeconomic context. A theory of management is, in effect, a kind of soft technology, intersecting with the environment and the challenges it poses organisations, relating to their performance. These environmental features include, as indicated above, technology, economic and social trends, but also elements such as the competitive and financial market place, or the changing dynamics of world or national trade. As these factors change, so does the prevailing portfolio of tools, theories and techniques which managers use to achieve results.

A helpful analogy may be drawn with music. The theory of western music, as currently conceived, has been built up to help composers and performers in those countries produce a *certain kind* of music using a *certain range* of instruments and opportunities. *Notes* are defined in a way to facilitate the construction of keyboard instruments which can play equally well in any key (so called 'even-temperament'). *Time* is conceived and structured in a way to facilitate the easy communication of non-repetitive rhythmic patterns, especially where large groups of players (like orchestras) may come together relatively infrequently. The whole idea of *melody* has developed out of the use of the singing voice.

Musical theory has thus evolved symbiotically with available resources, technologies and changing practices. New practices, such as the introduction in the twentieth century of the so-called serial method,[8] arise due to the availability of certain levels of resource and technology, and generate new theories. It is commonly accepted that this body of theory is not adequate to help with the performance or composition of music from other cultures or traditions – blues and jazz rhythms, for example, are only imperfectly captured in classical western notation. Even a brief consultation of music in a non-western culture emphasises that the different theoretical perspectives are not universal, but are closely intertwined with different practices, instrumentation and technology.[9]

So theory, in practice-based subject areas such as management – or music – has to be understood as a response to the availability and potentialities of resources, the challenges presented by the environment, and the portfolio of existing practices. Where one of these changes, so theory itself changes. The steady erosion of competitive advantage which the western economies witnessed in the fifteen years or so up to 1990 informed much theorising. Peters and Waterman's classic explicitly drew parallel after parallel between excellent US companies and Japanese management practices (as they were then perceived). Diminishing margins provided the backdrop for the theoretical basis of downsizing, a practice characteristic of the late 1980s. When the Dow Jones index went over the 10,000 mark, this idea ran out of steam, and new trends of thought supported buildback. There is a time-bound aspect to management theory which is rarely acknowledged.

Theory in management is thus dependent on several factors – individual, organisational and industry wide. Because of this we cannot see management as being a simple shared arena for debate. And we cannot view management ideas as being simple contributions to knowledge.

1.2 'MANAGEMENT' – A HYBRID CONCEPT

We need to establish how far the idea of management is particular to individuals and how much is common. I shall argue that there is a central core element to management – if you like, the basic definition – but that this basic core meaning can be amplified in various ways. The level at which individuals place their own interpretation of the management task is one, therefore, which has inherent limitations of transferability. By contrast, the basic core meaning is generalisable across all managers. Figure 1.4 illustrates this.

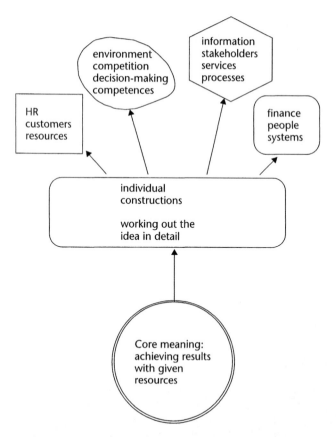

Figure 1.4   Core and peripheral conceptions of management.

Here we see a central core meaning, and then a range of different ways in which this is amplified by individuals. A purely functional or analytical analysis of 'management' makes the assumption that management is the same for all individuals. What has been argued so far is a counter to that. But it would be misleading to call this a *subjective* account of the idea of management. It has elements which are intrinsically linked to the needs, perceptions and capabilities of groups and individuals, and it has other elements which are applicable to wider ranges of people. But this does not mean that the subject is subjective. Rather it implies that some aspects of management have an individual-dependent component.

Whilst there may be a central unified meaning of the idea of management, the way that individuals bundle together the various factors is very much their own construction. The terminology is sufficiently plastic for one bundle – for example, HR, Customers, Resources – to cover much the same areas, but with a different kind of emphasis, as some other bundle, such as finance people and systems. The *elements* which influence how individuals place their own construction on the management task may be common to many managers, but *how they put them together* is variable – hence how they conceive of the management task is also variable.

So the perspective which will be taken in this book on the idea of management is that has a wide variety of component elements – different roles, tasks, activities and responsibilities. There *is* a unifying theme with all of these: management is concerned, as we noted above, with the achievement of certain organisational goals with a set of given resources. But this is a pretty thin definition (and not itself terribly original), though what shall be argued is that the devil is in the detail of the way individual managers flesh this out: the central core of the idea of management is common, but what really matters is the way this is worked out in detail. Specific versions of it vary quite dramatically from one person to another. Probably the main failing of most overarching theories of management is to overlook this feature. What this says about *knowledge* of management, and the management *research process*, is that a search for a single over-arching model of management knowledge is likely to miss this degree of variation in the way people think about management, and the range of factors affecting it. But also it suggests that management knowledge is not simply an outcome of a process of investigation – a point we shall come back to.

▪ 1.3 ANALYTIC DEFINITIONS

Let's look more specifically at what we mean by 'management'. The first issue is the generalist presumption – that is, 'management' identifies a set of concepts, skills, techniques and the like which are broadly applicable to all and any organisation. After all, we speak in English of managing a company, a sports team, a household; of having office managers, client managers, account managers, general managers, marketing managers, and so on. The sheer proliferation of the word suggests that it is a broad based concept, applicable in a wide variety of contexts. And this is without taking into account secondary meanings such as managing in the sense of being able to cope, or when one talks of 'managing to do something' as almost a synonym for achieving.

But we need to be careful where we start with definitions of the term 'management'. Even languages which are closely related to English, such as French, do not have a single term which directly corresponds to it. It is worth bearing in mind that Henri Fayol's major book on organisations used the French term *'administration'* – which most English translations have rendered as 'management'.[10] French and Italian both seem to have at least three terms which could plausibly be translated in English as 'management', these being – *'gestion'* (Fr)/*'gestione'* (It) (association of getting things done); *'administration'* (Fr)/*'amministrazione'* (It) (organising); *'direction'* (Fr)/*'direzione'* (It) (leadership). Once one gets to a language which is only a bit more remote, such as Russian, there appear European borrowings such as *'administratsiya'* and *'directsiya'* but also indigenous terms such as *'upravlenie'* (with a nuance of control) and *'zavedovanie'* (with a nuance of organisational leadership) – perhaps unsurprisingly, the Russians have, since the fall of Communism, taken to borrowing 'manager' and 'businessman' almost literally, as a way of reflecting western capitalism. And when one reaches East Asian languages there is no clear correlation to be made at all.

The linguistic discussion makes a minor point, but it suggests that the generalist view of management is not a universal idea. Arguably, it represents a form of intellectual colonialism, imposed on the global economy by the English speaking nations.[11] Be this as it may, the traditional approach is to analyse down the whole idea of management into a small set of key generic tasks or activities – organising, planning, motivating are usually included,[12] plus one or two more. A modern version of this switches focus from the function to the individual carrying it out. So in recent years there has been a spate of models of management competences and skills (see Figure 1.5).

The two examples of skills indicated in Figure 1.5 have overlaps, and some points of difference.[13] Both lists are non-situational – they specify skills or attributes which someone might demonstrate in any one of many situations. In this respect they both contrast with the approach of the UK management development body, the MCI,[14]

two models of management skills	
most frequently discussed skills of effective managers	*attributes of successful managers*
verbal communication	command of basic facts
managing time and stress	relevant professional knowledge
managing individual decisions	sensitivity to events
recognising and solving problems	analytical, problem solving, decision/judgement-making skills
motivating and influencing others	social skills and abilities
delegating	emotional resilience
setting goals	proactivity
self awareness	creativity
teambuilding	mental agility
	balanced learning habits and skills
	self knowledge
Whetton et al. (1994)	Burgoyne et al. (1994)

Figure 1.5   Management skills.

which breaks management down into a series of functional areas – finance, people, resources, information, etc. The MCI model seems to miss entirely the synthesis which is at the heart of the management task as I have depicted it earlier, but worse than that, it seems to package up discrete areas of management without regard to their interrelationship. In practice many people problems are also performance or quality problems, and many finance problems are also operational problems. The MCI approach is more or less silent on this aspect.[15]

The Whetton/Cameron/Woods and Burgoyne/Pedler/Boydell models are superior to the MCI in the respect that they leave open the issue of how a manager synthesises concepts, theories and knowledge as being a part of the way a manager meets challenges effectively. But this remains at an implicit level. It would be easy to think, from consulting either of the two lists given above, that management was simply the performance of a wide range of activities. This is in line with the findings of the empirical researchers referred to earlier – managers do lots of different kinds of things, with different skill needs, different timescales, and usually all under a great deal of pressure. But this focuses on the *phenomena* of managerial behaviour, not their underlying rationale or significance. As argued above, there is an underlying connecting thread, which can be best summed up as the requirement to help the organisation perform at an appropriate level using the resources available to it. All managerial activity should be devoted to this end, in some way or another.

Both sets of writers referred to above acknowledge this issue in the detail of how their models are applied, but their models stated in simple forms leave this out – suggesting at least that the overall purpose of a manager's role is less crucial a priority than the specific activities which are carried out in fulfilment of that role. On the view I have presented above, though, these are operating at different levels – specific personal attributes or skills are *tools* only. Management itself is *how those tools are used jointly* to achieve the ultimate end of performance.

Keith Grint has presented a contrasting view to this latter point.[16] For him, there is much less clear a definition of what management is. The very title of one of his books 'Fuzzy Management' underscores the uncertainties which, for him, lie at the heart of the manager's role. In one sense I do not want to disagree with the methodological point, that there is a great deal of uncertainty in management know-ledge (indeed that is really the whole theme of this book). The point of difference is that I am emphasising the central feature of manage-ment – its point of stability, if you like. That stable feature is the need to achieve results within an environment and with a clearly limited set of resources. It is this which binds together the variety of different skills and abilities individual may use to meet that underpinning requirement. The fuzziness which Grint emphasises should be kept at the periphery – at the level of the tools, techniques and qualities which managers may need to draw upon.

Now look at a contrasting view of the manager's role, as depicted in Figure 1.6.

This is a very different kind of approach to the question of what management is than the examples we have seen so far. It also depicts a *different conception* of management than the versions we have considered so far. Here there is a definite equalisation of the roles of manager and managed. The view presented in the analytic approaches

The manager is a sarathi, the chariot driver. He does not bear weapons or fight but a great proportion of the warrior's success depends on the vision, skill and ability of the sarathi to manoeuvre him through the battlefield and take the best advantage of various opportunities. The warrior is the executive; the sarathi the manager. It is the manager who plans, guides, directs and takes a holistic view of the arena to decide where his executives may operate and how.

A. E. Chakravarty

Figure 1.6 A hindu view of management.[17]

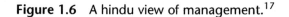

so far considered are more conducive to a top-down approach. In other words that managers are 'higher' – in status, responsibility, risk, intellect (rarely stated but often assumed) and ultimately gaining greater reward. Here the role of a manager is to achieve results by creating the opportunities for an individual to exercise their particular skill effectively.

'Didn't Taylor say just as much?' someone might say. Yes, he did, but bear in mind that his idea of someone exercising their particular skill was not the high level of professional competence implied by the warrior metaphor, but a manual labourer shovelling coal (and depicted in very patronising tones).

Two other points should be noted about the material of Figure 1.6. Firstly, it represents an attempt to link management to a completely different kind of study, away from disciplines such as sociology or economics, and explicitly closer to poetry – even to theology. But secondly, it still reflects the unified view of management which I outlined earlier. These two points emphasise the argument given earlier that whilst management has a clear central core, the manner in which people may link this to concrete practice is highly variable. This core connecting thread underpins the wide variety of activities and disciplines which form part of the whole field of management – there are many ways that the underlying stable aspect of management relates to the widely variegated range of activities and discrete tasks which make up the surface phenomena of management.

We are trying to understand what the term 'management' really means, in order to understand what can be said about management knowledge. So far we have seen that: (a) management is a particularly Anglocentric term; and (b) analytic approaches which break down management into a series of tasks, functions or skills fail to capture or explain how the connecting thread gets turned into so many different kinds of approach.

This is not a prescriptive definition of management. It broadly encompasses the wide range of behaviours and activities which can fall to a manager. It will provide a framework which makes it possible to discuss the range of different ways that individual managers achieve the linkage between this central stable idea and the component elements of their management experience – the various activities as well as specific contributions from different disciplines which inform their thinking and behaviour. As argued above, this is an individual phenomenon. How someone constructs their own model of management is a result of how they see the relationship between their over-riding role and this variety of ideas, tools, activities and the like which form the day-to-day content of their experience of being a manager.

▉ 1.4   IS MANAGEMENT WHAT MANAGEMENT DEVELOPMENT DEVELOPS?

Can we learn about management by looking at how people can be developed as managers? Perhaps management is transparently *the subject matter of management development*. So one might be able to construct an idea of management from the work of writers on HRD and similar areas. One intriguing view in this area is the use made by Stephen Fox of the distinction between formal and informal management processes – what he calls '*M*' management and '*m*' management respectively.[18]

Fox's innovation is not in the distinction – which is itself well established – but in the idea that one can turn the distinction on itself, so that there are four separate forms of management:

(i)   *MM formally managing management*: for example, formally defining a new corporate philosophy

(ii)   *mM informally managing the formal*: ways in which individuals work within the formal structures of the organisation

(iii)   *Mm formal attempts to manage the informal processes of the organisation*: for example, culture change initiatives

(iv)   *mm the interaction of informal management*: activities and processes

This highlights some interesting issues, for example:

(a)   *culture/nationality specifics*: are some cultures more attuned to one of these four types of management?

(b)   *priority*: are the four types of management equal in importance, or will this vary organisationally?

(c)   *certainty*: is knowledge about management more easily attained for some of these kinds than for others?

(d)   *dynamics*: how consciously do managers move between these four kinds, and how far do they interact? (for example, so that a formal attempt at developing a company mission may be more or less successful depending on how skilful managers are at playing the system)

Some aspects of these will recur later in this book. In general the answers to them will reflect the overall sceptical approach: (a) there *is* cultural and national variation, as well as (b) organisational and even individual variation in importance of the four types, (c) the more highly formal an element of management is, the more likely that clear knowledge may be available for it (but the less use it will be) and above all (d) the dynamic interaction between the types makes management knowledge highly situationally specific.

So the reference to management development has some relevance to the idea of what management is. But there is more to it than what we have seen so far. I have argued above that there is a central underlying element of the idea of management, out of which the variety of activities, roles, and tasks grow. Nevertheless, whilst this central aspect may have a degree of stability, what surrounds it changes, not only with time and when moving between organisations and cultures, but also via an interaction with management development processes.

Let us look at this hypothetically, creating a somewhat fictional history of the development of management.

Suppose that at some time the key conception of management was knowledge driven (for example, about economic trends, formal organisation and production techniques). At this time, then, the main task of management development would be seen as getting the relevant knowledge into aspiring or practising managers – up and coming managers attend class based sessions on 'what you need to know to be a successful manager', and formal management education is greatly in demand.[19]

This in turn would create a cadre of 'knowledgeable' managers, who have themselves formed the idea that management is about knowledge, and they then decide to develop the next generation of young managers by helping them acquire the key knowledge. So what we have here is a process of development which mirrors a conception of management but then consolidates this conception by creating managers who reflect this process.

Continuing this hypothesis, along comes a competing view of management – maybe sensitivity to the needs of the customer. This comes from outside the existing generation of managers (who have all been brought up on the above). Usually some combination of business failures and a new wave of management theorists/champions are the main catalysts. Management development processes are then redesigned to take account of this – so it now includes customer care, communication skills, and so on. A move away from a knowledge basis to a skills or attitudinal one means that a new repertoire of development techniques are constructed and put into operation. Personal development and inter-personal skills become the central focus – development activities are less sit-down-in-class based and more active, involving an attention to individually defined needs and capabilities. The next generation of more senior managers are thus well educated in recognising needs of customers, and regard this as the central feature of the management task. Development processes are refined to be ever more effective at delivering this outcome, so the next generation of managers are long on these skills, and tend to act in ways which reflect their development (because that is what they think management is all about – what they have been trained in). Then yet another management imperative comes along – say strategic analysis. Intellectual, rational and creative thinking skills come to the fore, and development processes are redesigned to deliver this in turn, and we end up with a succeeding wave of strategic creative thinkers.

Why this is not the real history of management and of management development is that change in the understanding of management is imperfect. Business is a broad front and many organisations still work with the dogmas of the 1950s – some are even still Taylorist. Also management does not simply swap one basic conception for another – there is some effort at growth, including the best of the old as well as the best of the new. Thus managers still need to learn some basic knowledge about economics, for example, need to enhance their inter-personal skills, and need to be creative strategic thinkers as well. It all builds up (which, incidentally, makes the task of being a manager ever more forbidding a challenge – the difficulty of juggling so many balls has always been there, but it was less recognised in the past and so less awesome). Additionally, there are styles and preferences – organisationally and also in terms of business schools, which have a strong influence on management development standards and orthodoxies. So we have not only Harvard style management education, but also Harvard style managers, noted for keen analytical alertness but not so strong on reflection.

Another side to this is that certain techniques for developing managers are more effective for some aspects of development than others. So it is easier for individuals to learn quantitative analytic tools on an MBA than via some form of on-the-job experience, whilst it is far easier for an individual to pick up what Richard Pettinger has called the Realpolitik of management[20] via direct experience or mentoring than through case studies or classroom role plays. The sheer existence of certain delivery methods and mechanisms of management development means that certain aspects of the management role are selectively emphasised, to the detriment of other aspects. Some management development delivery systems have their own inertia – no one is going to shut down business schools overnight, so even if they generally were perceived as of little use for business and for managers in the field, what they provide will continue for quite some time to have a significant impact both on the theory and the practice of management.

Let us recap. Though there is a central conception of management which is relatively stable, what surrounds it is changeable. Management as a subject matter changes, not just in terms of specific items of knowledge but also in terms of the territory – in terms of what is a suitable object of management knowledge (and hence of management research and investigation). The kinds of change result from an interplay between the (semi) profession itself, the developmental processes used to create new managerial expertise, and external catalysts of conceptual change.

This implies that conceptual changes in this field are not solely down to increases in understanding. The inertia and selective effectiveness of development mechanisms, not to mention the non-intellectual factors influencing the emergence of new management ideas, create the environment within which the *idea* of management, as well as its practice, changes. Before the Hawthorne experiments and the associated revolution in management thinking, managers did think about the needs of individual workers. Probably every canny industrial foreman knew the importance of understanding his labour force. But it was not seen as part of the management task – it was an extra, that shrewd operators added on to the 'official' conception. Equally, one can look back a long way and find references to ethics and business – at least as far as the time of the Koran, if not further. But as recently as twenty years ago Peter Drucker was making a *radically innovative* comment when he said that 'It is vision and moral responsibility that... define the manager'.[21]

Another aspect of this is that the impact of management development on managerial behaviour takes a long time to take effect. As we have seen there is a *double enforcement* of the dogmas of a particular time – once, when these are taught to a generation of managers, and a second time when these people, later in their career (and thus usually with more influence) continue to use the concepts they were exposed to often decades ago.

It is not simply that trends in management thinking take a long time to work through to practice. It is that practice is itself understood in terms of the content of management development – because this has a significant impact on the behaviour of managers. New practices are slow to take root because of the inertia of the past, and the way people conceive their role as managers is profoundly affected by their development experiences. Even theory which is meant to *describe* the management role changes it.

1.5   THE MANAGEMENT RESEARCHER

A final point to consider, which will recur in different form in later discussions, is the issue of what a management researcher is and what they actually do. There are two ways to construe the role of the researcher, and they embody two different conceptions of what management research is and what it can achieve:

(a)   management researchers are trying to discover the reality of management

(b)   management researchers are trying to develop a greater understanding of management

The first of these depicts the management researcher as a seeker after the truth of organisational management. It covertly presumes a sense that there is a single truth, and hence that the issue is how to get to it. We shall see this idea crop up when discussing approaches to management research which try to emulate the methods of natural science.

In contrast the second presents the issue as less convergent. It does not carry a sense that there is a single end point which could be agreed by all as 'the' truth about management (though it is important to emphasise that it does not obviously carry a assumption that there are equally viable alternative 'truths').

Beneath these two views is a cluster of related issues, such as the independence of researchers, or the extent to which material drawn from one context may be generalised across a whole range or category of management contexts. Evert Gummesson[22] presents a strong argument in favour of what we shall later call participatory research (see Chapter 8), but on a different basis to the argument given in this book. In effect his claim is that access to management reality is best achieved by a degree of participatory involvement of a researcher in the processes of an organisation. Simple 'dip-in' surveying, for example, is not likely to be effective in gaining access to the reality of an organisation because of the extent to which the process can be subverted, and because of the limits to the depth which a researcher can reach in a brief encounter with the organisation. Gummesson suggests that the best role for a management researcher may be better labelled as a researcher/consultant, drawing the strength of the process consultant's deep involvement whilst maintaining a focus on developing generalisable knowledge.

At the end of this book I shall present a view which undermines the idea of generalisable knowledge in its current form as being the appropriate model for management. But in addition there is one interesting point to consider regarding Gummesson's position – it implies that *there is a single reality of management which can be accessed.* He assumes that the more closely one is involved with an organisation the more deeply one sees into its heart. But – the more one is involved with an organisation, the more one is also drawn into its own prejudices, the more one is captured by its own self-image and its own highly biased version of its history. The brand new entrant to an organisation has a fresh perspective, from which they can see things which the older members of the organisation cannot. Of course, the longer established members see other things that the new person cannot. So who has the best access to the reality of management in such an organisation? Neither. Each can see something which the other can't. The 'whole' truth about an organisation is not visible to either party. It is rather like a steep mountain – the person at the bottom sees much at the bottom, but can't see the top, while the person near the top sees the overall form of the peak but the foot of the mountain is out of their view. It is not that there is *no* truth about the mountain – it is simply very difficult to get a single view of all of it at one point. Synthesising different views is a central feature of this.

So access is not a basis on which to differentiate levels of researcher involvement – though it is an important factor affecting what someone sees in an organisation, and how they see it. Whilst I will argue that the participatory style is maybe the central focus of the management research process, its local focus creates difficulties for the idea that current approaches to research generate management knowledge.

SUMMARY

In this chapter we have been laying some of the foundations for the later argument.

We have seen that management is a two layered idea – the inner layer is a central core that management is about achieving results with a given level of resources, the outer layer depicts the specific ways in which this is operationalised. The latter is the rich and useful concept which creates direct links with actual practice. It is not a discipline in its own right, though it draws upon the material of several feeder disciplines.

The outer layer is highly variable – affected by individual, organisational and global factors. So management theory cannot be seen as a stable body of knowledge. It varies according to circumstance.

We also saw that management development processes themselves lend a further degree of qualification to the image of a subject of study leading to stable, context free knowledge.

Lastly, we looked at the idea of the role of a researcher into management, and I indicated that the relationship between management research and management consultancy can be misleading. In particular the idea that the consultancy role brings a more true perspective on an organisation than the more independent researcher role is not helpful – greater involvement brings some awareness but only at the cost of obscuring other aspects.

The following chapters in Part I will explore the status of management research as knowledge, and will look at some of the *contextual* aspects of the process in detail. What we shall see is that these issues, too, will undermine the idea of management as a systematic body of knowledge.

NOTES

1 Though of course it might be excellent management judgement to ignore a set of factors *on occasion*.
2 Amongst the functional theorists most notable is Henri Fayol. The best known empirical studies have been carried out by Mintzberg (1973) and Stewart (1983).
3 Though regrettably until now no one has recorded this history. Alan Bray has however recently raised this as a question – see Bray (2001).
4 See, for example, Stewart (1983).
5 Of course, this is idealised. It pre-supposes, for example, that a manager behaves with sufficient consistency for their actions to have a pattern. The point is not whether this is factually true of all or most managers, so much as illustrating that some degree of conceptual activity is central to the idea of effective management. In other words, theory is intrinsic to management activity.
6 Handy (1993) Chapter 11. For non-UK readers, 'GP' refers to the role of the general doctor, working in the community rather than in a hospital.
7 An interesting example of this kind of argument may be found in the article 'To come of age – the antecedents of organisational learning' Harvey and Denton (1999). The authors present the development of the idea of organisational learning and the learning organisation as determined by the impact of social and economic factors on key groups such as management theorists and practitioners. A critical implication of this approach is that the *perception* of those economic factors is as important as the *actuality*.
8 A technique of composing where traditional harmony is replaced by a *series* of note relationships, each of which has equal importance.
9 See, for example, Massey and Massey (1993).
10 Fayol (1916). It does not really matter exactly what is the correct translation, so much that the different nuances and associations make absolutely exact translation difficult if not impossible.

11 Or, it could be argued, even more specifically by the USA, which spawned the growth in ideas about management since the mid-twentieth century.

12 This selection of two sources skims the surface of a wide range of approaches. A good summary can be found in Mullins (Chapter 12) and in other similar OB texts.

13 MCI – Management Charter Initiative. See, for example, their standards for Operational Management (1997).

14 Paradoxically, the MCI does make an explicit statement regarding the overall purpose of a manager's role, but fails to recognise that there is a substantial gulf between the over-arching purpose and the details of individual management interpretations of their task.

15 Grint (1997), especially Chapters 1 and 2. Many of Grint's ideas are closely linked to the argument of this book.

16 Chakravarty (1995) Chapter 1. Certainly not the only example where management theory has drawn on Indian religious concepts – see Parikh (1992).

17 Fox (1994).

18 Not quite the same as formal management qualifications, some of which may be skill or competency based as well as involving knowledge.

19 Pettinger (1994) Chapter 12 .

20 Drucker (1977).

21 Gummesson (2000).

Chapter 2

Knowledge and Utility

In Chapter 1 we tried to define management, in order to set the ground for the rest of the discussion. What we saw, though, was that even in defining the subject, there are problems in establishing how valid or useful management research is. Management, we concluded, is not a discipline in its own right (in the sense of having a shared ground for investigation and debate) but draws on material from a number of contributory disciplines. It has a broad central sense, which is pretty empty in itself. Surrounding this are the specific ways in which individual managers and management writers flesh out the basic definition. These ways are, though, highly variable – amongst other things, there is a clear *individual* element.[1]

Management knowledge is really soft technology, which has to be understood in terms of its relationship with other resources and indeed with reference to the challenges and tasks presented to an organisation or industry. This complex intellectual environment means that management as an idea is not a simple body of knowledge in the way that some subjects may be. The whole subject matter of management can vary depending on which organisation you look at, which industry, which national or multi-national context you consider, and especially which point in time is adopted as a reference point. As a result, individual managers themselves *construct their own understanding* of the management task.

So, in terms of the overall purpose of this book, the concept of management knowledge does not admit of the independent, context free conception that one can get with non-applied subjects. In this chapter we shall look more specifically at one particular cluster of these questions, namely the tension between validity and utility – how true something is as against how useful it may be. We shall see that these two do not often go hand-in-hand.

The main argument of this chapter can be summarised as follows. For an idea or concept or technique to be useful, especially to busy managers, it needs to be clear and easily grasped. So it should be simply expressed, and ideally have some motivating potential. Utility requires simplicity. But for something to be *true* about management, it needs to take account of a wide range of issues (because management is an applied human study). Truth thus requires complexity. So there is a tendency for truth and utility to go in opposite ways. The more easily understood and directly applicable an idea, the less likely it is to have a solid body of supporting evidence. The more precisely defined an idea and the more closely and soundly it is supported by evidence, the less applicable it is to general practice.

But before discussing these directly, we need to look more closely at what 'knowledge' in this field really means, and what kinds of product we can expect from management research. So the first part of this chapter presents a series of points contributing to the view that management knowledge is not scientific in nature.

Some readers may wonder – why bother? Is it not clear enough that management is not a scientific[2] subject? It may be clear to some readers, but this book would be incomplete if it explored the senses in which management knowledge can be both useful but not scientifically based, if it had not established whether or not it is scientific. In any case, the point is not that management *happens* not to be scientific – as if with a bit of effort we could make it so. The real question is whether management is a subject about which scientific knowledge can be had at all. In exploring this we will learn more about what kind of enquiry management research is and what kinds of value it can possess.

2.1   THE IDEA OF KNOWLEDGE

In Chapter 1, and in the above introduction, I have assumed a view of how management ideas relate to practice. I initially want to explain this in more detail. We start with a discussion of the intended product of research – knowledge.

Once one starts trying to explain knowledge the prospect of a full scale philosophical discussion rears it head. It would be reckless to think we could settle the matter in one section. Nevertheless, some discussion is necessary, if only in order to forestall any misconceptions.

Perhaps the most important feature of knowledge, of any kind, which management research activities must ensure if they are to have any kind of validity at all, is that of stability. An idea or result which changes unpredictably over time or when different researchers or research communities follow the same line of investigation provides nothing which can be shared. Such a result cannot enter into any arena for debate or discussion, still less be the foundation for management action, because there is no confidence that it will persist. We end up acting on, or discussing, something that has passed.

A degree of persistence and of repeatability are therefore important basic requirements of sound research. This is different from saying either that there is a specific level of stability which is required, or that these two properties are *sufficient* for something to be regarded as sound knowledge. The history of natural science is littered with ideas and results which were repeatedly obtained time after time over long periods, and only were shown to be false via an innovative twist – such as a new kind of experiment, or a new instrument of observation, or even a new domain of data collection.

So, to take one example, the speed of light was presumed for at least two hundred and fifty years to be just like the speeds of other phenomena of which people were aware: in particular that its speed would be relative to other bodies in motion – as could be calculated by adding or subtracting the speeds of those other bodies. The failure of a new experiment (not designed to *test whether* light had a speed incidentally, but simply to *measure* its speed) led eventually to the recognition via Einstein's theory of relativity that the speed of light was a unique limit:[3] a new experimental design had led to the overturn of a long held assumption. Similarly, the collection of data by Darwin in a new location led to his rejection of the traditional Christian view of the origins of life,[4] and the invention of the telescope revolutionised the study of space – indeed precious little *direct* eviden was collected by Galileo before the scientific world became convinced of the falsity of previous ideas about planets and stars.

This polarisation between the need to have stable results and the fact that many of these turn out eventually not to have been what they seem is a fundamental feature of all research (it can hardly be called a problem because it is irresolvable). In physics or biology as much as in management, we could always be wrong – the apparent stability of evidence in one direction may be at any time confounded by unexpected and conflicting results. There is no certainty in any science, whether pure or applied, whether natural or human related, which is not ultimately open to question and thus to possible refutation. The fact that there is no certainty with regard to questions which we solve by utilising external evidence – material that in some way or another we collect, rather than simply invent in its entirety – does not destroy the possibility of knowledge, either in the purity of disinterested natural science or in the more complex and more easily compromised area of management. On the contrary, it defines what kind of knowledge is possible.

Proof which excludes any possibility of error in research-based knowledge is not possible, and no amount of evidence or analysis can ever insulate an idea or theory from challenge. Any approach which makes it look as if there can be some kind of certainty, as a sort of absolute barrier against the sheer frailty of human knowledge, as if incontestable statements can be made about organisations, social trends, or subatomic particles, is searching for a pot of gold at the end of a rainbow, and the reader is strongly advised not to waste any time on such an idea.

Much of the above is over-simplified. For example, the idea that it is central to scientific knowledge that it be stable is accommodated in different ways by different writers. Similarly, it is misleading just to talk of the possibility of being wrong. In different approaches to knowledge, 'being wrong' can bear a number of different senses. Until the time of Karl Popper it was presumed that truth or falsity in science was primarily a logical issue – did the available evidence support the conclusion drawn? Largely as a result of the controversies stirred up by his work, the explanation of why something is accepted as true or rejected as false is recognised as having some social elements. In other words, whether or not a scientific claim is right or wrong is not a simple matter of someone going to see if what you said is really out there. It involves an element of balancing different intellectual requirements, revising ideas, communicating and maybe agreeing these with others, judging along with other individuals the merits of competing ideas, etc.[5]

f truth is not the same as the pursuit of certainty. ᷄ be had at all in management, or indeed in any ᷄es the collection of material via some kind of ᷄nal events. As a corollary of this we can say that ᷄᷄᷄ a theory *might* be wrong does not undermine its claim to ᷄aving been validly arrived at. Additionally, the possibility of error is not a specific aspect of management research, or even of applied research – it is an aspect of all knowledge of the world around us.

There are two further issues which need to be considered – firstly, the ontology of knowledge (what sorts of things are the products of research), and secondly, the range of purposes which are drivers or triggers for research activity.

What are the products of research? Research in the natural sciences produces results such as theories, laws, correlations, as well as explanations of specific events such as the extinction of the dinosaurs. There tends also to be an accretion of knowledge – one result is then taken as a given for further investigation. So results in the study of visual perception are used to help construct more in-depth accounts of the way the brain processes visual information. Theories and results about fossils interplay with those of geology, building on each other and/or refining the scope of theory.

A cursory glance at the literature of management theory yields the striking fact that whilst there are many *theories* in management there are no *laws*. Theories abound, though it is rare in the extreme for one of these to build upon the work of others.[6] Of course, in one sense this is a tribute to the good sense of management writers that they do not go off making wild generalisations about the necessary connections within so complex a subject matter.

But this absence of laws is not merely a matter of complexity. It is also a question of the context within which management knowledge exists. A law of management would have to make a statement that is expressed in completely general terms, something of the form 'All organisations of such-and-such a kind follow so-and-so a trend of behaviour.' So, for example, we could imagine a 'law' stating, say, that individuals working in small- and medium-sized enterprises (SMEs) tend to have worse employment conditions than ones working in blue-chip companies. But this is not a 'law' in the sense of, say, Ohm's Law, or even the so-called 'Iron Law of Oligarchy' advocated by Michels in sociology. It states a regularity, not a necessity. The regularity would be significantly different given the different politico-legal systems of various countries. Changes in the labour market, such as changed expectations of employees and a consequent drift away from SMEs, would also affect this connection. So the idea of a necessary link, bearing some degree of stability in the light of changes in social and economic conditions, which seems to be at the heart of the idea of a scientific law, is not present here.

Interestingly, one organisational writer *has* proposed a regularity which he explicitly compares with Michels 'Iron Law'. William Evan[7] has discussed whether the presence of hierarchy in organisations is so prevalent that it might be considered an invariant law of organisations in general. Whilst he does not come to a definite conclusion regarding this issue, he does make some claims which support the argument of Chapter 4 of this book – that cultural variables underpin management concepts to a sufficient extent that they may be regarded as the conditions under which such concepts can be applied. In other words, management theories are culturally conditioned.

Returning to the main argument, natural science describes laws which appear to be in themselves stable – the laws themselves do not change over time. Social sciences, applied or not, describe a world which changes irregularly. The very basis of the social world changes constantly – as a result of globalisation, technological improvements, population shifts, and so on. And unlike pure social sciences such as sociology, management involves not just how individuals and groups interact with this changing environment, but which tools and techniques are appropriate to a situation. So the aim of management research as a totality is not just a description or explanation of what happens in and to organisations, but also the devising and evaluation of methods and tools to help managers achieve organisational ends more effectively. What is appropriate now may be inappropriate in fifty years' time (and may have been inappropriate for the challenges of fifty years ago).

As mentioned above, whilst there are few if any laws of management, there are lots of management theories. The most important feature of this proliferation we need to note at this stage is their relative lack of evidential support – few published studies in management have very sound methodologies. It is tempting to call this an *underdetermination* of theory. But this states the point in the wrong way. It assumes that there is an appropriate level of evidential support which theories should have and that anything which has this level is in some way superior to anything which does not have it. In the second part of this chapter we shall see good reasons for stating that some theories which have no explicit supporting evidence may well be much superior to some which are very well evidenced.

There are also lots of cautiously designed studies in the field of management research, presenting neither theories nor laws but more limited results. These tend to have extremely tentative conclusions, such as 'The evidence suggests that xyz is an important factor in the way in which organisations deal with ABC problem'. Sometimes the results are presented in deliberately specific form: 'Our study demonstrated that R&D expenditure in the PQR industry was driven as much by home markets as by the need to internationalise'. In some cases the results are made quite specific – case study analysis, for example, usually makes no generalisable claims, though it may raise important general questions. Some studies do add more generalised conclusions, but not in a way which resembles the growth of knowledge which natural and pure social science presents. And the idea of an accepted necessary connection – that is, a 'law' – which subsequent writers could take as a given and use to build further knowledge is just about completely absent.

2.1.1   Critical Theory and Management Knowledge

It can be claimed that the above presents far too narrow an idea of what science or knowledge is. Jurgen Habermas has isolated three quite different kinds of enquiry, each driven by a different kind of interest, and each of which could be legitimately described as resulting in knowledge:[8]

1 *empirical-analytic sciences*: driven by the interest to predict and control phenomena, whether natural or human
2 *historical-hermeneutic*[9] *sciences*: driven by the interest of individuals and groups to explain and understand phenomena, and communicate this effectively between each other
3 *critical theory*: driven by the interest of individuals to exercise and develop their own freedom

On this view, all legitimate knowledge falls into one of these three categories. The first is concerned with developing know-how and technology to predict events and to regulate how and when they occur – for example, how better to predict the severity of the weather phenomenon known as El Nino, how to avoid major stock market crashes, etc. The second is intended to explain and facilitate communication and understanding between individuals – for example, to gain an understanding of what it feels like to be the victim of racial discrimination. Critical theory, the third and most controversial form of knowledge, is rooted in the potential of knowledge to empower individuals. Hence it involves an understanding of what underlies people's actions, concepts and beliefs, which in turn provides an emancipation from the implicit controls generated by ignorance of the conditions of thought and investigation. For example, an understanding of what underlies inter-personal conflicts at work can help people learn how to avoid them or use them to the best advantage (my example, not Habermas').

It should be recognised that Habermas' first two categories are not simply a jargonised version of the distinction between arts or humanities and natural science, but a division between subject matter which admits of a close linkage with externally collected supporting evidence (empirical-analytic sciences) and that which is not so much supported by evidence as a means of presenting and communicating evidence (historical-hermeneutic sciences). It is less, therefore the actual subject matter and more the means of investigation and style of explanation which are relevant. So some social sciences, such as experimental psychology, would fall into the empirical-analytic bracket. Other pure social science disciplines, such as social anthropology, would fall into the historico-hermeneutic.

By contrast, the critical theory category might make use of either empirical-analytic or historical-hermeneutic methods of investigation. It would add to this also what Habermas calls 'critical self reflection'. So this form of knowledge involves understanding how one's own behaviours and thoughts arise out of and are conditioned by the forms of life we lead, the types and sources of knowledge we are exposed to, and the interests – both individual and group based – which drive the creation of knowledge. Emancipation derives from a recognition of how one is involved both as a creator and a creation of a body of knowledge.

As a classification of human inquiry, this approach runs counter to the discussion of the earlier part of this section. For it raises the possibility that there might be forms of knowledge which do not retain the possibility of refutation. Empirical-analytic sciences are, roughly, what would naturally be regarded as natural science and thus would be subject to the possibility of being confounded by adverse research data. Also, what Habermas calls the historical-hermeneutic sciences require a degree of communicative interaction between individuals, which in itself involves the possibility that a communicating individual or group may check, counter or revise an idea developed by someone else.

But it is possible for just one individual, on their own and without reference to any other, to be emancipated by an idea. I may find a particular concept extremely illuminating and enlightening but be unable to communicate it to others, or when I do, others reject it. Nevertheless, this does not automatically mean that I cannot derive a sense of freedom from it, or that I am wrong to believe that I am thereby emancipated. Something may create a great deal of freedom for me and me only because of some specific features of my own history, or psychology, or spiritual state even, though it has no resonance for others, or does not meet the needs of the majority of humankind. This idea of extending one's freedom via critical knowledge and reflection fails to recognise that these can be personal and private, at least as much as they may be shared social events.

In general, the theory has as much of a political agenda as an intellectual one. Habermas and other similar writers would probably regard the fact that they have brought this aspect of social explanation to the fore as a strength of their approach. Many discussions of Habermas' ideas have focused on weaknesses such as the overlapping nature of these three senses of knowledge, or the apparent anomalous nature of critical theory compared to the other two forms of knowledge. I want to make two points, one recognising the value of such an approach, and the other critiquing it.

Firstly, the great value of critical theory for management is that it separates out three different kinds of overall impact which a piece of management research might deliver. Control, understanding and emancipation are all benefits which can be obtained from good management theory. Nevertheless, too great a reliance on one range of research methods is likely to reflect too great an emphasis being placed on one particular interest – for example, a high demand for large scale surveys which include very technical statistical analysis may reflect a misplaced expectation that management research should always facilitate our prediction and control of organisational events.

In keeping with Habermas overall conception as applied to management knowledge, it is probably the case that emancipation involves both control and understanding to be really effective. In Parts II and III of this book I intend to indicate how the discussion of research methodologies has become a form of constriction on management thinking and action. Different research philosophies become themselves tyrannies over what is accepted as legitimate knowledge about management. The consequence of this is that it is essential that management research maintain a high degree of eclecticism in its research methods. If you like, this would be an emancipatory discussion of its own. Right at the end of the book, we shall revisit Habermas' view, and we shall see that it can form the basis for a fresh approach to the questions of the nature and value of management knowledge.

The second point critiques critical theory. The idea driving Habermas' classification is that there are three basic types of human interest, and these define the three kinds of knowledge. But are there not other kinds of human interest, which themselves could define different kinds of human enquiry and knowledge? Habermas' tripartite model reads a little like one of the classical theories of motivation – for example, MacLelland's threefold division of human needs into achievement, affiliation and power.[10] As with these approaches, it over-models the phenomena it deals with: the approach is fine if it is merely intended as one convenient distinction amongst many others, but it is too restrictive if it is intended to be *the* basic categorisation of human interests.

One could imagine a number of different alternative interests which do not neatly fit into Habermas' three categories. For example, the interest in *harmony*, which can have social manifestations in terms of social cohesion and absence of conflict, individual manifestations in terms of people wanting to feel relatively at peace with themselves, and natural manifestations in terms of how the human race interacts with the rest of this planet without destroying or significantly diminishing the breadth and depth of biodiversity. So it straddles Habermas' three types of interest. Another example might be an interest in *creative expression*. This too cuts across the three Habermas categories. Maybe Habermas would say that these can be accommodated in each of his categories, but in doing so he is simply choosing to take his categories as more fundamental. There is no reason why we could not say that different aspects of the interest of control and prediction can be seen as aspects of creative or harmony seeking interests. There is nothing especially basic about Habermas' three types of interest.

The views of Habermas have been discussed at some length, but it is important to recognise that his approach has spawned a wealth of theory relating to social explanation (very little of it is directly linked with management – which has the complications of being both a *human* study and an *applied* one[11]).

This section has not delivered a specific conclusion regarding management knowledge. What it has done is evaluate some key elements of knowledge – the possibility of refutation being one central requirement. We have also looked at one of the more recent approaches to knowledge and social explanation, though that has had mixed value for the question of how valid management research is.

2.2 TRUTH AND COMPLEXITY

In this section, we shall look at what would be necessary if, management theory is to be sound, or valid and in the next we shall look at what is necessary for ideas to be useful to practising managers.

Management is a highly complex phenomenon. Just to list the key elements with which a manager works should convince of this – people (a wealth of different entire subjects in themselves), operations, finance, the multiple facets of the external environment, etc. To be successful as a manager someone inevitably deals with all of these consciously or unconsciously. So the management task implicitly or explicitly involves all of these.

To establish anything true about management, therefore, should involve a wide range of research methods, and lead to conclusions which are either expressed in very complex terms or consist of simple statements which then have to be qualified by a host of conditions relating to this or that factor. Take a fictitious example. A researcher develops a hypothesis about, say, how strategic managers perceive and respond to initiatives taken by their competitors. Consider the range of factors which could be included in the modelling of this hypothesis.

The point about Figure 2.1 is that each box itself refers to a complex cluster of phenomena. For the competitive environment and the psychological areas this should be plain enough. But mapping the internal environment of an organisation needs must include its decision-making structures, its reporting and communication systems, employee relations climate, and many other factors. Similarly, the range of factors affecting how an initiative taken by one organisation is communicated to a rival is influenced by very many factors. For example, traditions of open R&D within an industry vary widely, as does the availability and quality of industry publications.

A research study which took account of all of these would of necessity be long and multi-disciplinary. If it were to yield general conclusions then these would have to take account of many of the factors alluded to above. To the extent to which a study does not do this it

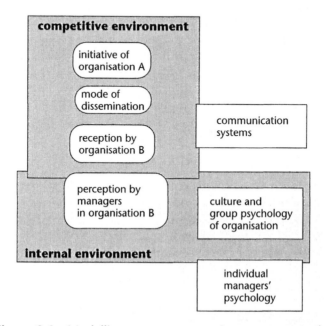

Figure 2.1   Modelling a management issue – an example.

becomes progressively more and more restricted in scope. So a result in management research is pulled in two directions – towards the complexity necessary to reflect the general business context, or to the narrowness which reflects the specific context in which research was carried out.

In practice researchers are rarely allocated the time, finance or human resources which would allow them to explore the issue in both directions. So in general researchers would see what they do as involving some kind of cutting of corners – taking greater account of the broad context at the expense of the more narrowly defined issue, or vice versa. But this does not avoid the point made above. However large the resource available there is a conflict between the volume of material necessary to reflect the wider context within which the research question is framed, and the compression necessary to focus attention on the key issue in which the researcher is interested. This is not a feature of the kinds of question being studied. It arises out of the psychology of attention – humans just cannot deal with much detail, they have to abstract or simplify.

There are two ways in which the conflict between context and hypothesis can be handled, but each has its difficulties. One option is to create a range of *contextual hypotheses*.[12] Thus the transferability of a result in management can be mapped out by making hypotheses about the similarity of one context to another. Suppose I start with an idea which may have been developed and tested, for example, with publishing houses in the US. I now want to apply this idea to the Italian clothing industry. So I need to make some justified hypotheses concerning the different dimensions in which these two industries and national economies may be similar or different. In all likelihood, the two industries are relatively similar in some respects, less similar in others. For each dimension considered, a probabilistic assessment can be made – that is, a statement that probably the two industries are sufficiently similar for the transfer to be made, or that they are probably too different. The totality of these provides an overall indication, and an overall qualifier, as to how far the analogy may be made between the two industrial contexts.

Of course, such hypotheses are only as good as the rationale behind them. The rationale for making such an assessment at all is based on a model of business as a whole, and of those businesses in particular, and so will only be as good as that model. In addition, though, there are several points where the analogy may fail, despite the best efforts of those who formulate such contextual hypotheses:

- the range of dimensions on which the issue of difference or similarity is judged may be too narrow

- the multiplicative effect of probabilities in the various dimensions progressively diminishes the degree of reliance that can be placed on their totality
- current knowledge may be inadequate to provide appropriate modelling of the situation
- there may be unseen factors which have contributed to an appearance of similarity
- the similarities may be changing, unbeknown to the researchers

These may look like incidental flaws – the kind that could be expected of any research stratagem. But there is more to them than simply the perennial possibility that we can get things wrong. It is that there is a weakness in the logic of how a contextualising hypothesis may be used. When a management idea is tested, this happens within a specific context, and hence the results may shed a light on: (a) the idea focused on; or (b) the contextual hypotheses employed; or (c) the way that the idea is being contextualised. So it is unclear what needs to be revised if we get an adverse result – is it the concept, is it a hypothesis, or is it the way the contextual hypotheses have been used with respect to the subject matter of the research?

So the idea of a contextual hypothesis, whilst often useful in practice, does not provide an unambiguous method for dealing with the complexity inherent in management research.

The other approach is to concentrate the research focus on producing closely defined industry or even organisation specific results. In effect this is to concede that the complexity issue cannot be eliminated, and to decide to work within it. Now if this is the approach to be adopted – and many management research studies seem to do so – then it is clear that it can reduce the *degree* of complexity involved in the research effort. But does it reduce the *scale*? We still have the multiple internal factors, and we still have to have some perspective on the external business environment – dealing with this is part of the management task, after all. No doubt the latter requires a much smaller amount of consideration, because here it only figures in terms of how a small set of individuals acted in the light of their perception of the external environment, but a shadow of the issue still remains.

But there is a more important problem here which, strangely enough, bears a close analogy with the problems faced by the idea of contextualising hypotheses. A research project which stays narrowly focused on one organisation, like a case study, for example, may well reduce the chance that its general results are disconfirmed by external evidence (on the basis that if it refers to fewer companies, then there are fewer companies which might conflict with its claims). But any conclusions of such a study which go beyond the merely descriptive themselves implicitly make assumptions, for example, about the typicality of the organisation and its processes. These assumptions implicitly include the very generality which this approach attempts to avert.

A case study which makes attributions that some event x happened, and as a result some other event y occurred, is in effect stating that event x *caused* event y, at least in the context of a specific organisation. And in doing so, the case is making a presumption that other factors were *not* the cause. In one sense this is obvious, but it raises two important issues. Firstly, this presumption involves an implicit attribution of laws – assumed necessary connections which imply that it is reasonable to conclude that a given set of factors will cause or bring about an event. These are the very things that we saw were not too prevalent in the management research sphere – so in management research we implicitly use ideas of which we have little systematic evidence. Secondly, the multi-dimensionality of organisations means that some interaction with other factors is *the very mechanism* by which a given cause can achieve its effect. For example, if the conclusion of a case study is that the leadership style of the manager led to a deterioration in employee satisfaction, then it is not just that it *happens* that various other factors were involved (for example, communication systems, external competitive pressures) – it is that without these there would be no linkage at all. These other factors are the medium through which a causal connection operates. If they are not there, then neither is the connection. There is no leadership style without it being relayed through communication systems. There is no direction to lead if there is no business environment. These are not incidental to the process of leading, they are how leadership is enacted.

Where such factors are not explicitly described, they are being assumed – and the usual assumption is that they are typical for the industry or type of organisation. In our example, if a key factor is not described or discussed, say the financial condition of the company, then the presumption is that this factor was operating 'in its usual way' for that kind of organisation, or maybe that it was non-existent. These may well be fair assumptions to make on occasion, but they are *assumed laws* – the absence of explicit reference to them should not be mistaken for their non-existence. So the attempt to restrict the scope of a research study does not eliminate the need to take such assumptions into account when drawing conclusions.

What this discussion shows is that although researchers may attempt to avoid being drawn into the complexity inherent in management concepts by researching on a narrow front they *cannot avoid* it. *Any* level of explanation necessarily involves reference to general laws and principles – even though these may be left as implicit assumptions they are still part of the overall package which is subject to empirical test.

Clearly, someone might try to go even further, and be entirely descriptive in their case study, making no statements at all about causal connections. One problem here is that it could well end up as a pretty vapid kind of study, but more importantly, even this will not do. *Description is itself loaded with covert explanation.* To identify a statement made by a manager as an expression of corporate strategic policy, for example, looks like a simple description of the kind of communication they made, but implicitly there is a range of linkages with other factors such as the strategic decision-making process, change management, etc. To call it instead a memo from the MD creates different links – for example, with corporate communications systems, employee relations practices, etc. To describe something is also to partially offer some explanatory links. So the common idea that social scientific research can be divided into descriptive and explanatory is fine as a working rule, but ultimately false in principle.[13] This issue is explored again in greater depth when we come to consider approaches to research such as the concept of 'grounded' theory.[14]

Restricting the scope of a study, therefore, does not take away the issue of complexity. So we are left with the problem of how a management researcher can successfully deal with this and produce conclusions which truthfully sum up the range of factors involved in their study. Ultimately a researcher 'solves' the problems we have discussed above by making a choice as to what will be focused on and what will not. In doing so they choose what kind of approximation is being made of reality by their research. In other words there is no mechanical process by which a researcher can divide the range of possible factors into those which will be taken within the research study and those which will be excluded.

The reader might think this is nothing special. In essence this also happens in the purest forms of natural science. Assumptions have to be made about equipment, experimental conditions, and so on. But the key difference with management research is not in the *quantity* of assumptions which have to be made, though that is significant in itself (for example, a study of the sources of staff conflict in an organisation involves a higher level and quantity of variables than the observation of bacteria in a petri dish). It is that the nature of the assumptions is different.

To test a theory in natural science, it is a reasonable assumption that unless there is some evidence to suggest that something is in a state of change it may be assumed to be static. Suppose I am studying the dispersion of certain infectious illnesses through a certain population. I will assume that the general level of health (other than the infection being studied) in that population is more or less what it has been in the recent past. I will only question this if, for example, I have heard of research which suggests that this population's health is in the process of changing.

But this kind of presumption is triply more open to challenge in the case of an applied social study. Firstly, the key elements are much wider in number and, in the case of research involving people, a far wider range of values can be taken by each component variable. Secondly, simply because of this greater complexity the phenomena are much more sensitive to minor changes in their environment. A minor nuance in the way a message is communicated can change its interpretation from being accepted as a reasonable request from management to being a duplicitous attempt at fooling the workforce. Complexity theory reigns supreme in human studies. But thirdly, the interaction between theory and subject inherent in all human studies means that researchers themselves undermine the stability of the phenomena they attempt to study, both in terms of their research activities and in terms of the fact that the aim of much management research is to help enhance people's practices.

In this section, then, we have looked at some problems of generating true conclusions for so complex a field as management. Some of the problems are not specific to management – they crop up with other applied studies, and even in some so-called pure disciplines. But the main point to note is that whilst the problems of a complex environment are not unknown to researchers in this field, it is rare to see these reflected in the way that much management research is presented to the academic community (still less the public). Research *designs* are developed at least sometimes with this complexity in mind, but research *reports* rarely reflect it. In effect, every conclusion of a research study should be prefaced by a list of qualificatory assumptions about the context. The tendency for researchers to provide cautious conclusions such as 'the study suggests that...' is laudable in spirit, but self-defeating in practice, because there is no explicit explanation for the level of caution displayed by the researcher. It is essentially incomplete.[15]

So the truth of management research is complex – usually far more so than can practically be reflected in the research activity itself.

2.3   UTILITY AND VALIDITY

We have seen some of the difficulties which the issue of complexity raises for the truth of management research. Though in practice many studies abstract away from that complexity, they do so at the expense of the validity of their work. The simpler the result the less true it is in any unqualified sense.

In this section we shall look at the idea of what makes a theory or result in management *useful*. This idea will be explored in more detail in Parts II and III.

As we saw earlier in this chapter, one of the merits of the approach of Jurgen Habermas is to recognise that research can address a number of interests. It is not necessarily the case that every item of research must address all interests. A piece may be very helpful from the point of view of predicting and controlling events, but not easily communicable (perhaps because of its own complexity). Similarly, an approach might be illuminating without yielding easily testable predictions. Freudian analysis, for example, is often cited as being an easily communicable and highly illuminating theory which has not succeeded in yielding generally accepted predictions about behaviour. As Michel Foucault has said, it is a theoretical framework which has created a discourse (or as he calls it a 'discursivity') which goes beyond the truth or falsity of its claims.[16]

So to talk of a piece of management research as having some utility is not to identify a single dimension and say that the research is above a certain threshold on this one dimension. It is rather to indicate that it is above a certain threshold in *some* direction.

What kinds of interest or need may be met by a piece of management research? This question is probably best answered by conducting a brief review of those agencies and parties which have an influence on management research and knowledge (Figure 2.2).

This is a wider frame than the one presented by one of the leading texts on management research – that of Easterby-Smith, Thorpe and Lowe.[17] They see the research arena as affected by two main groups – academic community and commercial sponsor, with a further influence provided by 'the subject itself'. In practice, however, the examples they give of the last are further influences driven by academic researchers. Although these writers are clearly aware of the wider social and governmental influences on management research they do not present them within this framework.

In any case, Easterby-Smith, Thorpe and Lowe call their approach a stakeholder analysis, which is misleading. Stakeholders do not necessarily have significant power to influence what happens. They have an interest or a stake in what happens, *whether or not* they can exercise any strong influence on events. Hence a mapping of stakeholders, in the full sense of that term, would have to include groups which in themselves are relatively powerless to influence the course of the research, such as employees, individual retail customers, individual

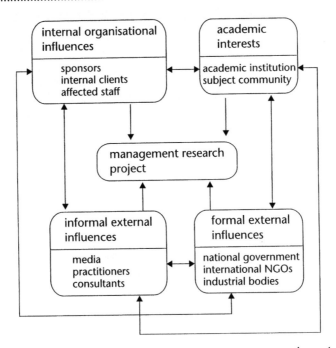

Figure 2.2   Key influences on a management research project.

members of the local community or local economy, and independent users of the products of the research (for example, managers working in other organisations, business and management students who subsequently read reports of the research). All of these have an interest in what the research questions are, how the research is conducted, what the proximate results are, and/or what kinds of professional action will be taken by organisations as a response to the results.

But note that I said these groups are *relatively* powerless. Their interests and needs are often presumed by other influences, especially by media and politicians and sometimes also by industry bodies and organisational sponsors. So it is not that their interests are not addressed at all, but that these are subsumed, for better or worse, in the needs and interests that other influences have.

Generally, the groups identified in Figure 2.2 are likely to have an influence on at least the following areas of the research:

- the choice of subject area
- the specific form of the research question
- the kind of data collected
- the style of the conclusions drawn
- the style and forum for dissemination of the research

There is much to be said regarding each of these areas, but for the present purpose, the last of these is the most relevant. Different interest groups have different expectations of what the results of management research will achieve. Clearly, an academic subject community will expect to see research which is related to current academic interests. Material which is too innovatory simply finds no handle to enter the intellectual debate. On the other hand, the media are more responsive to their perception of what their public is interested in. So newspaper reports of research, naturally enough designed to help sell papers, will focus on research with striking, curious or controversial conclusions. Published books represent a much more segmented market, though recent years have shown signs of a desegmentation. The volume end of this market tends to cater for the needs of professional practitioners. Hence, just as practising managers tend to be solution driven, so too the books on management that they buy often are solution driven. So research based material which is incorporated into such texts needs to have clear, definitive solutions – inconclusive research tends not to be much publishable anyway.

So where does this leave the point about utility? One key point to draw is that there is no single sense of utility which predominates. The immediate temptation is to presume that how far a piece of research addresses the needs of professional managers and organisational sponsors should provide the litmus test of management research – if the people who actually have to put something into practice don't think much of it then it must be defective to an extent. But: (a) professionals are hidebound by their own prejudices, just like the rest of us, and therefore cannot be taken as a simple authoritative touchstone on issues such as industry relevance; and (b) research is often seen as a means of *changing* the views and perspectives of its audience, rather than reinforcing them. Remember also the point of Chapter 1 – managers create theory, to an extent, so they are not simple touchstones, they have their own theoretical pre-suppositions and prejudices, as much as academics have.

The point of the last paragraph is perhaps stronger when talking of so-called 'pure' disinterested research when the interests and needs of an audience are generally regarded as secondary to the desire of the researcher to discover something new, to '...force the lock, batter down the door, outface, defy, disprove the oracle' to use Lawrence Durrel's somewhat heroic language.[18] But nevertheless, there is still some truth in it for applied research as well. If management research never uncovered anything which challenged our current preconceptions every company would still be based on models such as that of the Roman Army (or even earlier forms of organisation). The difference perhaps is in the contact which the management researcher needs to

establish between their work and the needs and concerns of practitioners. A pure researcher need only consider the needs of one of their
key influences to establish their ideas – the community of their
academic peers. Management research has to take account of how
their work relates to practice (which is quite different from only
researching subjects which have a clearly foreseeable practical
application).

But this suggests that there is a clear agreed sense of what is relevant to practice. In fact it is not that simple. Go back to the metaphor
of the mountain. I see it from above, and miss the details at the
bottom. Someone else sees it from the bottom, and cannot see the
top. Clearly there is no one perspective from which we can say – this
is the *real* view of the mountain. It goes beyond this, however. There
are some perspectives from which you can get a full description of the
mountain. You could,[19] for example, have a complete description of
the mountain in physical terms – a long list of statements about the
mountain's components, say, particles, strata, rock formations, etc.
Someone could regard this as the 'real' account of the mountain, and
the other perspectives – from the top, from the bottom – are simply
incomplete versions of this. But the key point is that this kind of
account does not represent a picture of the mountain at all. It is of
value if you are a geologist, or someone wanting to work out the
magnetic pull of the mountain. But it is not of itself any use if you
want to know the easiest way to climb the mountain, still less if the
mountain will be a pleasant sight for a group of stressed executives
wanting a restful weekend away, or if it is a worthy subject for a
painter. 'What's the best way to see or to get to know the mountain?'
therefore, is a question which is defined in terms of people's interests
and intentions. *Knowledge is in part defined in terms of our purposes.*

Utility for the practitioner is after all a central requirement, but that
it needs to be recognised as not a single idea – useful for whom, and
for what purpose? Additionally, utility has its own limitations: other
requirements of management research are not automatically determined by the practicality test.

So the original statement of my argument at the start of this
chapter is only partially true. Truth about management, that complex
phenomenon discussed in the earlier part of the chapter, is therefore
not *necessarily* in conflict with the utility which some interest groups
seek in the results of management research. But it remains the case
that there is a conflict with the prime user group – managers, practitioners, and professionals. For these consumers of the results of
management research, it is certainly the case that they require simple
ideas, expressed in a manner which wears its applicability on its face.
Without this, they cannot be used. Research based material which

reflects the underlying complexity of the issue accurately is likely to be so detailed as to be cumbersome, and to blur a clear understanding of the relationship between theory and context.

We shall come back to what practising managers are looking for, and how they incorporate management research into their practice, in Parts II and III.

SUMMARY

In this chapter, we have looked at the two central criteria by which management research is judged – truth and usefulness. It is clear that truth is hardly accessible in this area. When it is, it is either overly approximated or too heavily conditioned by the contextual elements of the research to be very clear. Utility is multi-faceted – depending on the needs and perceptions of a variety of interest groups, but nevertheless, if practising managers are taken as a central party, then it is clear that their needs, to put ideas into direct practice to solve problems, work against the complexity of accurate, truthful, research material. Knowledge is best understood as being not so much an independent picture of reality so much as an interaction between the needs and purposes of individuals and that reality.

In Chapters 3 and 4 we shall look at two key factors which can provide a major limitation on the idea of management research as providing generalisable knowledge – culture and ideology.

NOTES

1 Which is not to say that it is necessarily subjective.
2 'Scientific' is itself a controversial term, as we shall see in Part II. As a working definition I mean here the systematic collection of information from the observable world from which may be inferred knowledge – here, then, the term includes social as well as natural science.
3 Arguably we are in a similar period of crisis in physics at the present, with standard presumptions about mass, gravitation and other related issues being challenged by the apparent evidence that a huge proportion of the mass of the universe is not directly visible.
4 Though in itself this rejection did not *directly* lead to the formulation of Darwin's theory of natural selection.

5 We shall discuss Popper in more detail in Part II, but the interested reader is referred to Lakatos for a good account of Popper's ideas.

6 A refreshing exception is the cluster of ideas which David Kolb and Peter Honey have developed out of the work of the great pioneer of applied psychology, Kurt Lewin: both of these have built their views on learning up on the foundations provided by Lewin.

7 Evan (1993) Chapter 1.

8 Habermas (1972).

9 We shall discuss the idea of hermeneutics in detail in Chapter 6. For the moment, the reader unfamiliar with the term should construe it as the way we come to an interpretation of concepts because of how they fit in with the rest of what we believe (individually or collectively).

10 McClelland (1961).

11 Though the two best short introductions to management research both have useful, if brief, discussions. See Easterby-Smith et al. (1994) and Gill and Johnson (1991).

12 A modern parallel with what used to be called induction by analogy (see Keynes (1921) for an account of the latter). I have benefited greatly from discussions with a colleague, Tony Emerson, in my understanding of contextual hypotheses.

13 Cf. Hart (1998) where he divides social research into exploratory, descriptive and explanatory. He talks (p. 47) of the first two of these categories as both involving the how or what of a phenomenon, without recognising that the answer to a how question cannot but involve an account which links in with general laws and principles, for without these there could be no explanation at all.

14 See Part II, though as a preliminary, a very clear account of grounded theory can be found in Bloor (1976).

15 Add to this that when the conclusions of research studies are made public, the degree of epistemic caution expressed by researchers tends to be thrown to the winds by the demands of media reporting, which of necessity focus on the most striking types of result, without any of the conditionality which surrounds them – for there is no soundbite to be had in the enumeration of the potential drawbacks of a theory, only in its excitement value.

16 Foucault (1969).

17 Easterby-Smith et al. (1994).

18 Durrel 'Clea'.

19 This is a thought experiment, hence its somewhat far fetched nature.

Chapter 3

Distortion and Bias

The first two chapters have set out the bones of an argument concerning the extent and kinds of value which can be expected from management research. In general the conclusions so far have been largely negative – management research does not measure up very well to the canons of pure scientific research, and in the absence of these there is a serious question as to what level of validity can be expected at all. This is neither a new nor a particularly startling view in itself, but it is set out here as the necessary backdrop to ascertaining what can be said about the merits of management research.

In this chapter we shall look more closely at the way in which different interest groups can influence the progress of a management research project. What we shall see is that at each step there are distorting mechanisms.

One preliminary point is the question of management theory as *ideology*. This presents management concepts as specifically tools of one particular cluster of interest groups – basically an owning/ruling social class and a subordinate managerial class which does the former's biding. The idea that management ideas carry a surreptitious political agenda, inclining managers and workers alike to perceive their relationship in terms which ultimately benefit the interests of managers and owners, is attractive but can only be substantiated to a limited degree. The word has a quasi-Marxist ring which suggests the *deliberate* acts of a group (class) who make choices specifically to foster their own interests as a group.[1] In other words, this version of the ideology argument would hold that a particular class in society deliberately defines and controls management knowledge in such a way that their own interests are thereby enhanced and their control over others is also increased. As Clegg and Dunkerley put it '... the most important aspect ... of management education, generally, is ... [its] role in reproducing ideology.'[2]

Sympathetic though I feel to this view, my argument below does not substantiate it. Rather the view is more that groups and individuals make atomised choices which collectively create a bias in management knowledge independently of the conscious intentions or interests of any specific group, though in fact the bias tends to create a solution orientation to management writing which only superficially benefits the managerial class itself.

This argument relates specifically to the radical conception of ideology. Furusten, in his very original discussion of the impact of popular management books, regards ideology as any presentation of one set of concepts as a vehicle for projecting a hidden further set of ideas.[3] This is a broader idea, and while the argument of this chapter is highly relevant to this approach, the point made above relates primarily to the idea that management ideas are a way of the political right smuggling in covert establishment-partial ideas under a smokescreen of apparently universal ideas such as leadership, division of labour, etc.

Let us return to the model of influences on management research discussed in the previous chapter – the four key categories of influencing agents (academic community, corporate sponsors, formal external bodies such as governments and NGOs, and less formal external factors such as communications media). We shall start with an indication of some of the likely sources and reasons for bias for the different categories of interest group. By far the largest group of issues affects the academic researcher him- or herself.

3.1 ACADEMIC BIAS

At first sight this seems the obvious location of bias, for these are the people carrying out the research (note that this category includes not just professional academics and their research assistants, but also individuals following academic courses and development programmes and required thereby to conduct research into management). The prime potential source of bias in this category is the traditional image of an individual having already made up their mind about the conclusion they are expecting. In one sense this is only human, in another it is distortion (when the expectation interferes with the way that data is collected or analysed).

This sort of bias is well known and there are many ways it can be contained. More important is the bias which has pre-dated the specific research question being formulated. This may be content related or methodological in nature. We shall look at the content related bias a little later.

3.1.1 Methodological Bias

Central to the idea of methodological bias is the concept of a research *stance*. By this is meant the tendency for each individual to be more easily persuaded by one kind of research than another. Specifically, the traditional polarisation here has been between so-called 'hard' and 'soft' data. People are often depicted as being more comfortable *either* dealing with material which is numerical, explicitly structured, quantified or easy to convert to quantification, *or* with material which reflects the essentially personal nature of management. In the former case, large quantities of statistically analysed data are the type, if not the norm, whilst in the latter the ideal is in-depth personally generated material, interpreted sympathetically by the researcher. One could perhaps over-simplify this difference as being between left-brain and right-brain styles respectively.

Gill and Johnson, as a clear and instructive example of how this kind of bias is handled, provide a quick questionnaire for their readers (bearing in mind that their book is essentially a piece of instruction in research methods rather than an analysis of these), intended as a way of focusing their readership on the issue. They take a consciously eclectic approach to management research, describing it as 'methodological pluralism'.[4] Individuals complete the questionnaire as a means of recognising their preferred approach to research. As was mentioned in the introduction to the book, an easy conclusion to draw from this (despite the author's laudable intentions) is that there is an element of *style* or *choice* here.

As an advice to the intending management researcher, especially those on accredited management development courses, this approach has its heuristic points. But the uncritical reader is apt to draw the false conclusion that this is *all* a matter of style.[5] If this were the case, then what is to be made of different research studies applied to the same phenomena but using different approaches? If this is just a matter of style, then that suggests that different approaches are of equal value – so studies using different approaches, and leading to different results would still be of equal validity (presuming that they had both been conducted appropriately).

Compare one study which collects hard data with another which involves so-called soft data. The point is not that the results are just going to be *different*, though it would be surprising if these two approaches produced the same *kind* of result. It is rather that they arrive at their conclusions in so different a manner that it is difficult to see how they can be compared at all. 'Style' therefore, seems to mispresent this variation. It is not a question about what someone characteristically chooses – now hard data, now soft. It is more a matter of what picture can be built up out of the material collected.

3.1.2 Triangulation

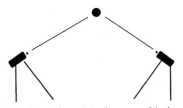

triangulation – the original geographical meaning
two or more exact parallel observations are
combined to allow a calculation of position

Suppose two studies of the same phenomenon are both well conducted according to the canons of their respective methodologies, and yet conflict in their results – what is to be said? Neither has any obvious superiority in their claim to being true (except maybe to people who are instinctively pre-disposed in favour of one approach over another). The disparity adds nothing to either study – it cannot even be the case that doubt is cast on one by another, for there is no guarantee that *either* is false.[6] It is just that neither supports the other. In the unlikely event of *three* or more sources of triangulation being used there is the possibility that two studies agree and one conflicts. As we shall see below, the concurrence of two or more studies is not in itself a certain indication that the two must be closer to the truth than the one, but where there is this majority verdict the question which must be raised is – how come one study was wrong?

the modern meaning
different *kinds* of evidence are put together

In simplistic terms (in order to focus the issues more sharply) one might say that if two studies indicated one result and one indicated another, then one is only 33.3% probable and the other two are jointly 66.6% probable.[7] 'Jointly' is a nice term here. It is certainly not the case that this means that one can simply add the probabilities, for that would suggest that each study has just a 33.3% probability – which would imply that each study *on its own* is no better than either of the other two, whilst what is being claimed here is that the fact that two studies concur gives *each of them* a greater likelihood than the one which is out of step. The analogy of *a priori*, mathematical, probability (of the kind which deals with cases such as three balls, two green and one red) breaks down at this point, which is exactly where it gets problematic. What kind of confidence do we have, that because two studies indicate one thing, then that is more likely than the single study suggesting the opposite?

Clearly if by some accident the studies all came to the same conclusion there would be a great temptation to say that this was well grounded – this is supposedly what 'triangulation' is all about. But notice that in the previous sentence I used the phrase 'by accident'. As mentioned earlier, it is natural in social research to presume that different methods will produce different results, so as a safety measure triangulation has a low presumed probability of success – the likelihood is greater that different approaches will produce different results. So as a measure of determining validity, triangulation is an odd step to take – given that it is more likely to lead to disconfirmatory results than confirmatory ones.[8] This contrasts with the original source of the idea of triangulation, geography, where the use of two vantage points provides compatible data which can successfully be combined. It is not in that context a check but more of an observational device in its own right. But more important than the doubtful progeny of the concept, *it is not at all clear how studies with radically different methodologies could arrive at the same kind of result at all*. And if the kinds of outcome of studies using radically different methodologies are themselves radically different from each other, then there is no virtue in trying to combine them to generate some kind of 'weight of evidence' argument. For the combination would not be coherent. The following subsection will elaborate this argument.

Before turning to that, however, it is worth noting another aspect of the idea of triangulation. There is a further presumption that because some different perspective has been taken, then that automatically generates a viable form of triangulation. But in the original meaning of triangulation, *there are good and bad triangles*.[9] A triangle which is too acute, or too obtuse, is not much use for geographical triangulation. Extending the point behind this analogy, we could say that the sheer fact of two separate methodologies being used is not sufficient to provide the additive support it is hoped for (even if all other doubts were dispelled) – there must be a suitable fit between them.

3.1.3 Content Bias

A large amount of researcher interpretation is needed to establish that for example, a set of in-depth interviews or a cognitive mapping exercise is saying just the same thing as a large set of statistically analysed data obtained from a highly structured questionnaire. In the field of management there is a significant and crucial gap between the precision necessary to establish results clearly and the flexibility of the language used commonly in day-to-day organisational interactions. Management researchers tend to bridge this gap unconsciously, but in doing so they reintroduce the very kinds of bias that their chosen methods are designed to exclude.

Suppose we are researching a subject such as, say, managers' reactions to disasters and emergencies. A hypothesis may be formulated on the basis of prior research – say that the effectiveness of disaster management is more dependent on the degree to which staff have internalised the appropriate procedures via training than on the design of the procedures themselves.[10] One study collects highly personal, eye-witness style accounts of what managers felt when placed in disaster situations, comparing cases where a disaster was well handled or even averted, another carries out a controlled simulation of disaster or near disaster situations and observes behaviour, and maybe a third sends a structured questionnaire to a large number of respondents involved in disasters or near disasters and asks about procedures, training, and similar matters.

Let us suppose that each of these is as well constructed and administered in itself as it can be (so there were no overtly or wilfully leading

65

interviews, the simulation was fairly designed to allow positive as well as negative outcomes, and the questionnaire was well designed). Clearly this would be an exceptionally well triangulated piece of work – it is not usual for a study to make use of more than two sets of data as sources of triangulation. What kind of result is established by each of these approaches? For the first, we hear about what people felt, what they believed about procedures, what training had sunk in with them, what they expected others to do and similar issues – personal views which themselves need to be closely compared to see where there are trends or patterns. The second will give us a clearly defined set of events carried out in a safe (that is, non-real) situation, and will draw inferences about what would happen in a real life situation, whilst the third will present actual correlations between events and independently identifiable issues such as presence or absence of explicit procedures, training events (and some formal evaluation of these), etc.

The nearest equivalent to having three studies indicating the same thing might be, for example: (a) where the first study ended up with a number of interviewees saying that they felt that their training had helped them cope with the emergencies; (b) where the second had a close correlation between training prior to experiencing the simulation and performance against some separately defined target behaviour; and (c) where the third indicated some large scale pattern of coincidence of training activities and specific disaster outcomes.

The difficulty of establishing that these are three different studies which demonstrate the same connection is best revealed in the contrast between the data which is collected and the significance which is then placed upon it. The simulation provides a clear, pure, linkage – these events happened in this order. Simply because of that purity it is difficult to set up a clear relationship with managerial reality. The real world is awkward, gritty in places, fuzzy in others.

The grittiness: disasters don't happen in an event free universe, they happen when I'm settling in for the night reading a book, or when the critical negotiation over the annual pay round with the unions is in its most difficult phase. Good simulation will cover the simple surprise factor, but it cannot replicate the entirety of what is running through a manager's mind each and every day.

The fuzziness: training does not always come in nice neat packages; one person goes on a course and learns nothing, another talks to a more experienced colleague and learns a whole lot (and vice versa). The specific events used in a simulation as 'training' fit incompletely with what is done in the actual business world.

A similar point can be made about the questionnaire based survey – 'training' is such a broad term, and covers such a wide range of activities and outcomes, that it is not at all clear that the extent of what is done in an organisation can be satisfactorily captured in a short set of questions. Not only learning activity, but also learning outcomes would need to be explored in some detail. This is not an impossibility, but unless it is done in detail one cannot even start to suggest that the survey has established the same result as the simulation. *Separating out the key factors from a carpet of possible causal elements is itself a critical methodological choice.* As Julienne Ford says '...the methods and techniques of science are devices for making decisions about truth.'[11]

A high level of detail *can* be covered in in-depth interviewing, on the other hand. Someone can recollect what they learned and how they did or did not put it into practice during an emergency. Of course, they may have only a limited degree of insight into their own learning, so that they fail to appreciate the contribution of their own latent understanding to their performance. And equally they may have an imperfect view of the learning processes which the organisation puts in place to deal with this aspect of their operations. But more important than this is the fact that, in guiding an interviewee who strays off the point back to the required subject, the interviewer, in this kind of case at least, *cannot but reveal what they are looking for.* The image of a sensitive interviewer as being able to eliminate researcher bias is a myth.

An interviewee who is asked about training might give the required kind of answer, but equally they might go off on what (for the interviewer) is a tangent – they might for example start talking about how far the organisation fulfills legal requirements for training, or about the different kinds of training activities which are used and whether these are in-house or out-house, etc. The interviewer has to bring the respondent back to the area of inquiry, and *in doing so, they will be unable to conceal entirely their intentions.* It is all to easy for an interviewer to believe that because they have: (a) avoided any loaded language; and (b) not made any gross emphases of voice then they have therefore eliminated the possibility of bias creeping into the interview. In fact, though, what has happened is that bias has been made subliminal, and therefore all the more difficult to spot.

Reflect back on the basics of non-verbal communication. A huge amount of the communication between individuals is not in verbal form. A large amount of the non-verbal is under some degree of our control – so we can satisfactorily dissemble, lie, deceive, pretend, and so on (we may be doing this unconsciously). Even more telling is the consequence of this – there is a wide range of subtleties which we pick up on in the interpretation of people's communicative behaviour. The difference between a convincing actress and an unconvincing one is for all practical purposes ineffable – one just is convincing and the other not. Similarly the difference between people's self presentation and credibility when cross examined in a courtroom is microscopic – impossible to be tracked with any degree of control.[12]

Ann Oakley, writing from a feminist perspective, has argued strongly that the classical interview is strongly conditioned by male–female power relationships and the ways in which these have been institution-alised in forms of research.[13] Karl Rogers, the doyen of non-directive interactions, has also talked about the impossibility of eliminating one's own feelings about a client, and about how it is inappropriate to try to do so.

It is also impossible to eliminate one's attention and pre-conceptions about a certain subject of enquiry, and self-defeating to try to do so, because the respondent will form their own views (well or badly founded) about the subject matter and build speculative hypotheses on top of these, for right or wrong. Amongst those will be a presump-tion that the researcher has some view about the subject. A respondent will therefore react to subtle elements of the researcher's behaviour and take these as cues indicating the researcher's views – true or not.

Content bias is not the attempt to impress a certain belief in an individual's mind. Rather it is that we cannot avoid subtly influen-cing the respondent to have the same view about the link between a term (for example, 'training') and the concrete way it might get actual-ised in the real world. In other words, the fact that certain individuals in an interview discussed their training and its contribution to their performance in an emergency or disaster situation may be as much a consequence of the interviewer imposing their interpretation of the term on the conversation as it is that the individual construed the issue under investigation in a certain way. It is one step before the specific result.

Arguably, this is an example of how most of the key methodological problems occur before anything really methodological is considered.

The point about this discussion is not that there are many areas where studies can be faulty, though this is one obvious conclusion. It is rather that the attempt to adduce more evidence, even of a different form, does not by itself create a greater level of likelihood for the phenomenon in question. For if the evidence has been collected in certain ways then one may doubt whether they represent the same phenomenon at all. Bias intrudes, not simply in the construction of results, but in the formulation of methodology and the influence this has on the conduct of the research.

3.2   VOLUMES OF EVIDENCE

I can imagine the following objection: 'Surely it is obvious that if we have lots of evidence which indicates a certain phenomenon, then we can have *some* confidence that somehow that evidence is on the right track? Even if there is a small amount of evidence pointing in the wrong way it is natural and rational to accept the pre-ponderance of evidence pointing in a certain direction. No researcher ever claims 100% certainty. And it is well known that no method of collecting social data is foolproof – all your argument shows is that there are possibilities of error, some of which look pretty remote. If the terms of the research have been clearly and fairly unambiguously defined then it is reasonable to acknowledge some degree of correlation as a legitimate guide to what is the reality.'

There are two points here. One is the suggestion that since the flaws in social research methods are well known, then they do not matter; people have been using them and generating results for decades so why are we fussing now? The main reason is that the problems and weaknesses in those methods mean not that researchers should stop using them, but that they should try to get an idea of what is established by the use of these methods. What do we mean when we say that a study has shown this or that? How true *is it*, or *could it* be? That is the key question, and decades of use of social research methods does not change it. So what if our imagined protagonist supposes that many researchers have not been worried about it in the past – that makes it OK?

The second is the more important point that in practice people *are* convinced by large aggregations of evidence, even if there might be flaws at the periphery, because the presumption is that there is something there after all. There are two rejoinders to this. Firstly, there is the practical point that in fact we are not talking about small digressions from perfect correlation but in many cases correlations which are as low as 0.3. There must be a serious question as to the legitimacy of such linkages (where 1 is a perfect positive correlation, and 0 represents a completely random correlation).

The second, more principled point, is that what has been argued above is not that there is the 'standard' level of uncertainty, to be expected of field results ('standard' because the world is simply not a perfectly certain place), but that this uncertainty can be found in the structure of the methodology used – in the way it is planned that results obtained by means of different research methods will be compared and combined, and in the very operationalising of key management terms. The key point is that the establishment of a phenomenon which is described in the ordinary language of everyday life, such as 'training' is too gross to be simply reflected in the precision of well designed research instruments. Defining the relevant concepts in operational terms is often presented on an analogy with cleaning the windows – we clear away some of the less relevant aspects in order to see clearly what we mean by a term such as 'training'. But in reality this is not refining the concept – it is *redefining* it. Change some elements of an idea and you change the idea.

The volume of material collected is only partially relevant to the validity of a study. If I have a glass of stagnant water there is no advantage about collecting a bucketful of it – it's still undrinkable. A single glass of clean water represents a drink – the other water does not, however much of it there is. A large quantity of flawed material is not a large amount of evidence – it is just a bunch of irrelevant material. A small collection of well researched material is therefore much more valuable.

The divergence between the precise data collected and the concrete – and rather rough – phenomenon reflected in ordinary discourse has to be bridged by taking quite large methodological decisions. It is notable that the natural sciences have progressively moved away from such ordinary terms as 'heap', 'green', or 'cold' and replaced these with more precise terms. In the case of social science, especially of an all embracing applied social science such as management, it is difficult to see how this can be done in such a way as to allow the pure perceptions of ordinary managers to play a central role in research of providing testimony – respondents talking or writing about their experiences and actions, as a key source of uninterpreted data. For precision breeds technical language (that is, jargon), and jargon takes people away from what they normally say into a rarefied and acquired language, which itself prejudices research. People who are familiar with such a language cannot be regarded as 'normal' subjects, but are already pre-disposed towards certain kinds of responses by the sheer fact of their acquisition of that technical language (for this brings with it its own shared presumptions about behaviour, about norms, about what is accepted as true, etc). We do not collect from such respondents their own views, but views which have been created by their exposure to existing management ideas.

Anthony Giddens has dubbed this problem that of the 'double hermeneutic'.[14] By this ungainly phrase he means that there are two levels where interpretative decisions have to be made – one level is that of the degree of consensus and agreement between researchers over the use of technical terms of social theory, but the other, and more difficult, level, is that of the relationship between technical language and that of our ordinary discourse about social issues.

The upshot of this double hermeneutic, though, is that managers become theoreticians in a different sense from that outlined in Chapter 1. There it was argued that managers develop their own theory-in-use (as Argyris would call it[15]) as they deal with their day-to-day problems. Managers become theorists in the sense of becoming familiar with the language and jargon of business schools, and accept this as a legitimate means of interpreting their experience as managers. Management theory then becomes a self-fulfilling prophecy. This self confirming nature of management research therefore undermines its validity. Managers attend courses and become knowledgeable in the theory of their occupation. They learn terms such as culture and strategy, and this leads them to structure their thoughts in these terms. So a researcher who uses these terms finds kindred spirits everywhere. One example of this, anecdotally, is the use of the team role types of Meredith Belbin.[16] Just about every individual who has attended a post-experience development course at a business school in the UK is familiar with the Belbin model. So the Belbin terms – 'plant' 'complete finisher' 'shaper' and so on – have passed from being theoretical terms which are treated with some caution to become 'ordinary language' terms which are accepted without question. A researcher who wishes to test the application of Belbin's model in a given context will find that it is accepted as second nature. But this 'ordinary language' has not stood the test of time that our really 'ordinary' concepts and discourse have. It is a couple of decades old, hardly to compare with ideas and terms which have developed over centuries, and thus one has to question whether this is a durable addition to our understanding or a fashion which will wither as its current circumstances of usage die away.

To clarify the argument of this section: bias in field research is a standard issue for all researchers, and it is not in itself a major problem that that kind of bias can exist (even research methods in some natural sciences, such as medicine, are explicitly designed to handle one kind or another of researcher bias). What is problematic is that this extends *before* the act of data collection, into the methodological choices made by the researcher, and then reaches *forward*, as a result into the way research is carried out, into the act of interpreting results. Unlike some areas of study, management involves an essential reference to the language in which issues are perceived and acted upon. The creation of a theory laden 'technical' language then is a substantial influence on people's conceptions of the management task. Hence academic bias is endemic in this area.

There are other aspects of academic bias: Gunnar Myrdal has pointed out the sheer institutional inertia in a subject discipline, so that it cannot properly conduct its own critique: 'The structure of economic theory has been determined entirely by the need to protect itself from its own radical premises.'[17] In other words, academic subjects create a need to maintain their own existence, so anything which threatens that – even the contradictions of its own subject matter – must be repressed, at least within its own world-view.

3.3   OTHER DISTORTING MECHANISMS

The other main sources of bias affecting management research projects principally stem from its existence as a social process of creating and communicating ideas. We shall look at two groups which influence by means of their control over the dissemination process and one which is concerned with the initiation and institutional evaluation of management research. There is a clear correlation in the direction in which these groups tend to influence the research process. Whilst this is not an intentional conspiracy to restrict the research process or anything of that kind, the effects are not too dissimilar from what such a conspiracy might lead to.

3.3.1   Publication Bias

The first separate key source of bias is the publishing mechanism for management research. The point here is not that publishers have their own personal sources of bias, though one may presume that human nature being what it is this is the case to some extent of other. Rather it is that the *process* imposes bias on research, independently of the intentions of individuals, be they managers, researchers or publishers.

The key forms of published management research are:

- *commercial*: research monographs, textbooks, (some) academic journals, professional literature such as magazines or trade newspapers
- *academic*: research monographs and textbooks, academic journals
- *professional*: consultancy or research reports, professional magazines
- *State/NGO/lobby*: consultancy or research reports, policy papers

Clearly these represent different types of players in the market, and with a different share and position in the market. Not all will be discussed in this section. The most important sources for the purposes of this discussion are the commercial publishers, who have the largest share and thus both the biggest influence and also the biggest degree of leverage acted upon them – hence they will be the main focus here.

The issue here echoes some comments made in Chapter 1. Management research is part of a wider market of business and management literature, and hence it is affected strongly by the features of that market. How a piece of research is perceived by potential buyers of management books is a crucial element in the choices made by researchers, the choices made by those who commission management research, and the ways that the results of management research are presented to that market.

One crude and clearly false way of expressing this would be to say that management researchers only produce, and publishers only publish, material which is regarded as 'attractive' to their public. But a subtler, and perhaps for that reason much more insidious, aspect of this is in evidence.

As stated earlier in this book, management ideas can easily be seen as a sort of soft technology, a way of thinking which can lead to improved practices, different and better ways of working, etc. Hence management research, which contributes to and creates these ideas, is seen from the point of view of what will enhance management behaviour. In other words, it is generally approached from the perspective of what will aid managers – what will help them operate more effectively. This inevitably tends to create a management bias in the research. What will help management become (or at least appear to become) more effective crowds out the study of management in its own right.

Books sell because they are attractive to an audience. There are far more individuals wanting to know the best way to motivate unwilling employees, handle management buyouts and so on, than there are those wanting to hear about management failure, about discrimination and harassment of employees, about unethical behaviour in organisations. Unsurprisingly, then, modern management literature is awash with 'thinking positive', solution-oriented material, and there is a relative dearth of exploratory, problem raising writing. Managers are likely to feel that they have problems enough without their gurus creating more.

The bias created by commercial book publishing, therefore, is anti-reflective, pro-solution and pro-technique. This is not the only kind of effect which has been claimed follows from the role of publishing and media in the creation and dissemination of ideas in social science. In a semi-messianic work published over twenty-five years ago, the sociologist Stanislaus Andreski[18] argued that the commercial element in academic research (coupled with an inappropriately over-professionalised approach to research organisation and academic life) inhibited good original creative work, and led to safe but uninspired non-controversial work. I disagree with this view – creativity and risk taking are not eliminated by the publishing industry (indeed in some ways these can contribute to *too much* excitement in management writing). Rather what happens is that the risk and creativity is severely constrained. So long as the work produced is solution oriented, then there is room for a researcher or writer to be creative and original.

The effect of this technical non-reflective tendency is: (a) to depress work which raises more questions than it solves; (b) to emphasise elegant design of presentation; and (c) to neglect practical day-to-day managerial implementation.

We have seen already evidence of (a). The point made in (b) is that punchy persuasive ideas which have a clear motivating potential and an original resonance are almost by definition liable to appear attractive to managers, giving them an advantage (often – because this is after all a commercial environment – a competitive advantage) over less dynamic alternative approaches. The point behind (c) is that any management idea which presents a tool or technique does so in abstraction from its implementation. The incarnation of a pure clean idea inevitably exposes it to a variety of complicating and often unforeseen elements, such as application of a model of commitment in a multi-site organisation rather than a single-site application which may have been implicitly assumed by the writer.[19]

3.3.2 Dissemination Bias

A further aspect of the way the public presentation of management knowledge can distort the process of creating that knowledge is the medium by which a management idea concept or tool is made known to its public. It is commonly supposed that the mass media are the sources and causes of 'spin' – of placing a clearly understood but possibly simplistic interpretation on a story which may be itself ambiguous. This is a consequence of the points made earlier in this section and in Chapter 2 regarding what makes a piece of management writing attractive to an audience.

It is doubtless the case that a piece of research from any discipline or area of study will have a much greater chance of being publicised if: (a) it says something very striking; and/or (b) it creates an image of a new future or a new opportunity. In the management field, papers or books which combine an appearance of empirical ('usually construed as' positivist) study with a controversial or suggestive result will be more likely to receive publicity in the press radio or television than qualitative work (which is not understood publicly as being of equally 'scientific' value), or material which is not expressed in so striking a manner. The latter is a standard consequence of the news process: what makes news (and thus publicity) must have some arresting quality – the unusual (for example, man bites dog rather than dog bites man), or 'well I never' types of story, or stories which have developed their own soap operatic plot line, such as the continuing unfolding of a drawn out political scandal (for example, the Clinton–Lewinsky affair in 1998) or saga like continuities such as a sequence of events in some extended foreign policy story (for example, the oscillating demonisation in western media of certain Middle-Eastern leaders).

But the issue of 'spin' is more complex. Knowing that media operators will place a spin on a piece of work means that an astute and
publicity conscious academic will pre-empt the work of the media by
doing it themselves, principally in order to give their work a good
chance of receiving publicity. Publicity sells books, creates a name for
the researcher, and gives them a cachet as a controversial figure (and
hence likely to gain other benefits such as being invited to give papers
at conferences). So the academic conducts 'spinnable' research.

The influence of the media is perhaps less uni-directional than the
publishers. In the latter case the commercial imperative tends to force
publication of material which addresses the conscious needs of the
audience (the managers, who tend to perceive their needs generally
in terms of how to solve their immediate problems). The media, by
contrast, will try to project material which will be of interest to all
their public. Hence whilst some of their influence will be towards
solutions to managerial problems, they will also give prominence to
material which finds a personal resonance with their audience (or
which can be presented, accurately or not, in these terms). Nevertheless,
whichever direction the influence takes, it is away from a longer
drawn out, thoughtful consideration of issues involving ambiguity
or uncertainty.

So the overly solution oriented bias in the public presentation of
management research is doubly enforced – both by the disseminators
and by the producers. We shall now look at a third influence tending
in the same kind of direction.

3.3.3   Sponsorship Bias

The last kind of bias to be considered is that created by the issue of
who sponsors management research. Again this is not a crude conspiracy theory analysis: there is no evidence to suggest that management
research is directed in the way that some have alleged certain tobacco
companies have deliberately directed or influenced research into the
health effects of smoking (for example, by only funding researchers
who commit themselves to finding results which minimise or question the orthodoxy that smoking is a prime cause of cancer and other
major life threatening diseases). Rather it is the now familiar point
that the structure of the 'management knowledge industry' (for want
of a better phrase) creates conditions which work against reflection
and tend to encourage a solution orientation.

Sponsors of management research generally come from the following:

- academic institutions' own research funds
- state funds

- individual companies or corporate consortia
- private foundations

Academic Institutions

Academic institutions tend to take decisions on a collegiate basis, often (though not always) drawing together the opinions of teaching staff from various subject disciplines. This would suggest a tendency towards academically orthodox research, and away from mould-breaking work.

State Funds

The state – any state – cannot help but conceive of research in terms of how this might contribute to policy aims. Hence the degree of bias here is likely to be quite self conscious. As Kurt Lang puts it 'Social research operates against a background of vested interests...'.[20] Prime amongst these are the interests of the state itself, and the various economic/political power groups surrounding it, such as major industry lobbies.

Company Sponsorship

Companies, operating individually or in consortia, may fund academic research for two reasons: (a) reducing tax liability via charitable donations; (b) contributing to their own R&D operation; and more insidiously (c) for PR reasons, either to offset criticism of their own processes (for example, tobacco companies and smoking research) or to create a positive image as benefactors of the academic world (the 'Sue Grabbit and Run'[21] Chair of Legal Ethics type of phenomenon). The first of these reasons may be presumed to carry yet again the regression to orthodoxy which we have seen. The second is by its very nature solution and technique driven, carrying the more widely encountered type of bias. The third perhaps most acutely of all is addressed solely to an organisation's own needs, without reference to any external idea of what is independently true.

Private Foundations

These too are likely to carry both types of bias – more likely the academic orthodoxy kind, though depending on the nature of the foundation there may be a restriction of research to specific subject areas.

The net result of these is that sponsorship brings two kinds of potential bias. Firstly, it reinforces the solution driven approach in that some of these funders are looking for specific questions to be answered (few would be funding research to create problems). Secondly, it creates a pressure towards research projects which manifestly cohere with current academic orthodoxies. Work which strongly challenges orthodoxies, methodological ones especially, is likely to find few supporters. This is a general result – which affects microbiology as much as, if not more, than management. But it clearly applies to management research as well.

SUMMARY

In this chapter we have considered the potential areas where management research may be subject to bias. Returning to one question posed at the start, is there an ideological element to management research? The argument of this chapter has been to look beyond this. Doubtless there are potential spaces for ideological bias to intrude – such as in the provision of state funding, or the choices made by directors of publishing houses to suppress or encourage certain kinds of work. But that is not the largest or most problematic source of bias. Though I disagree strongly with the overall argument of Lex Donaldson over this issue, the material of this chapter would give some support to his view: 'Organisation Theory: occasional ideological use, but not an ideology.'[22]

Far more significant is the traditional area of researcher bias, operating not in a specific result-seeking manner, but in the ways that research questions are formulated and that the ordinary day-to-day conceptual framework in which organisational activities are carried on are translated into a researchable format. A second key point is that the key influences which are external to the researcher her- or himself generally tend to encourage non-reflective, technical solution based work.

NOTES

1   Marx suggested that the ruling class(es) had a conscious perception of their own interests and took deliberate steps to enhance these. They were, in his terms, a 'class *for* itself' as opposed to the working class – which was only a class *in* itself – and which needed political action to recognise its own interests and needs.

2 Clegg and Dunkerly (1980).

3 See Furusten (1999) Chapter 5.

4 Gill and Johnson (1994).

5 Which is not to say that writers such as Gill and Johnson make this mistake, but that individuals reading their work can easily make it. I have encountered many postgraduate management students who have fallen into this trap.

6 Though there would be a guarantee that not both can be fully and unequivocally true in their entirety.

7 Of course, rounding up 99.9–100%.

8 It is true that on the kind of approach adopted by Karl Popper and others (see Chapter 5) this suggests that when triangulation is used and does lead to parallel results then that is very strong evidence that the different studies have uncovered something real. It still seems odd, though, to adopt a practice which is not likely to yield the results one wanted. The logical extreme of this would be to take a test which could only just conceivably yield the result one wanted – then if it happened it would be especially strong evidence. In fact of course investigators do not do this. Looking at something from different perspectives is used as a check but not as a source of proof.

9 I owe this point to a former colleague, Laurence Solkin.

10 This is a fictitious example, but hopefully it displays the logic of my argument.

11 Ford (1975) p. 91.

12 Impossible given the limitations of time and resource available to us, either in the research process or the courtroom. In *principle* this all could be cleared up, but that term is tantamount to saying that one *believes* that it can without being able to *demonstrate* that it can – an act of faith by another name.

13 Oakley (1981).

14 Giddens (1982).

15 See Argyris (1992) where this idea is a central part of the argument of almost every chapter.

16 See Belbin (1993).

17 Myrdal (1969) p. 102.

18 Andreski (1972) Chapter 3. Andreski's book contains on almost every page an important point about the weaknesses of social research, but it is written in an exhaustingly apocalyptic, cassandra-like tone, which seriously obscures his argument.

19 See Chapter 12 of my previous book 'Managing Values'.

20 Lang (1975).

21 A mythical unscrupulous law firm depicted in the satirical UK magazine 'Private Eye'.

22 Donaldson (1985) Chapter 9.

Chapter 4

Cultural Relativity in Management Research

In Chapter 3 we looked at various sources of bias within the process of management research. What we saw was that ideology as an *intentional* distorting mechanism is less important than the biases created by the fact that management research is a social process which exists in a partially commercial environment.

In this chapter we shall look at factors external to the research process which undermine the possibility that management research creates universal knowledge. Chief amongst these is the possibility that national cultures provide a major limitation on the transferability of management ideas.

4.1 THE IDEA OF NATIONAL CULTURE AND THE CONTEXT OF MANAGEMENT RESEARCH

The term 'culture' is a construct. It depicts the different ways in which groups of people behave together, think together, feel together. Sackmann[1] has identified three different perspectives on the idea of culture:

1 *holistic*: whereby culture is seen as an *integration* of artefact, emotion, cognition and behaviour
2 *variable*: whereby culture is seen as the range of behaviours as *expressions* of different and varying meanings

3 *cognitive*: whereby culture is presented as the *underpinning knowledge* or belief element which lends meaning to an organisation's practices or artefacts

The lesson she draws from these is that there is no simple unified definition of culture (n.b. she is talking primarily about organisational culture, but the point here is a generic one). Each approach is itself only a partial view of the phenomenon. Therefore cultural studies for organisations are necessarily limited by the incomplete standpoint taken by any particular researcher.

Each of Sackmann's three perspectives on culture seems to recognise that culture includes both a surface element (ritual practices, symbols, standard behaviours, etc.) and a depth element (the meanings attributed by cultural participants to the surface elements for example, religious or political ideologies). What is not specifically pointed out, however, is that the depth element defines the surface element. Acts or objects which do not carry an underpinning meaning have no cultural significance, and hence can easily seem not to exist at all. The specific way in which an individual expresses assent, for example, is often overlooked, because the culturally important aspect may be that assent is expressed in a specific form. Figure 4.1 provides an example.

The issue here is not that the leader of the meeting, Alan, does it badly (he does!) but that the opinions of the different individuals can all be taken as expressions of agreement, when they may all be tacit ways of disagreeing. Possibly non-verbal aspects are relevant. The stock in trade of political style communication is to use non-verbal elements of communication to deliver a reassuring message whilst maintaining

---

An agreement

A: Right, then, are we going to change the date of the launch? John?

J: Yes, Alan, I suppose we could, so long as we are sure that all of us can make the new date.

A: Great. Sally?

S: It seems that the old date has got a lot of problems with it.

A: Yes, so we really can't stay with it can we? Robin?

R: Yes.

A: Arshad?

Ar: If we go with the new date we can be sure that the publicity material can be revised in time can't we?

A: No problem. So that's it, then. We're all agreed.

Figure 4.1

a deliberate precision in the verbal expression of a statement: 'I want to REASSURE everybody that we will take this issue VERY SERIOUSLY.' [the capitals indicate verbal stress] Of course nothing substantial has been said here, but an emotional message has clearly been conveyed – reassurance, seriousness.

In any case, John expresses a conditional, 'yes–if' which is just as well expressed as 'no–unless'; Sally simply makes a point about the disadvantages of the previous date; Robin provides so bare an answer that one might question whether there is anything he is refusing to share with the group, whilst Arshad asks a question. The cultural context of a decision-making meeting defines communications in terms of whether they support or reject an action. A manager acting effectively will (or at least should) see through this and seek to clarify the under-lying needs or thoughts of the protagonists, but in practice lots of fac-tors can incline even a good manager towards a swift decision – when it's the end of a meeting and everyone wants to go for lunch, and things have been very strained, and no one quite understands all the arguments properly, etc. – so a decision is rushed through. The point is not managerial ineffectiveness – it is that context defines certain fea-tures of communication out of existence, and where context can do it, so can culture. A well known stereotype depicts the more tradi-tional Japanese person as characteristically avoiding outright dis-agreement because it involves the other party losing face. So discussion may be peppered with 'yes, so long as . . .' or 'I agree, and in addition we should . . .' and similar phrases to indicate that the use of the word 'yes' is not intended as a simple and unconditional agreement.

This issue itself has a major significance for the conduct of inter-cultural research. For the researcher has to use specific concrete modes of communication, and for each of these there is a cultural element. Cultures differ in the way that written or oral responses are treated. In one the written is all, in another it is nothing. So the researcher work-ing in their own country relies on their own cultural commonality with the subjects of the study to support their assumption that the act of communication has been a genuine transfer of ideas from one person to the other. Where one of the communicants is from a different culture, then the act of communication itself is problematic. For many western countries, globalisation has meant that they have become multi-ethnic nations. Hence even a standard local survey into, say, company budgeting systems, cannot escape being within an inter-cultural context, with all the attendant problems of communication.

Let us look further at the role of culture in organisational research. The models of national culture developed by Geert Hofstede and Fons Trompenaars are well known, and need no extensive explanation, though they are summarised in Figure 4.2.

Hofstede's dimensions of culture:

power distance	i.e. degree of difference based on social status
uncertainty avoidance	i.e. risk aversion
masculinity	
individual–collective	
long–short term focus	

Trompenaars cultural constructs

achieved–ascribed status	i.e. what you do as opposed to what you are
synchrony–sequence	i.e. attitudes to time–past and future vs. present alone
individual–collective	
universal–particular	
neutral–emotional	
diffuse–specific relationships	i.e. holistic vs. contractual business relationships
self determination–fate	

Figure 4.2   The Dutch school of cultural analysis.[2]

Differences between national cultures can undermine the ability of a member of one to properly understand the behaviour of the members of another. This represents a stark contrast to the study of organisational cultures within a single national culture. For in that case the protagonists carry similar pre-conceptions about key elements such as attitudes to risk, time, gender equality and so on, which form the framework within which, for example, managers in one company may be more or less decisive than another. But in comparing how an organisation in one country operates with another in a different country, there are far fewer points of connection.

The methodology of participant observation, so often offered as the solution for this is: (a) expensive and difficult to interpret in transferable terms; and (b) defined in terms of a researcher from a 'home' country stepping out 'into' another culture – so the experience of the researcher is essentially one of strangeness, essentially alien, in contrast to the individuals s/he studies, who are acting in the manner they see as natural and normal (perhaps perceived by them as the *only* natural normal way to behave). The researcher is incapable of truly sharing the experience they participate in. This may not always be problematic for the researcher – it depends what exactly they are researching into. But it delimits the technique as having only a partial answer at best to the issue of cultural difference.

Knowledge itself carries a burden of its cultural origin. Perhaps the strongest type of contrast here is between non-western knowledge of the medicinal effects of naturally occurring substances and the modern western health care industry. There is no doubt that some ailments have been successfully treated by modern medicine. The virtual eradication of smallpox, for example, has been trumpeted as a great success for modern medicine. It is unclear, though, how far this ravaged pre-urban populations, if at all.[3] Furthermore, it is now evident that many natural medicaments previously written off by the western medical establishment as 'magic' (with the imputation that they were therefore of no serious medical value) have come to be recognised as incorporating valuable beneficial effects. This was not a case of *refusal* to accept a potential treatment as effective. It was rather a *failure to understand* that a natural treatment could possibly work, which in itself stemmed from a failure to understand that people (and especially people who looked and behaved so differently – there is racism here as well) could develop medical knowledge which did not spring from the rational model of investigation which took hold of European thought about five hundred years ago.

In an analogous manner, modern management theory looks almost exclusively at the ways in which organisations in western economies operate – where other cultures and economies are considered it is usually as a source of contrast. The methods and styles of organisation required in non-western style activities is largely ignored.[4] So management literature is full of discussions of mergers and acquisitions in large corporate bodies, but almost completely silent on the ways in which people living in rural subsistence economies organise themselves, take decisions, develop and make effective use of skills within the group, allocate resources, maintain morale, compete with other similar groups, and so on. At the very least there must be a suspicion that this parallels the medical example mentioned above. We shall return to this in Section 4.3.

▨ 4.2 CULTURAL ASSUMPTIONS AFFECTING MANAGEMENT RESEARCH

A key feature of the results of natural science is that they are understood as being of universal application. What is true of gravitational attraction in southern Egypt is regarded as equally true in Los Angeles or on the other side of the moon. Is social knowledge equally so? This underlies the main question of this part of the present book – is an applied social study such as management capable of generating material which can be called science? Can it be said to bring universal knowledge at all? Or is the result of management research always conditioned in space and time – fit for a time and place but not telling a truth about all ways of managing in any situation?

This is not merely an academic debate. It is also of great practical importance as well. The influence of management ideas in the last part of the twentieth century and the dawn of the twenty-first has generally been via an emanation which starts from a small group of post-industrially developed countries such as the USA, France, and the UK, and slowly is transferred to other regions – the Pacific Rim early on, then later affecting developing and restructuring economies such as the Czech Republic, Poland, India, Brazil, and so on. A simple corollary of the question of how far management knowledge is culturally dependent is: why should these countries seek to learn from the post-industrial economies? Is there a justification for the assumption that the 'knowledge' which has been developed in those latter countries is transferable to other environments which have different histories and traditions, different national stereotypes (and hence different approaches to what issues are problems needing a solution, as well as different ways of creating and implementing those solutions), different styles of education (and therefore differently structured labour markets), not to mention different current economic problems?

The idea that social knowledge may be context dependent is certainly not new, but in recent years it has become a more pressing issue for the status of management research. As long ago as 1967 Peter Berger and Thomas Luckmann talked about the differences in what would be counted real in New York City as opposed to rural Haiti.[5] Lincoln and Guba[6] over a decade ago identified a 'naturalistic paradigm' of a non-positivist[7] approach to inquiry which includes the idea that hypotheses about human behaviour are time and context dependent. Marshall and Reason,[8] writing more recently, quote this with favour, in the course of their argument that explanations in management research need to acknowledge cultural and individual perspectives more overtly (amongst other things).

One difficulty with assessing arguments concerning culture dependence of management ideas is that this concept is often woven in to a more general anti-positivist package of methodological claims. So Lincoln and Guba put their claim together with ideas such as the value-bound nature of inquiry, the dependence between researcher and researched, and the multiple nature of social realities. But the cultural dependence argument can be considered independently of other anti-positivist views. In the following discussion I shall be looking specifically at the contextual claim. The ideas of Lincoln and Guba regarding value-dependence and researcher non-independence have been aired earlier and will be explored in Part II of this book. But the idea that there are multiple realities is not tenable. However difficult to understand, and however many complications this creates for an understanding of knowledge in management (as elsewhere) *there can only be one world to study –* without this idea debate collapses into non-transferable self expression.

Perhaps the first issue to acknowledge is the inter-causality of different delimiting factors. A piece of management research is created by an individual (or occasionally a group of individuals), with their own perspective on the issues studied. But beyond that such an individual works inside an organisational framework, which itself exists inside a set of national or international cultural influences. Figure 4.3 indicates the nesting of factors likely to qualify, delimit or condition the potential universality of management research. This delimitation I shall call the degree of *parochialism*.

The idea of parochialism is that a concept, however universally expressed, may still be strongly conditioned by unrecognised local factors. The point is that localisation is itself a relative concept. A research project is likely to be conditioned at all these levels at least. An individual's personal perspective may constrain the questions he or she asks, the types of research method they employ, the kind of answer they would consider to have any kind of meaning at all. This is not quite the same as bias, for it is not in itself an inclination toward a specific result, or even a specific kind of result, but a boundary around what can be accepted as a result – clearly there is a grey area where it is not that clear whether what we have is constraint or bias: this should not undermine the following argument.

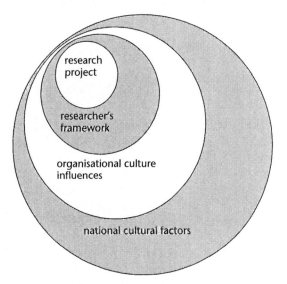

Figure 4.3   Layers of context – different sources of parochialism.

The individual is placed in an organisational setting and this is located in a context of national culture (not necessarily a single culture – it may be some combination of several, for example depending on the workers employed in the organisations studied, the multi-nationality of the organisations involved in the study, or the degree of multi-nationality of the intended audience for the research). This contextual complex they will naturally try to transcend, if they are making any effort at all to generate knowledge. But the transcendence works only up to a point. A researcher can only generalise in terms of the model they are using – this is a point we discussed in Chapter 1. Hence their attempts to create a universal result will depend on *which local values of variables they recognise*. By definition, if a researcher does not acknowledge the influence of a factor, then they cannot control for it. If someone does not realise that individuals from the Indian sub-continent are more likely to be quick at mental arithmetic than their European counterparts, they will not be able to assess the differences in the way Indian managers respond when faced with a table of complex figures and a short decision time, compared to say English managers. The variable is not part of the researcher's model, hence it cannot be controlled for – so if the study is enquiring into links between decisiveness and other personality factors, for example, it will miss a crucial trick.

An instructive example of how a researcher may fail to recognise a key contextual variable may be found in the literature on social research itself. Janet Finch, in writing about the special character of social research interviews with women being carried out by women, writes the following:

> '...where a woman researcher is interviewing other women, this is a situation with special characteristics conducive to the easy flow of information. Firstly, women mostly are more used than men to accepting intrusions through questioning into the more private parts of their lives, including during encounters in their own homes. Through their experience of motherhood they are subject to questioning from doctors, midwives and health visitors; and also from people such as housing visitors, insurance agents and social workers, who deal principally with women as the people with imputed responsibility for home and household.... Secondly, in the setting of the interviewee's own home, an interview conducted in an informal way by another woman can easily take on the character of an intimate conversation.'[9]

This passage makes an important point which refers back to the arguments of chapter 3 and earlier in this one. The interview process, however hard someone tries, is not a neutral act. Given the levels of difference and inequality in modern societies, social perceptions cannot help but play a part. White interviewers with black respondents, men interviewing women – these cannot but influence (and often interfere with) the process of collecting information, whether the researcher adopts a positivist or anti-positivist research stance. Janet Finch goes on to illustrate her argument with some telling examples of interviews carried out with women – the way in which the women interviewees responded was much more open (and hence facilitated the collection of data much more validly) than if a man had conducted the interview. In this she is surely correct.

Finch's examples, however, are all of a western style welfare economy. It is true that medical treatment is, more or less around the world, western style to some extent these days, so the first part of her argument is moderately true today of the globe in general (though would not have been a hundred years ago). But the latter point, about social workers, insurance agents and housing officials, has a distinctly western style ring to it. And the image of a woman's home providing an intimate setting for an interview again suggests (though this is more speculative) an atomised nuclear familial context. True, there are parallel practices, roles and functions in non-western societies, so the point is not to suggest that Finch is wrong in what she is claiming. Rather it is that her analysis is couched in western-centric terms. So if her assumptions about other societies are incorrect, then her analysis is true only for the west.[10] Given that this is an argument from an individual trying to extend understanding about the impact of context on the research process, one can assume that other researchers are likely to be generally less aware of this limitation on their work.

The above turns on gender, which is one specific cultural element. It is, though, intended as a key illustration of a general pattern – that researchers may well be unaware of assumptions they are making about the broad context of their work.

4.3   CULTURAL CONTENT OF MANAGEMENT THEORY

How far is the *content* of management ideas culturally dependent? The argument here will be expressed in terms of the strengths and weaknesses of the key potential alternatives – this discussion will thus define the extent of cultural content in management writing.

The range of views about the level of cultural content in management knowledge can be put on a scale, thus:

1   properly conducted, management research produces entirely *culture free* knowledge

2 some *cultural elements may be introduced* into management knowledge due to the assumptions of the researcher[11]

3 *cultural elements are imputed* to management ideas due to the presuppositions of the audience

4 there is a shared and possibly even semi-conscious *degree of cultural assumption* between researcher and audience; this in turn creates a culture dependent theatre for interpretation of the concepts involved, which, nevertheless may have a general application

5 management ideas *depend on the assumptions of a specific culture* to derive their full significance, though some elements may be culturally transferable

6 management ideas *only gain meaning within a given culture*, though this can be translated into something transferable

7 management knowledge is *entirely knowledge about one culture*, and hence intrinsically non-transferable

Apart from statements 2 and 3, which almost run in parallel as versions of what might be called soft absolutism, the rest of the list proceeds in a sequence from a hard absolutist to a hard relativist position, with 4 and 5 representing mixed (but not neutral) approaches. Note the comments made earlier – this scale is not identical with a positivist to anti-positivist dimension. For one thing, there is no such single scale. As we shall see in Part II of this book, there are several directions in which a methodologist might go which count as anti-positivist. For another thing, such a scale would literally mean nothing more than from positivism to non-positivism, which is not a substantial dimension at all in this context. Positivism and its alternatives are *all equally capable* of being represented as culturally determined. It is arguable that positivism is nothing more than the expression of European rationalism taken into the twentieth century. Equally arguable is that anti-positivist approaches have evolved out of (what have been claimed to be) the limitations of positivism as identified, tested and evaluated within European culture and its derivatives.

Statements 1 and 7 are placed here for completeness, though they are not likely candidates for acceptance. The difficulty with statement 1 is that it rests on the crutch of what counts as a properly conducted piece of research. The phrase is vague, and therefore flexible, and too easy an answer to an objector. 'So this piece of research was culturally biased? Well it wasn't properly conducted then.' The positivist cannot rely on this type of response. A clear criterion of what counts as proper research conduct needs to be outlined.

In a different way statement 7 is not acceptable. Statements about management are made in general terms, and therefore they are distinct from ones which are explicitly qualified by cultural reference. It is semantically incorrect to say that a statement such as 'Sound competitive strategy requires an organisation to decide between cost leadership and differentiation' is really just *about* western economies. It may only be *true* of these, or more precisely it may be progressively less easy to maintain the less developed an economy is, but this is quite separate from the question about where the statement draws its meaning from. Even if the management writer has certain economies in mind when they make such a statement, this does not mean that they are only talking about such economies. If they were, then there would be no semantic difference between the above statement and one which started with a prefixing phrase such as 'In European and North American economies. . . .' Statements about management which do not explicitly relativise themselves to specific cultures should not be construed as such.

In considering the other statements, it is useful to refer back to Sackmann's threefold division of holistic, variable and cognitive models of culture. These relate differentially to statements 2 to 6. Basically, one can say that they link in inverse order – the statements which give a higher priority to the role of culture are best thought of as embodying the holistic model, whilst statements 2 and 3, which indicate a more limited influence of cultural elements on researcher and audience, reflect the more limited cognitive model of culture.

The holistic view depicts surface manifestation and inner meaning as inextricably interwoven, too far integrated to be distinguishable. Arguably the extreme version of this is statement 7, which we have seen fit to reject. Statements 5 and 6 above depict the results of management research to be essentially connected to culture, dependent on it for their meaning. This is not to deny some degree of transferability, but only in virtue of the source of the meaning – that is, the 'home' culture of the researcher or audience.

The variable model depicts culture as that which is expressed through a variety of surface manifestations. Here meaning itself is to an extent distinguishable from its expression, albeit incompletely. Statement 5 shades into this view – dependence could be taken to imply that the *significance* of the management idea is separately identifiable from its cultural *expression*, but that the former depends in some way on the latter. So a researcher conducting interviews in the USA on the attitudes of first line managers to the motivation of their teams might find that the subjects interviewed (male ones, at least) may well draw on their sense of the significance of the word 'team' from their experience of sports teams. This does not mean that the term has no significance for the subjects outside that association, but it does imply that their grasp of it is dependent on this connection. Statement 4 (which represents a more complex phenomenon than the others) explicitly projects culture as the mechanism for interpreting concepts, and thus as the means of expressing significance via surface phenomena.

The cognitive model separates the surface and underlying meaning even further, so that external phenomena (what I have called the surface manifestations of the culture) are no more than the vehicles for presenting a separate meaning or belief. There may well be problems with this kind of model – how far can we talk about a meaning or belief which is independent of its expression, for example? A researcher trying to establish the role of the dress code in an organisation, for example, would seek in vain for a link between the behaviour and some external meaning, for the meaning is defined in terms of the practice – without the practice there is no separate significance.

The question of how far culture impacts on management research resolves itself into the question of which of the three models Sackmann outlines is most accurately a reflection of culture in general. The above discussion indicates that the cognitive model is suspect – distinguishing the surface cultural forms from the underlying significance too strongly may undermine the whole idea of practices having any meaning at all.

Both of the other two approaches present a picture of culture as a conjunction of explicit acts and behaviours and an associated meaning which somehow underpins these. This conjunction is clearly closer than simply the former being a vehicle for the latter. Whether it goes so far as a total integration is doubtful. If that were the case then we would be in the extreme hard relativist position, which would depict all communication and behaviour as being a reference to a single culture only. How one could ever break out of this is difficult to see. If all we can understand or recognise is our own culture then it seems impossible even to recognise that other cultures exist at all. Each individual would measure everyone else's behaviour in terms of a home culture (which clearly would make a lot of other people's behaviours pretty strange indeed). In practice it seems clear that we acknowledge that people who live very different lives to us have a different cluster of meanings which are intrinsically associated with their behaviour. But it is also fairly clear that if we are to recognise other cultures as culture at all we need to have some ideas which stretch out beyond our own circumstances, as somehow transferable.

Some thirty-five years ago Peter Winch identified a cluster of concepts which he claimed were limiting concepts for any human society or culture.[12] His cluster included the concept of life, and its close relatives, birth and death, and the polarisation of humanity into two genders. Vague though these terms are, there are ways in which individuals (such as the author) from a European derived culture can see how they can apply differently in different cultures and still represent something transferable between those cultures. I would want to add to these the complex of attitudes regarding work roles and relationships. Every culture has to create the opportunities for its members to provide for their most fundamental personal needs – shelter, food and warmth. These interlace with Winch's own list – gender most obviously, but also the idea of what a life is, of which kinds of death are acceptable and which are not.

To take an example, much has been made of the Trist and Bamforth studies of miners in the north of England, or of the 'affluent worker' studies of car workers in central England carried out by Goldthorp and Lockwood.[13] But their discussions of these workers has focused on the descriptive elements of how they preferred their work to be organised, how far they worked in teams, what their own attitudes toward remuneration and effort were. Little has been said about *why* the miners worked most effectively in teams, or *why* the car workers retained a sense of being working class despite their increasing economic position, or about the attitude of either group towards their work as a contribution to a household, and the associated implications for gender, childhood, working life and quality of working life which all this implies. Of course, one should not criticise studies for what they did not set out to do. In Goldthorp and Lockwood's case, they had a very specific idea they wished to test (the idea that growing affluence of manual workers would lead them to adopt more middle-class values – the so-called 'embourgeoisement' thesis), and test it they did, very successfully. The point is to locate these examples of research in a cultural context. That context involved a clear separation of gender roles, a conception of physical work – the acquisition of material necessities – as being an essential part of a man's life, and in the miners case a conception of work relationships as being a defining element of natural community life.

From a distance of but a few decades, these seem less rigid so far as life and work in the UK is concerned than they did at the time of the studies. Work is no longer solely done 'at' work – but very often at home nowadays. Physical labour is no longer the exclusive preserve of men, still less are other roles, such as professional practice or management, a male preserve. Social relationships are no longer so closely dependent on a local economy which often was dominated by a small set of major employers. Above all the conception of work as 'bringing home the bacon' (to use an archaic English phrase) is less obviously the source of job or career orientation – ironically, since unemployment in the UK is currently much higher than it was during the times of the two studies mentioned above.

These two studies, carried out at a similar time, throw into focus the idea of culture and management research. For it is clear that much in these studies is still of general interest – in the Trist case the whole idea of organisations as sociotechnical systems could be thought as having started with this study. But it is also clear that the separation of only a few decades indicates how temporally parochial they were. One only needs to imaginatively project a few more decades into the future and the disintegrity between work and home, which was a fundamental feature of both studies, may well have disappeared for a large section of the working population of the developed countries. And equally, one only needs to look at rural communities in many parts of the less developed countries here and now to realise that the idea of organisation, competition and management applies in very different ways to that pertaining in the UK, France, Germany and other developed nations. For one thing, some activities directly connected to the carrying on of a business may be engaged without any explicit concept of a transaction at all.

■ SUMMARY

In conclusion, in this chapter we have seen that culture does provide a major limitation to the universality of management research. I have spoken most of the time as if here is a researcher coming from a monocultural background confronting subjects from another, different, monocultural background. In practice, it is far more complex than that. Few of us today are simply single culture individuals (no one living in the UK currently could be seen in that light). So the cultural impact is more complex and more subtle. But it remains a key feature of management research which is underrecognised.

Cultural assumptions mean that applied social research such as the management field can virtually never step entirely outside itself and view the work at a distance. Always we are observing through our own cultural filters. This does not mean that we cannot make any transfer from one culture to another – if this were the case, we would have no idea of inter-cultural comparisons at all. But it does imply that there are serious limitations on the generalisability of any piece of management research.

NOTES

1 Sackmann (1991) Chapter 2, but note that the use made of this classification in this chapter goes beyond Sackmann's own view.
2 Hofstede (1980) and Trompenaars (1993).
3 As a tangent, it is worth noting that the thesis of Jared Diamond is that these diseases were not just importations of western European city states, but actually formed one of the key factors which enabled Europe to colonise so much of the rest of the world between 1400 and 1900. See Diamond (1998).
4 An indication of the cultural conflicts this can lead to is illustrated in Muller (1998).
5 Berger and Luckmann (1967) cf. p. 197.
6 Lincoln and Guba (1985).
7 Positivism – in this context the idea that social science should mirror exactly the methods of the natural sciences.
8 Marshall and Reason (1997).
9 Finch (1984) reprinted in Hammersley pp. 168–9.
10 I suspect that these assumptions are true in some respects of other societies and not true in other respects. But the real point is that these assumptions are made. Whatever, this comment is not intended to undermine the basic spirit of Janet Finch's work.
11 This is the view considered in the previous section.
12 Winch (1964).
13 Trist et al. (1963) and Goldthorpe et al. (1968).

Conclusion

In this part of the book we have been looking at some of the broader underpinning issues relating to the validity of management research. Some of the key points are as follows:

- management theory is as much a creation of practising managers as it is of professional researchers
- the complexity of the context within which management ideas may be tested undermines claims to its truth
- the utility of management ideas is not a monodimensional issue of what practitioners can use, but covers the needs and interests of a wide range of stakeholders
- management theory bears a definite slant towards non-reflective, solution-oriented material, but this is less due to ideology than to the specific features of the context of research and its place in the publishing market
- there is a significant degree to which management theory is culturally biased

These are not in themselves major mould-breaking results, but they jointly contribute to the overall answer to the question of what value-management research can bring. The cumulative effect of the above points is to incline more towards an image of management research as *presenting*, rather than *representing*. The difference between these is that representation suggests the production of a stable unitary account of the reality of management, while the idea of presenting suggests that the role of the presenter is central.

What we need to do now is look in detail at some of the philosophical approaches to social research, in order to establish what they can and cannot demonstrate about the management research process. To this we shall proceed in Part II.

Four Characteristic Research Paradigms

INTRODUCTION

Earlier I identified two contrasting beliefs in methodology: one as a mechanism for securing validity, and the other as a relationship between researcher and researched. The substance of the main argument of Part II is to explore this contrast in terms of some of the classical approaches to methodology.

There are many approaches to social research methodology, some of them based on very fine distinctions. An account of the whole of this range could easily produce 'ism' exhaustion, where there are just too many similar but not identical views for the reader to form a clear overview. We shall look at four broad representative areas. Each of these areas is characterised in terms of the way in which it resolves the contribution/creation issue.

One group comprises the approaches which liken management research to natural science – positivist and related schools of thought, such as critical realism and grounded theory. Another is the group which rejects the analogy with natural science, but retains the idea that research leads to an agreed depiction of management reality. This includes approaches such as hermeneutics and phenomenology. Beyond these, however, is a dimension which takes the interrelationship between research and practice as a critical feature. Into this category we will put post-modernism and deconstructionism. Finally, there is a category for the approaches which extend the idea of practice further, and present the research process (and the key value in management research) as essentially an interaction between researchers and respondents – this category covers participatory and action research.

So in Chapters 5–8 we shall look at these key approaches to management research. In each case we shall encounter difficulties with the idea that these methodologies on their own provide a secure route to knowledge. The key conclusion which we shall argue in Part III is that these different methodologies reflect different *complementary* aspects of the process of discovery about management. In other words, they are not alternatives at all, but reflect different aspects of the process of developing management knowledge.

Central to the question of how far management research is valid is the position on the link between social and natural science. The debate concerning validity starts from the way in which this link is evaluated.

One model relating to this which is often espoused is a linear depiction of methodologies, stretching from a strongly positivist position at one extremity over to a strong subjectivist position on the other. Figure II.1 below illustrates a cluster of different polarisations which embody this linear image of methodologies. Such polarisations over-simplify what many writers say, but this kind of modelling under-lies much of the critique of naturalist approaches such as positivism.

This way of looking at social research methodology is severely misleading. Some of the key terms here, such as 'hard information' are maybe less clear than we presume. Some other ideas here are fairly vague – in what way might knowledge be a creation? Clearly not in the way that *fantasy* is a creation. Also most of these are highly relative terms – some items may be more or less objective.

This approach tends to work from a stereotyped idea of a 'trad-itional' approach, rooted in the natural science analogy, and then defines methodological positions in terms of how they react against this. The very word structure of some terms, such as *'post'*-modernism, demonstrates this: a concept that depends for its existence on the position it attacks. It is convenient to divide concepts into two opposing types, but in the case of social research methodologies it has the effect that the variety of non-naturalist approaches get lumped together,

social science should parallel natural science	social science is fundamentally different from natural science
hard information	soft information
independent researcher	engaged researcher
focus on facts	focus on feelings
theory grounded in external evidence	theory imposed upon evidence
objective	subjective
quantifiable data	unquantifiable material
knowledge mirrors an external reality	knowledge is a creation

Figure II.1 The traditional opposition.

when they actually have significant differences. Admittedly, the division I give below is itself an over-simplification, but it does have the merit of demonstrating the range of non-naturalist approaches.

In contrast to the one-dimensional depiction of methodologies, I want to use a two-dimensional model based not only on the division between acceptance or rejection of the analogy with natural science, but also on the relationship between theory and practice. There are two elements here. The first is the extent to which the research approach is focused on *the material itself* or on *the researchers*. The second is the nature of the research activity – as providing *foundations* of knowledge or as a dynamic process of *investigation*.

I shall call these four approaches paradigms as illustrated in Figure II.2. The term has been much misused. What I intend by it is that they represent, not *specific theses* about management knowledge so much as *directions*, or trends, in people's thinking about knowledge in management. It is the general *style* of an approach which matters here – we are looking at characteristic approaches to methodology, not the specific views of individual writers.[1]

One view on paradigms of methodology is that they should answer three different kinds of question:[2] (a) a question of what kind of thing a piece of social knowledge actually is – and what kind of reality social knowledge represents; (b) a question of how we can know this social reality; and (c) what are the most appropriate ways of finding out about this reality. Lincoln and Guba call these the *ontological* question, the *epistemological* question and the *methodological* question respectively.[3] In Chapters 5–8 we shall move between these questions

focus on knowledge	focus on knowers	
naturalism: social science methods should parallel those of natural science	*interpretavism:* social knowledge is an interpretation of data	focus on data as foundational
deconstructionism: social knowledge can only be understood in terms of the concrete practices of those who possess it	*participant inquiry:* social knowledge comes about through collaborative investigations of its stakeholders	focus on the dynamics of investigation

Figure II.2   Four methodological approaches.

fairly fluidly. At times any one of them could be of central relevance, and at other times any of them could be less important. Hence the discussion will focus on those issues which are important for a particular paradigm, rather than systematically evaluate each paradigm in terms of each of these three questions.

So what you can expect in Part II is a presentation of some key approaches to research methodology (keeping in view the applied nature of management) plus critique in the best sense of the term – identifying strengths as well as weaknesses.

There is, though, an ambiguity in the way we shall look at these four approaches. The main reason for us examining these approaches is to get a feel for the primary ways in which current researchers in the management field construe their task, and whether there is a rationale or underlying justification for adopting one approach rather than another. However, these approaches also reflect a certain kind of historical progression of approaches to social science. The order in which we look at these approaches will (roughly) recapitulate their appearance as theories of social research. It is as if the current range of approaches includes the key developments which led up to the present day – in my view a healthy sign that the theory of social research has not lost sight of its roots.[4]

As a very rough and ready illustration of this development, here is a brief indication of the key stages in the historical development of social methodology (at least as it applies to management research).[5] Until the late seventeenth century, there was no formal intellectual sense of the development of societies as a field of potentially scientific study. In 1725, however, the Italian thinker Giambattista Vico in his book 'A New Science' propounded a new approach to the study of history and humanity, one which he placed explicitly in parallel with natural science. Although there were other writers who (in retrospect) implicitly raised similar questions at around the same time, the idea of a science of society did not catch on, and Vico died largely unrecognised as the grandfather of social science.

Over a hundred years later the French writer, Auguste Comte, returned to the issue of how we could have a science of society. In the middle of the nineteenth century he advanced the idea that human society could be studied in the same way that natural phenomena could – coining the term 'positivism'.[6] Whilst the methods of collecting information about people might be different, the main purpose of such study was the same – to establish the laws of human behaviour. Comte's ideas had a lasting impact on many later nineteenth century writers, amongst them Marx, Durkheim and Weber,[7] three of the most important of the early sociologists (though it is arguable that Vico's earlier work had as much influence, but went unacknowledged).

At the same time, almost in parallel, was developing the science of biblical interpretation – which went by the name of hermeneutics. During the nineteenth century writers such as Friedrich Schleiermacher and Wilhelm Dilthey began to apply hermeneutic techniques to fields such as history and literature, but it was in the early twentieth century that interpretative techniques began to be recognised as offering an alternative approach to the study of human behaviour. Partly this was political, as positivist theory began progressively to assume a more structured and formal appearance, and became rather too like natural science for the likes of some social thinkers. Partly it was due to the influence of philosophers such as Martin Heidegger and Edmund Husserl, who in their different ways emphasised the 'internal' nature of human experience. It was argued by interpretavists that human behaviour could not be understood without an account of its meaning in human terms – that is, in relation to texts and utterances. The idea of identifying and establishing laws of behaviour thus were replaced (in the hands of some writers) by the need to understand what such behaviours signified for those who acted thus. Such an approach took the study of societies away from such 'hard' subjects as economics and closer to 'softer' ones such as anthropology.

But this was not a simple revolution. Many social researchers were unconvinced, and continued to conduct large scale surveys, collecting large amounts of data and submitting these to statistical analysis. In the USA, for example, this more empirical approach went from strength to strength.

The rejection of natural science as a model for social science sparked a great deal of intellectual interest in Europe. Other approaches were developed – one notable one was structuralism – whereby researchers tried to identify underlying structures within which social events gained their meaning and significance.[8] In France this attracted great interest, and a subsequent spawning of successor approaches, such as post-structuralism, post-modernism and deconstructionism.

There was a political inspiration here too, more overt. French intellectual life in the middle and later decades of the twentieth century was dominated by the discussion of Marxism. Whilst the positivist/realist approaches were decried as simply reflecting the ideological backdrop of capitalist societies (and thus not so much analysing but reflecting the pre-suppositions of such societies), the interpretavist approaches were also seen as essentially conservative – not presenting any challenge to the dominant ideology of the ruling class but acquiescing in it. Writers such as Derrida, Foucault and Baudrillard were concerned to illustrate the depth to which human thinking is entrenched in its social context (which for them was almost synonymous with its political context), and the difficulties this creates for any attempt to get a fix on social phenomena. In Foucault's hands this became the basis for a different way of approaching the interpretative task, whilst in Derrida's it became almost anarchic.

None of these three approaches was developed specifically in relation to management – or indeed to any applied social study. They were mainly theories relating to 'pure' social science – sociology primarily.

Almost at the same time as the last of these was emerging, there was a different approach developing in the USA and UK, specifically in the applied social science fields – that of participatory research. This, in the hands of Chris Argyris or Peter Reason, grew up out of their practical experience of trying to conduct small scale research and consultancy projects, and represented an attempt to create a research framework which went even further away from natural science methods (with their emphasis on the separation of observer and observed).

So the current position is that we have positivists, realists, hermeneuticians, phenomenologists, Foucauldians, and more, all researching and writing about social phenomena (some of which have lost any intellectual touch with each other, which is not a healthy sign). In Part II, then, we will consider these four different approaches (and others which are not discussed here) as reflecting both the *history* of the subject and its *contemporaneous* aspect. As we shall see, though, this does not mean that the earliest one (the analogy with natural science) is in fact archaic and less worthy of attention than the later ones. Far from it – all have their value as well as their drawbacks. Each of them has remained popular with some communities of researchers and writers about organisations (whilst there are no Derridan management theorists, there is a Foucault inspired school).

The reader for whom this is familiar territory may well wonder what has happened to the idea of critical theory and the work of Jurgen Habermas, briefly mentioned in Part I? His approach is considered in more detail in Part III, and adapted to take account of the issues raised by Part II. For although some may depict critical theory as an offshoot of hermeneutics, this is misleading. Habermas (especially amongst critical theorists) is an inclusive writer, whose approach has provided a model for the account developed in Part III.

NOTES

1   Although we shall in fact discuss the views of specific writers, it is less a matter of what they as individuals say so much as the implications of *a view of that kind*.
2   See Lincoln and Guba's contribution in Denzin and Lincoln (1998).
3   Which is not really more than giving them their appropriate philosophical jargon names.

4 Would that management theory itself had preserved a sense of history, of where it has all come from.

5 Readers who are familiar with the history of sociological thought may easily skip the rest of this introduction. Readers who are not should read it with another very big health warning – this is not a definitive account of the whole of the history of thinking about social research; it is only meant to give the reader a feel for the main trends.

6 His second choice term – he initially wanted to call such a science 'Social physics' but was under the impression that it had been used to express a different idea.

7 Though Weber at least, and in some ways Marx and Durkheim also, began to allude to some of the issues which crystallised into interpretavism in later decades.

8 Generally linked to the great French social scientists Levi-Strauss, though arguably the work of Anthony Giddens could be considered as in this tradition (though he uses a slightly different term – 'structuration'). Structuralism is not discussed in this book not because it is not important or interesting, but because the key issue for the methodology of management research are captured by the discussion of interpretavism.

Chapter 5

The Positive and the Real

The first paradigm which we need to consider is the idea that social science does not in any serious way differ from natural science. Its origins go back at least as far as Auguste Comte. But it is important to point out that there is at least as much management research going on that attempts to mirror natural scientific methodologies as uses approaches specific to social science. It is alive – at least in the hands of its adherents.

There are two main versions of this view – positivism and realism. In subsequent chapters, when either of these approaches is referred to, the term 'naturalism' will be used – as marking the link with natural science.

'Positivism' is the term often used as the basic starting point for discussions of the validity of research in general, not just applied social research. Most positions are defined in terms either of consonance or conflict with 'positivism'. This is misleading. For one thing, outside of the discussion of management research, it is generally acknowledged that there are several different versions of the idea that social science should be closely modelled on those of natural science. As a result, positivism, a strongly expressed, highly controversial, and easily refuted idea, can easily crowd out realism, a more subtle idea, less readily grasped and less easy to conclusively reject. For another, the term 'positivism' itself has gone through changes since its original formulation, with the result that one is not so clear about what the word means any longer.

In this chapter, then, we shall: (a) examine the idea of a close analogy between the methods of natural science and those of management research; (b) look at the some of the formulations of the two main versions of this idea, positivism and realism; and (c) consider and evaluate some of the objections to these two approaches. What we will see is that positivism makes only a very limited contribution to an understanding of management research, but that realism, though limited in what it says, has rather more value in it.

5.1   THE ANALOGY WITH NATURAL SCIENCE

We need first to see what is it that is being analogised with. Probably there are five key elements which are common to all modern approaches to natural scientific investigation: empiricism, reduction of concepts to more basic elements, natural laws, independence of observation, and the accumulation of knowledge.

5.1.1   Empiricism

The term empiricism derives from the Greek word 'empeiria' which means experience. The philosophical movement bearing the name empiricism is the view that all knowledge (with the exception of our understanding of reason, mathematics and logic) is derived from our experience – what we take in through our senses. The natural consequence of this is that all investigation and enquiry should be driven by experience rather than by speculation or abstract reasoning – theory arises out of what can be experienced, and is therefore entirely dependent on experience.

This idea certainly goes back to the seventeenth century English writer, Francis Bacon, who talked of different kinds of fallacy people fall into through not following experience. He called these errors *idols* – a kind of idolatry of pre-scientific approaches to knowledge.[1] Roots of the idea that the evidence of one's senses should be the sole or most important basis for knowledge can be found even earlier – in the writing of William of Ockham, a twelfth century philosopher, and indeed as far back as Aristotle.[2]

The idea evolved into two separate concepts. On the one hand was the philosophical idea that all knowledge was derived from experience. This was dealt a major blow in the eighteenth century when Immanuel Kant showed how some of the key concepts necessary for knowledge, such as cause and effect, or the idea of time and space, cannot be derived from sense experience.[3] Then, in the twentieth century philosophical empiricism encountered further major problems, even by such sympathetic Anglo-Saxon philosophers such as Willard Quine, who argued that the totality of our knowledge even in natural science remains partially undetermined by the evidence of our senses.[4] The stripped down reports of 'pure' experience proved to be inadequate to explain even a claim such as that the liquid in a test tube turned blue, let alone anything more substantial. And some philosophers, such as Ludwig Wittgenstein (in his later work) and John Austin, undermined whether such 'pure' sense reports are even intelligible.[5]

On the other hand the emphasis on experience as the primary source of knowledge also evolved separately into a central principle of the methods of practising scientists. So although empiricism as a *philosophical* view has fallen into disrepute, as a *pragmatic approach* to scientific method it has continued in most areas of natural science to the present day. Experiment and observation remain the cornerstones of how natural scientists go about their business, and it is hard to see how they could do otherwise.

Note that I said – in *most* areas. Some aspects of natural science do not easily fit into a simple concept of evidence from experience. The best known example comes from advanced physics. It is accepted that there are competing theories of the origin of the universe, but that observation alone cannot arbitrate between these. In other fields, too, certain ideas are recognised to have significant evidential gaps, but this has not in itself resulted in their rejection. One example of this is the status of the Darwinian principle of survival of the fittest, upon which most of modern evolutionary biology is based. It is acknowledged as a limited model which cannot entirely explain the whole of evolution, but in practice scientists continue to work with it. It underlines that an idea in natural science can be a useful tool for further investigation and explanation irrespective of how comprehensive is its evidential support.[6]

Note that the presumption of just about every writer in this area is that natural science is the clearest and most explicable kind of knowledge. So if this paradigm encounters difficulty in making sense of physics or biology, how much more likely is it that it will fail to account properly for management?

5.1.2   A Reductionist Programme

Another key tendency in the work of natural science is to try to link results in different areas together. We discover an aspect of the way cheetahs compete for territory, for example, and there is an immediate question as to whether this has a genetic basis. Say investigation demonstrates that there is some genetic basis, then geneticists search for the actual gene on the DNA of the cheetah. If that is found, then there may be a new research programme devoted to the chemical mechanisms of the gene, which leads to the fundamental chemistry involved, which in turn may then raise questions about the underlying physics which makes such reactions possible. And it is not solely a matter of going to a smaller and smaller scale. There may be important questions raised by the original study which bear on ecological models, or on models of open systems, which may mean that part of the explanation also reflects the role of larger scale factors such as group behaviour.

The natural scientist is caught in a continual loop of asking 'why?' We find one thing out, and we ask – why is that? And in general the kind of answer that natural scientists look for is to subsume the result under a more encompassing theory or law. In other words, they try to *reduce* one kind of phenomenon to being a subclass of another.

But this is a *programme* – not a simple belief. It is more like an intention or pre-disposition. Natural scientists, like the rest of us, ask why and look for certain kinds of answer – this tendency helps them do their work. But there are enormous areas where it simply has not yet been put into practice.[7] The elevation of such a tendency to becoming a rock hard belief that everything *is* ultimately reducible to laws of basic physics is an *intention* – an act of faith, almost a prejudice – which is not in itself founded on evidence.

5.1.3   The Idea of Natural Laws

The idea of reducing one set of results to being subcases of broader regularities pre-supposes that those regularities are more than merely correlations. It presumes that they reflect some underlying mechanism. If phenomena are brought about mechanistically then in some sense or another they do not just happen but *had* to happen in that way. In some way there is a sense of necessity about the link.

How to explain this sense of necessity has been a source of great debate over the last three centuries. The eighteenth century Scots philosopher David Hume denied it any reality, suggesting (in effect) that it was just a psychological association from our observing a constant correlation between phenomena – I see X followed by Y enough times, and I *think* there is a casual connection, but all that can be *observed* is the correlation. Opposing him, Kant said the general idea of cause and effect was a *precondition* of having any kind of knowledge from experience at all, not something we derived from experience. In the twentieth century the American philosopher Nelson Goodman tried to find a logical base to the idea of a necessity in natural science in the idea that a scientific law differs from a mere statement of correlation by the fact that the former can be used to predict what things *would* be like, projecting beyond what *happens* to be the case to suggest what has to be the case.[8] But whether this is any more than just an ingenious way of saying that the link is a law rather than a mere correlation is not clear – certainly it does not help us identify independently which links are laws and which are not.

This is an idea which is easier to be guided by than to explain. Although the simple version of laws as statements of cause and effect have been largely superseded by systems thinking, the underlying view that the natural world presents compelling linkages remains a key element in scientific investigation. The distinction between mere correlation and necessary connection is central to the idea that there is a mechanism to be investigated. There is no substantial question 'why?' if there is no forcing mechanism, for the answer comes back: no reason why – it is just a correlation, no more than that.

5.1.4   The Joint Ideals of Independence of Investigation and Repeatability

A corollary of the idea of law is that what we discover does not depend on the specific circumstances of the particular individual carrying out the investigation – it should be repeatable by others using the same methods. If the natural world reveals itself to us through our senses, then my experiences should be no different to yours. The test tube should turn blue for both of us. If it does not then how could we be said to have found some underlying mechanism? Why would anyone treat this as a discovery if I see blue and you see red?

It is a central principle in natural science that results obtained by one researcher are tried out by others, often trying to achieve the same result in the same kinds of circumstance before seeing how to test it more severely in extremis. Where results are not repeated, the presumption is that there is no lawlike connection – the example of 'cold fusion' of the last decade illustrates this.

5.1.5   The Belief in Accumulated Levels of Probability

A further consequence of the idea that the natural world runs according to lawlike, necessary, connections, is the confidence that steadily we can come ever closer to understanding those connections. In other words, as time goes on, more and more evidence accumulates in a certain area. We have seen too many apples fall to earth to expect the terrestrial form of the law of gravity to be just plain wrong.[9] Optimistically, we hope that over a long period of time we approach – if never actually reach – the certainty of how the world works.

But the optimism about getting ever closer to certainty presumes that the world is entirely deterministic. It has been accepted for well over fifty years that the model of observation used for normal sized objects does not work at the subatomic level – quantum theory dictates that the location of a subatomic particle is determined at the expense of its movement, and vice versa. This means that the more precise the measurement of one, the less precise the other. So some parts of the natural world may well not be completely explicable on a one to one event basis. Some fields of investigation may set a very definite upper limit on how close we can come to certainty.

We have seen here five key inter-related ideas. Basically the view that social science – and management research in particular – can be approached in the same manner as natural science implies that these five ideas apply equally well to social as to natural phenomena. What we shall see is that some of them do, and others do not.

5.2   THE MEANING OF POSITIVISM

As we saw in the introduction to this Part of the book, the term 'positivism' came into the language via the nineteenth century French philosopher-scientist, Auguste Comte, though some of its tenets may be traced back earlier, to David Hume, and even further back to Francis Bacon. And the idea of social study as having a similar potential to natural science certainly goes back to Vico. Comte though was the first to explicitly hold that human phenomena could be studied in an analogous manner with the natural world, and that therefore the methods of natural science are basically also of equal value in the study of humans. He coined the term 'sociology' as a natural science of human behaviour – interestingly, though, he preferred the phrase 'social physics' as an alternative.

For Comte, social phenomena could be investigated in a parallel manner to the physical world. Enquiry would be based on observation and experiment, which would lead to the formulation of laws which would allow clear predictions of the future and parallel explanations of the past. Writing some half a century later, another French writer, Emil Durkheim, took this approach further – he projected sociology as an independent science investigating the 'objective reality' and 'inescapable necessities' of society.

It is important to note the contribution of these early sociologists, as some of their key ideas were later discarded or overlooked. For one thing, Comte held very strongly that social phenomena could not be understood in isolation – that they only made sense in the context of theory (somewhat at odds with the empiricist trend in natural science we discussed earlier). For another, Durkheim, in his own sociological research practice, made free use of interpretation, and projected meanings and significances into human phenomena which would not sit easily with modern positivism, and would seem to be closer to an anti-positivist methodology, construed in more modern terms.

Positivism took on a more tightly defined guise in the twentieth century. Partially this was a result of the influence of a more analytically driven philosophical version of the idea, logical positivism, which held that language itself could only have meaning in virtue of its link with observable phenomena. Partially it was also the influence of American psychologists and sociologists, who took a keenly empiricist approach to the study of human beings, emphasising controlled observation and statistical analysis. This in turn was perhaps a reaction to the anti-positivist approaches which began to gain currency, so that the approach needed to be more distinctly defined. This led to a strong interpretation of positivism, as stating that social research had an identity of method with natural science.

Arguably, the key features of a positivist approach to research include the following:

- *'bare' facts*: the idea that there are features of the world which can be perceived or observed independently of theory, and are thus in some sense basic or bare facts; thus description of what we directly observe comes first, and then is used as a foundation for theory construction;[10] there is, then, a strong distinction between *describing* an event and *explaining* it

- *researcher independence*: researchers should not impose their theoretical prejudices on the facts; basic factual data on a certain topic which is taken from a specific source would be the same no matter who actually carried out the collection; analytical techniques should operate in the same way whoever uses them

- *theoretical reductionism*: theories are only constructs out of the observable phenomena they explain; they carry no added significance, and the kind of explanation they provide is primarily the prediction of observable events on the basis of prior observables; all ideas are ultimately to be understood in terms of what they say about the observable world

phenomenalism: the idea that there is nothing beyond what can be sensed, there are no 'hidden' essences of things which cannot in principle be investigated via our sense experience	*nominalism*: the related view that knowledge can only be about concrete objects, and thus apparently 'theoretical' entities must be entirely explicable in terms of what can be directly observed
unity of science: all investigation worthy of being called scientific follows essentially the same process, and thus all sciences use essentially the same methods	*value free study*: what is right or wrong cannot be determined by scientific investigation

Figure 5.1   Kolakowski's rules of positivism.

- *value-free research*: concepts of value are not found in the observable world; they are human impositions, and thus the researcher can (and should) carry out investigation independently of value judgements

The above links closely with the depiction of positivism given by Leszek Kolakowski, a relatively recent commentator, who has identified four rules of the idea (see Figure 5.1).[11] We can see here a definitive answer to the key questions which Lincoln and Guba suggest that a methodological paradigm should answer.

The positivist approach:

Ontology: only what we can sense exists
Epistemology: all knowledge is of what we can sense
Methodology: all science uses the same methods

There are other underpinning beliefs which we have already encountered that are associated with positivism. These are not central to the approach as outlined above, but they are commonly encountered in discussions of the idea, and therefore merit some discussion, such as the view that *every* knowledge claim can be determined (eventually) one way or the other via observation. Another is the idea that there is no causality in nature or society over and above those constant correlations between one event and another which can be directly observed.

Regarding the first view, when applied to social research it is possible to take a view that at least some knowledge claims cannot be determined one way or the other by observation – a positivist but indeterminist view. This approximates to the view which Blaikie has described as 'negativism' – that the only valid standards of research are indeed those of natural science, but that social science does not measure up to these standards, and hence cannot be regarded as providing knowledge at all.[12] Regarding the second view, stemming again from David Hume, it is (as we have already seen) itself highly problematic. Philosophers of natural science[13] have argued that the idea of law in natural science is valid, but requires a stronger concept than mere constant conjunction.

5.3   POSITIVISM IN MANAGEMENT THEORY

Derek Pugh, a leading OB researcher of the 1960s and 1970s, is a good person to start with in discussing positivism applied to management research – he describes himself as 'an unreconstructed positivist'. What does this assertion mean? So far as Pugh is concerned, it appears to indicate the following philosophical beliefs: (a) a belief in something he calls realism; (b) an assumption that people and organisations exist as relatively concrete entities; (c) a belief that the OB universe manifests orderly patterns or regularities, and (d) a belief that data collected can 'expose' these regularities.[14]

Pugh makes another comment which is worth noting. He says that knowledge is to be distinguished from wisdom, on the grounds that the former '... [when] generated through systematic, comparative, replicative, scientific study of the empirical world, consists of generalisable propositions that give insight and/or have predictive powers when applied to phenomena other than those on which they are based.' By contrast, wisdom is seen as deeper but '... riddled with superstition and incompatible beliefs and ideas'. This echoes the claims of Comte a century and a half earlier, who talked of subject disciplines going through an evolution from theologically dominated conceptions, to metaphysical speculation, leading finally to scientific investigation.

Pugh has set out what he presumably would regard as a clear statement of positivism, but in doing so he leaves a variety of unexplained ideas. His idea of 'realism' is not explained, so (a) is intrinsically problematic. Interestingly, it is the first time that this term has had a high profile in our discussion. As we will see later, realism is really a separate view, more subtle, but for that reason less often encountered in discussions of social research.

Pugh's point (b) is odd – has anyone ever questioned whether *people* are 'relatively' concrete? Are organisations as relatively concrete as people are? Presumably not, but this leaves us with a question as to what all this really signifies. What kind of 'concreteness' is possessed by people which is possessed to lesser degree by organisations? Even more puzzling is why he feels the need to state this – what is the great benefit about being 'concrete'? Against what is there a contrast – what things are relatively *not* concrete? What things are relatively *more* so? This point sounds more like a hope than a justified claim.

(c) and (d) are less problematic, though even here the slightly eccentric way of presenting (c) leaves the question – are there regularities because of some underlying factor, or are these regularities which 'just' happen? The positivist answer rules out any reference to anything substantial beyond those regularities, whilst a realist approach (as we shall see later) would imply that regularities exist because there is a single unchanging reality that underlies the phenomena investigated. This is a key feature of the realist approach – that there is a stable world independent of our perceptions, which we discover *by means of* the regularities which we observe. The key difference between the positivist and the realist view is this idea of how far the world is independent of our experience. Pugh seems to muddle this by trying to have the best of both worlds.

In any case, why a *belief* that the social world exhibits orderly patterns? Again this is elevated to an apparent article of faith to suggest that there is more to it than *just* the exhibiting of regularities – I suspect Pugh wants to say that these are really there, not just apparent to us.

Part of the problem here is that Pugh acknowledges his debt to the philosophy of David Hume, but he tries too hard to apply this to social phenomena – in Pugh's case, the study of OB. Hume subscribed to a view which cannot account fully for our belief in a single law-governed world – which he saw as merely an assumption, virtually a prejudice. It was Immanuel Kant, writing in deliberate rebuttal of Hume, who explained how some of our ideas (such as that there is a single world which is orderly) are not *beliefs* which we can prove by means of scientific – or any other – kinds of investigation, but *necessary pre-conditions* of any kind of science, rational thought or systematic enquiry.

This excursus into metaphysics is important. As we have seen above, there are points where Pugh seems to subscribe to a hybrid view, incorporating elements of realism as well as claiming allegiance to positivism. Paradoxically, in this he comes close to an assumption made by anti-positivist views, which seem to subscribe not simply to a rejection of the key ideas of positivism, but to go further and reject the underlying idea of an independent world which operates in a law governed way – that is, they throw realism out along with positivism. But realism is an independent view from positivism.

Some element of the realist viewpoint is fundamental to any attempt to explain any phenomenon. Explanation is the attempt to make things intelligible. We only make them so by showing how they arise from their circumstances. Simply to indicate a pattern within which a phenomenon fits is not to make it intelligible. Some reference to processes outside the phenomenon, which have some form of influence or impact on it, is essential for explanation. This is as true of explanations of trade union behaviour in terms of Marxist ideology as it is of explanations of managerial style in terms of the Myers-Briggs/Jung psychology, as it is of explanations of star movements in terms of relativity, as also it was of explanations of the weather by reference to the anger of the gods. They all explain one phenomenon in terms of others which brought them about. In doing so they all presume that there is a unified medium through which such 'bringing about' happens.

Returning to Pugh, I have suggested that he has confused positivism with realism, and that his self avowal would be better regarded as a statement of a realist perspective. Be that as it may, he has explicitly advocated something he calls positivism. As he has expressed it, it is not a consistent or especially clear view.

Another management writer who seems to advocate something like a positivist approach is Donaldson,[15] though this is based on indirect evidence. Donaldson does not in his main discussion on organisation theory make a simple statement of where he stands on methodology. Rather he defends a partially identified 'orthodoxy' against detractors, who mostly come from interpretative or hermeneutic style perspectives (see Chapter 9). The orthodoxy which he defends is not clearly set out, though he speaks with approval of empirical and quantitatively based studies, quoting Pugh and other members of the Aston school. He also seems to argue in favour of the primacy of factual data collection over theory building and testing.

It is therefore not easy to critique Donaldson's position in itself. It clearly has some affinities, at the very least, with the overall idea of drawing an analogy between natural and social science, and may be more explicitly positivist than that. But it is too reliant on an idea of orthodoxy which cries out for further explanation. Maybe this is not a great issue, especially as his main defence of organisation theory (as he conceives it) is at the time of writing, fifteen years old, and therefore already ageing quite significantly.

It is worth noting, however, that adherents of the positivist approach not only exist but are continuing to thrive. Any reader doubting this is advised to consult recent editions of the leading management journals, where they will find ample examples of research papers describing tightly controlled surveys, often with large bodies of data which are then submitted to statistical analysis. Not every researcher will happily acknowledge themselves to be positivists, but there is a stylistic format which is characteristic of positivist research: definition of a model or formulation of hypothesis; systematic data collection exercise; analysis of data; conclusion for hypothesis. What makes this specifically positivist rather than realist is the absence of methodological uncertainty – the conducting of data collection using a single method or instrument. For positivism there are no constructs beyond experience – hence on that approach the collection of data via one source *can* be completely valid. On a *realist* view, on the other hand, there is always the possibility of alternative perspectives, for the world being investigated is not dependent on one particular perspective or one particular line of enquiry.

5.4   CRITICISMS OF POSITIVISM

The preceding section has been largely discussed at a theoretical level. In this section we shall consider the criticisms of positivism in a more concrete context. Most of these points are well known – they are presented here for completeness.

5.4.1   Facts Cannot be Isolated from Theories

The early positivists, especially Comte, recognised that social phenomena cannot be identified in isolation. Even in natural science it is acknowledged that there is no clear dividing line between what is description and what is explanation. As we saw in Part I, so simple a matter as the description of someone's behaviour in terms of consultation rather than persuasion raises explanatory elements which go beyond the simple identification of what someone actually did. Someone might think that it is possible to strip away even this element of theory, and operate at the level of describing the manager's behaviour in purely physical movements, but this would be misleading. Someone's behaviour is not a set of mere movements of limbs, it involves an essential element of intention – so explanation of human behaviour has to go beyond the physically observable.

5.4.2   Researchers Cannot be Entirely Independent of the Subject of their Research

Data collection in the human sciences is a personal interaction, and thus personal dynamics come into play. We saw an example of this earlier – interviews are rarely if ever completely simple collections of information, as the researcher so often is giving clues about their research interest by means of unrecognised non-verbal cues. Again, another aspect we have already noticed is the influence of personal stereotypes – women carrying out interviews may well in general collect different kinds and depths of information than men, even when conducting the same kinds of interview.

Whilst interviews are a crucial example of this source of bias, questionnaire instruments are not free from the possibility. Question design is fraught with potential ways in which individuals may contribute more to a study than merely provide their overall underlying latent attitudes. For example, certain kinds of language can be objectionable or embarrassing. Certain terms may create in respondents a range of associations which change their emotional stance to the research. Even the visual appearance of a questionnaire can lead individuals to draw conclusions about what is sought and thereby adjust their response accordingly. In general, if an individual picks up a cue from the researcher that a study (of whatever kind of methodology) is likely to lead to policy decisions which might influence their own interests then they may well respond to the study in a way which they believe may improve their own position.

None of this is new – it is mentioned here because it illustrates the point that social researchers are not clean sheet agents of investigation, but bring something substantial to the process.

5.4.3   Subjects Cannot be Entirely Independent of the Theories which Explain their Behaviour

Karl Popper[16] has pointed out the simplest form of this criticism. A researcher's conclusions do not affect the behaviour of rocks, DNA structures, or galaxies. But a human being can be so influenced. Suppose I read about someone's theory of human behaviour. Once I have heard about this I may react to it. In some cases I may deliberately try to buck the system to prove the theory wrong, whilst in others I may passively accept the theory and adjust my behaviour towards what I am led to believe is normal. In each case *the theory has actually changed* the phenomena. There are also more complex versions of this point, such as that discussed in the previous sub-section, that researchers often inadvertently insert their own views into the investigation, and in doing so create a response from the subject which does not reflect their basic attitude, but their immediate reaction to the research event. As Roger Trigg puts it '...we cannot abstract ourselves from all societies and divest ourselves of pre-suppositions.'[17]

5.4.4   In Social Research, Values Cannot be Eliminated from the Investigation

There is a general point about social research here, and a specific one relating to applied social research.

The general point is that our language and concepts of human behaviour, whether individual or group based, are shot through with values. Simply to refer to human beings calls into play an implicit network of moral concepts such as political rights, and ethical duties. Moreover, certain concepts have an evaluative nuance which is inseparable from their application. For example, the idea of a workplace *team* is implicitly positive in value terms – people may argue about which is the best form of teamwork, but the concept itself has a positive 'glow' about it.

The applied point is that where research is likely to lead, in terms of organisation decisions, then by definition this is going to involve values. The policy options themselves only draw sustenance from the values which define their benefits. Consultation, for example, is a tactic which may improve organisational effectiveness. The benefits of which may lead to are ultimately things which are perceived to be valuable in their own right – such benefits may be measured in terms of, for example, improvements in profitability (which contributes towards the personal financial benefits which shareholders may expect – that is, shareholder *value*: a term not chosen by accident, despite its pseudo-economic gloss) or maybe in terms of employee satisfaction, self evidently a phenomenon valued by the individuals concerned. Organisations exist in order to deliver results which individuals value, so it makes no sense to try to separate organisational research from values – these lie at the heart of organisational existence. So the idea of a 'value-free' form of management research is not at all clear.

5.4.5 Theoretical Explanations are More than Mere Predictions of Phenomena

In natural science the prime test of a theory is what it will predict. Galileo's theories about motion were accepted because they predicted the behaviour of balls of different mass when dropped from a tower. Einstein's theory was eventually accepted because it successfully predicted the appearance of the eclipse of 1919. Positivism is committed to the idea that the same kind of process must be at work with social theory.

But recall the argument from complexity which we looked at in Part I. Human behaviour brings a multitude of factors into play. The behaviour of groups of people must cover a huge range of such factors. No two people are completely alike psychologically, and hence no two groups of people can be sociologically completely alike. As a result of this, there is a very restricted range of human phenomena for which we can make clear simple predictions which have much of a chance of being correct. One can make predictions about the behaviour of the majority of members of a football crowd when their team scores a goal, and hope for a good chance of being correct. But one may find it hard to predict with the same level of confidence about the behaviour of a crowd of angry political demonstrators.

I may successfully predict that a certain individual will object to my decision as a manager, but not be able to predict what form that objection takes – outright rejection, appeal to a higher authority, constructive confrontation, and so on.[18] In general social theories are not able to operate with the same degree of predictive success as much of the theory of the natural world (as we have to some extent seen earlier). The models used may help us identify the different options that individuals or groups have, but they have a very low probability of identifying which specific option was taken.

In the natural world there are only a few possible outcomes of an event – one stone falls on another, and the first is likely to: (a) stay still; (b) move a little; (c) move a lot; and (d) break apart. Not a lot else can occur.[19] In the social world there are countless significantly distinct options. Suppose I inform someone of a decision I have made. Amongst the very many different potential responses there are, someone may get angry about the decision. Within this one option, they may: (i) scream and shout immediately there and then; (ii) ask to speak to me in private and then scream and shout; (iii) wait an hour or so and then come and scream and shout; and (iv) come back the next day and scream and shout. And screaming and shouting is just one of very many crude behavioural responses, and within each of these responses there is the issue of the many different varieties of counter decision they make – such as threatening to resign, resigning, threatening to take the issue to the CEO, threatening to take the issue to the union, going and bad mouthing me to other staff, etc. Prediction is simply too tenuous when considering the complexity of human behaviour.

Positivism makes a strong claim about the parallelism between social and natural science. Even in the hands of two management research practitioners who are quite positivistically inclined, the idea is not easily expressed. But in any case it has severe limitations, as illustrated above. As we noted previously, this is not a matter of historical curiosity – there are many people out there doing positivistic management research.

5.5 THE IDEA OF REALISM

I indicated earlier that realism is a related approach to management research but one which may avert some of the key weaknesses of positivism. The discussion will be truncated relative to that concerning positivism, but many of the key themes will recur at later points. It is to be noted that I shall be discussing here a broad interpretation of the idea of realism, rather than looking in too much detail at the views of any one writer.[20]

Very roughly, realism is the view that there is a single real world which operates according to scientific laws, and which we incompletely know. It is discovered by reference to what we can directly observe and experience, but there are aspects of it which are remote and maybe not at all directly accessible to us via experience.

Realism again takes seriously the analogy between social and natural science. Perhaps the key difference between realism and positivism is that it recognises that there are limitations to this comparison.

Realism shares with positivism the empiricist approach without committing to an out and out empiricist philosophy – it depicts social knowledge as *relying* on experience as the ultimate test of theory, without being completely *reducible* to statements about experience. For the realist as much as for the positivist, a theory has no validity unless it has been tested rigorously against experience. But this is not the same as saying that every idea can be turned into a statement *about* experience. We noted in an earlier section that positivism tries to eliminate all reference to 'theoretical' ideas unless these are directly linked to experience. So for the positivist all knowledge is ultimately explicable in terms of our experience. 'Internal' factors, such as underlying causes or mechanisms which assure a law-like necessary connection between one event (a cause) and another (an effect) have no meaning for the positivist unless they themselves are describable in experiential terms. In contrast, the realist recognises that there are limits to what we can experience, and that there may be factors which we cannot directly experience which create the necessary link between one event and another.

The other key difference between the two ideas is that realism rejects the idea that all knowledge can be reduced to some basic level, for example, that everything is ultimately explicable in terms of the interactions of particles in subatomic physics. This does not exclude the idea that scientists rely on the technique of repeated 'why?' questioning. On the contrary – as Bhaskar says, for science, 'its essence lies in the move at any one level from manifest phenomena to the structures that generate them.'[21] The key point here is that the 'structures' which 'generate' (or in more straightforward language, *cause* or *bring about*) social phenomena may themselves be remote from what we directly experience.

Suppose a researcher finds that members of ethnic minority groups clearly occupy a smaller proportion of senior management positions than they would if these were distributed pro rata to the ethnic composition of the population in general. This would seem to be a clear example of a social phenomenon, directly based on what the researcher has experienced or observed. Now the researcher asks the why question, and tries to link this phenomenon with potential underlying structures. One of these might be the features of the labour market in the country or region being investigated, another might be the psychology of racial discrimination. But in either case, the structure or factor used to provide this explanation is significantly more remote from experience than the phenomenon to be explained. The idea that labour is best understood in terms of market theory is in itself a theoretical assertion – indeed the term 'market' is after all drawn from the metaphor of a group of street traders operating competitively in one place. 'The labour market' is therefore a construct. Even more so is the psychology of racism a construct,[22] distant from what we actually can observe.

A related point about 'theoretical' explanations is that realism takes a more flexible view of natural science. As mentioned earlier, positivism views natural science in a highly reductionist manner. In principle, for the positivist, all phenomena can be reduced to statements of what can be experienced. There are no meaningful ideas which do not *directly* connect with the observable. But the practice of natural scientists is not as simple as this. For one thing, models – 'theoretical' entities – sometimes turn out to be observable after all, and sometimes remain just theoretical. When Mendel proposed the idea of a gene it was a theoretical object: just as atoms were. Now we have directly seen photographs of genes, whilst the atom has proved to be a complex network of even smaller phenomena which we call particles for convenience, but in fact are bundles of energy which possess peculiar clusters of properties. Physics, supposedly the most fundamental of all the natural sciences, at this level, is less obviously 'real' than biology.

Related to this is the fact that for natural scientists prediction is more important than the precise semantics of the concepts and terms they use. Models, as Harre points out, are the central mechanism for this, but they are not necessarily tied to the observable world in the way that positivism would suggest.

Realism is ambiguous regarding the range of methods suitable for social research. Bhaskar explicitly rejects the idea that the natural and social world can be investigated using the same kinds of methods, whilst Harre explicitly affirms this.[23] This may be as much to do with what they regard as a method as anything – clearly we don't send questionnaires out to inorganic chemicals, and we don't try to carry out open repeatable experiments with people.[24] Each is equally inappropriate.

5.6   OBJECTIONS TO REALISM

5.6.1   An Improvement over Positivism?

How well does realism cope with the objections raised against positivism?

Regarding the issue of the integration of fact and theory, in the case of realism there is no excessive reliance on a categorical distinction between these two ideas, so a degree of greyness in the spectrum is not a significant problem in the way it is for positivism.

Regarding the questions of researcher independence and value free investigation, different proponents of realism may view these differently. Bhaskar's formulation of realism directly acknowledges researcher dependence and an element of value boundness. It is doubtful whether other proponents, such as Rom Harre, would agree with this. But it indicates at the least that realism is not intrinsically vulnerable to this objection as positivism is.

So far as the matter of the relation between theory and prediction is concerned, realism still maintains a close analogy between natural and social science, so prediction is still an important aim of the research process. Hence the problems of prediction, including issues arising out of the complexity of the management context, apply to realism as they do with positivism.

So overall, realism improves to some extent over positivism, though not completely eliminates all these issues.

5.6.2   Problems Specific to Realism

Perhaps the most significant issue for the realist to deal with is what exactly does the main claim of realism actually amount to? A world which is not entirely accessible to our experience? What can we say about it other than what we gather from that experience?

Those realists who want to emphasise the independence of the real world from what we perceive may appear to be committed to a concept of the social world as somehow 'beyond' what we perceive, but it is not necessary to go to this length. It is entirely consistent with the idea of realism to say that: (a) the world does not depend on our perceptions; (b) we have a limited contact with this world; and (c) this contact can change as the technologies of investigation change. This does not suggest that there is anything *intrinsically* remote or hidden. Some things may not be accessible now, but may later become so when a new technique of collecting information is developed. So we can approach closer and closer to reality, but we do not ever attain it entirely.

Another side of this issue presents a different kind of problem, one which is less optimistic about the possibility of objective social knowledge. If we start at a distance from social reality and then approach closer and closer, then it suggests that in some way what we start with, though imperfect, has some degree of rightness about it. But if we start from a position which is erroneous, how can we move from that to a more accurate position? Our most basic language about social matters is already theory laden (as we have already seen). So it is difficult to see how we can erect a framework which moves from a false view of management to a less false one – the very building bricks which we use to start off with already have that degree of falsity built in. This issue is not resolved by the conception of realism which has underpinned our discussion so far. In the next section we shall see a more radical version of the realist approach, which purports to side-step this problem.

5.7   CONJECTURE AND REFUTATION

Karl Popper[25] devised a dynamic alternative to the traditional realist approaches to natural science in the middle of the twentieth century, and later he and others claimed that it could also be applied to social science (though he restricted his discussion, as many have done, to 'pure' social sciences such as sociology and economics, rather than applied studies such as management). Basically the root of Popper's version of what has been called by some 'critical realism'[26] is that science is not about collecting data to *confirm* theories, but rather to *test* them. Hence the proper activity of a scientist, natural or social, is to formulate theories or hypotheses (or *conjectures*) and then try to refute them. Truth is never conclusively arrived at. All that happens is that a conjecture withstands refutation, but there is no further test which establishes it for good. This fulfils the realist idea that we can approach but never completely grasp the final truth of the social world.

Whilst this was a striking and challenging argument, Popper's views have not really found many friends in the social sciences. One issue is that as a result of Popper's work, there was an explosion of interest in the philosophy of natural science, and a host of contrasting views put forward. Amongst these, the views of Thomas Kuhn, above all, provided a great challenge to the hypothetico-deductivist approach, questioning whether it was even true of natural science, let alone social.

Kuhn, in contrast to Popper, identified different stages in the development of a science. 'Normal' science proceeds along different lines from 'revolutionary' science, which occurs when the dominating paradigm of the time is dislodged and refuted. In the normal period the emphasis is not on refuting ideas, but on slow and steady building up of solutions to peripheral puzzles. But in time there grows up an anomaly which cannot be so resolved, and then the dominant ideas of the field are rejected, leading to a period of relative uncertainty until a new idea establishes itself as able to solve many of the current puzzles, which then ushers in a new period of normal science, and so on. The great merit of Kuhn's views is that they seemed to fit the history of natural science more snugly, but the implication of this approach is that there is less of pretension to realism. There is no suggestion that we are even approaching a reality, but rather substituting one kind of perspective for another. This makes realism less appealing, and is more compatible in spirit with some versions of interpretavism (see Chapter 6).

5.8 THE IDEA OF A 'GROUNDED' THEORY

A final twist on the idea of social science as akin in style and approach to natural science is the idea of *grounded theory*. This was developed specifically in relation to social science, and therefore has a more direct relevance to the social world than the previous approaches. Nevertheless, I have included it here because it is closer in style and spirit to naturalism than to other approaches such as interpretavism.

Developed by two social[27] researchers in the late 1960s, grounded theory took up the question of where theories came from. Hypothetico-deductivism depicted these as subject to test and potential refutation, but did not explain where they originated. Nor did the Kuhnian approach make an advance in this respect. The advantage of grounded theory is that it purports to demonstrate how we can move from one level of interaction with social reality – the pre-systematic reflections of subjects in a study – to the more sophisticated conclusions of the systematic researcher.

Essentially the idea of grounded theory is that we start with the basic perception of social actors, and we slowly proceed from this via testing, reformulation, retesting, continually refining, excluding or redefining, as we move towards a more generalisable theoretical perspective on the subject matter. The claim of Glaser and Strauss was that this would remain closer to the perceptions of the subjects, and would proceed from their perceptions in terms which they would recognise. In this respect it starts to step forward towards the inter-pretavist tradition, but it is still an attempt to emulate the systematic methods of natural science. Often it is self-consciously linked with the pre-Popperian tradition of *induction* – the idea that knowledge arises out of the collection and analysis of data rather than the testing of theories.

Glaser and Strauss' work is not entirely isolated – there is a tradition of 'analytic induction' which includes other attempts to show how generalisable knowledge can arise from individual cases.[28] One of the main difficulties with this kind of approach is the issue of *transfer*. Suppose I start my research with one particular case, in which a number of managers in one organisation talk about their approaches to decision making. We have some kind of unified image or concept, which pur-ports to make the views of all these managers more intelligible. Now we move to another case – a new organisation. What do we now compare? *The very language in which decision making is couched is now based in a different setting.* It is the *imposition* of the researcher to say that this is the same phenomenon. The fact that the same words are used is no guarantee that the same experiences are being considered. What complicates this further is Giddens' double hermeneutic: the understandings of the individuals participating in the research have already been interfered with – they are not naive managers, but exist in a theoretically laden environment in which many experiences which they might well have explained in entirely different terms now become identified as decision making (or reengineering, or strategic intervention, or whatever buzz language they have been infected with).[29]

Another difficulty with grounded theory is that it proceeds functionally as if there are no false starts. But we may easily start with the responses of an individual who is confused, idiosyncratic – *or just plain misguided about their own perceptions*. It is not at all impossible that someone uses a language to describe their behaviour or perceptions which is not even their own real perception, let alone someone else's. Paradoxically, the more articulate a person is the more chance that this could happen: the articulate person is able to construct an elaborate verbal structure which may maintain the superficial verbal consistency of a set of statements which really does not reflect how they actually experienced something at all (but may represent a post hoc rationalisation of the experience, for example). Once we start wrong, the theory building of grounded theory proceeds to build up on this error. Grounded theory shares with interpretavism the presumption that when surveyed using the standard question and answer techniques of modern social research, people are basically correct about their own perceptions (though the treatment is rather different). But whilst this might be true in the main, this does not prevent us being wrong on occasion. And on grounded theoretic methods, start wrong stay wrong.

So as a description of a useful set of *methods* grounded theory may have its merits, but as a *methodology* – an explanation of how social research can provide knowledge – it has serious weaknesses. We shall see some of these problems replicated when we look at hermeneutics.

SUMMARY

In this chapter we have looked at the two most characteristic approaches to the analogy between natural and social science. We have seen that positivism is clearly too strong a claim – almost an eccentricity which imposes as much challenge at the feet of natural scientists as it does at the feet of social researchers. Realism is a more moderate cluster of views though this does not avoid problems such as the theory laden nature of social descriptions.

It was in the light of these difficulties that the second group of ideas, intepretavism, has gained great support in recent decades. To this paradigm we shall now turn. But before doing so, it is important to recognise that whilst some of the answers which naturalism provides may be suspected, the requirements it raises – such as that knowledge must in some way be independent of the investigator – retain an importance and value which will persist in subsequent chapters. And perhaps the most important element of realism which we will need to keep a hold on is that there is one world, albeit with many features. So investigation is not about finding *an* answer, but finding *the* answer. This issue will become crucial in our very last chapters.

NOTES

1 Bacon (1620).
2 For a discussion of the views of William of Ockham, see the internet Encyclopaedia of Philosophy. Aristotle's views can be found in various parts of his large oeuvre, but perhaps the clearest expressions of his views on this point are his scientific works, such as 'Generation and Corruption' (in McKeon ed.).
3 Kant (1787). The idea is stated right at the start of the work, though the rest of it is a demonstration in detail of how this is the case.
4 Quine (1953).
5 Wittgenstein (1953) and Austin (1962).
6 The point here is not that these are conclusive objections to the idea of empiricism (they are not) but that they indicate that more is going on than just the access to experience and its systematic explanation.
7 See Maddox (1998) for a fascinating discussion of how far natural science has gone and how much further it has to go.
8 Goodman (1955).
9 In its original range of explanation – that is, for objects not too much larger or smaller than humans (which in terms of physics means differing by a factor of, say, 10^4) and moving at less than about one-tenth of the speed of light.
10 Though this was not part of Comte's original vision.

11 Kolakowski (1972). It is crucial to recognise that what Kolakowski calls 'phenomenalism' is very different from the verbally similar but logically very different concept of 'phenomenology' which we shall discuss in the next chapter.

12 Blaikie (1993) Chapter 2.

13 Such as Goodman op cit.

14 Pugh (1981). Later quotes of Pugh's in this section are all from this work.

15 Donaldson (1985). Most of his main points come in the introduction and first two chapters of this work.

16 See Popper (1961).

17 Trigg (1985) p. 203.

18 The added complication here is that what I observe is the form – the external behaviour – which I have to judge whether it is a way of someone objecting or not.

19 Though there may be a range of different *ways* in which a stone may break, or fall over, or whatever. We are simply interested in *whether* it breaks (or falls, or stays still). In other words – *what we have an interest in* is a significant factor in what we regard as a phenomenon at all. The argument of the following paragraph in the text indicates that there are many more aspects of social phenomena in which we have sufficient interest to regard as distinct phenomena. But the smaller range in the natural world is not because of what is there but because of *what we find important*. This will become extremely important in Part III of this book.

20 So we shall not be considering some of the key ideas which some specific modern realists have presented as core elements of their views, such as the idea that there are three levels of what can be known (the empirical, the actual and the real). Interested readers should consult Outhwaite (1987).

21 Bhaskar (1978).

22 Though a construct with a very complex structure, incorporating spectra of reactions from out-and-out racial hatred through to liberal white guilt-ridden over-compensation, and involving a number of different responses to law, social trends, social acceptability, etc. To call something a construct is most definitely NOT to consider it a fiction. No one should interpret this view as suggesting that the experience of being discriminated against on account of one's racial origin is somehow not as real, in human terms, as non-constructed experiences.

23 Harre and Secord (1972).

24 Though it is conceivable that a closed (that is, non-disclosed) experiment with a group of individuals might be repeated. This, however, is not a very popular approach to the explanation of human behaviour in organisations.

25 The ideas of Popper and Thomas Kuhn are very well discussed and compared with each other in Lakatos (1974) – rather more illuminatingly than reference to their own works.

26 Though in discussions of the philosophy of natural science it is more commonly described as 'hypothetico-deductivism'.

27 Glaser and Strauss (1967). Though more recently there has been some falling out between the two of them, as could be seen in the early part of 2000 on Glaser's own website, where he made some very critical comments of Strauss' later work. The idea of grounded theory is well expounded in the article by David Partington – though sadly in the volume in which it appears, none of the other submissions display anything like the same methodological sophistication. Partington (2000).

28 A relatively recent approach in the same tradition can be found in Eisenhardt (1989).

29 This echoes an objection that Keynes raised to this kind of comparative induction – it still rests on the more basic analysis of cases into collections of features and qualities. See Keynes (1921).

Chapter 6

Management Theory as Meaning

In the previous chapter we looked at naturalism, the analogy between social science and natural science. Two main versions of this idea were compared. We found that positivism, the stronger analogy, makes too great a claim even for natural science, and encounters a series of difficulties. The weaker, broader version, realism, does not entirely escape all of these though overall it is less vulnerable.

I mentioned earlier in the book that the range of different approaches to applied social science has often been presented as a single dimension. At one end is often located a 'hard' position which depicts social and natural science methods as more or less the same – which I call 'naturalism', but is more often called positivism, although we have seen that this may not be the most characteristic version of the position. At another end is often placed a view which depicts social science as entirely concerned with meaning and interpretation – sometimes called (again, misleadingly) phenomenology.

One major error which I shall criticise later is the mistaken view that the difference between these two clusters of views comes down to a difference in preference for objective facts rather than feelings, sometimes misleadingly described as a preference for quantitative vs. qualitative data, or (even more simplistic) 'hard' vs. 'soft' information.[1] However, the kind of information someone works with is not the differentiating factor. Different researchers and theorists will take differing views about what counts as knowledge, but the sheer presence or absence of feelings is not a determining factor in this evaluation. The key factors relate, not to the kind of material someone collects, but to the way in which someone *uses* the material they have collected to make statements about an underlying reality. It is perfectly possible for a researcher to make use of long tables of statistical information, but treat them in an interpretative manner, and equally it is, if anything, even more feasible for a positivist or similar to collect data relating to people's feelings, and then draw categorical universal conclusions from that data. It is what someone *does* with all this which characterises their approach, rather than the material collected itself. The type of information dealt with by a researcher is quite separate from the way in which they deal with it.

This point is not brought out at all clearly by many standard texts in this area. There is a tendency to cluster together the *philosophical* issues of how a researcher conceives of social reality with the *practical* ones of what kinds of data someone works with.[2] Maybe there is as much a question of style as substance in this clustering. All the same, it is the philosophical distinction to be drawn here that greatly affects what we would accept as knowledge about management – the practical one is less relevant.

The strategy of distinguishing between 'positivist' and 'phenomenological' social research methodologies is only useful for presenting the distinction between approaches which do and approaches which do not try to mirror or resemble natural science methodologies (in other words, as a distinction it only really serves the purpose of helping elucidate and critique positivist/realist approaches). Even there, it fails to present a clear view of the nature of natural science, and thus only partially explores the difference between positivism and realism, let alone the wide range of approaches which reject the analogy with natural science.

When we turn away from this analogy, we will see that there is a wide range of non-positivistic and non-realist methodologies which are: (a) not always easily differentiated from each other; and (b) not obviously 'more' or 'less' interpretavist than others in the same over-all category (and so not easy to fit onto a one-dimensional model). Some of these differ from each other almost as much as they differ from positivism and realism. We cannot look at all of these approaches in this and the following two chapters. A quite different kind of book would be needed to do the majority of them justice – one which is more philosophical and even further away from management practice than the current discussion. The aim here is to present to the reader with a sample of the range of ideas in this area, to discuss some of the strengths which have been claimed for specific examples of these, and to indicate the weaknesses with them.

Before looking directly at these approaches, there are three import-ant cautions which the reader needs to take account of. Firstly, the original expressions of some of these approaches are often highly abstract, sometimes deeply obscure, and can conceal an array of assumptions which are common to philosophers in France and Germany in the later twentieth century, but not necessarily clear to management specialists, to non-specialist readers or to philosophers from the Anglo-Saxon tradition.

Secondly, few of these writers have discussed the application of their views to organisational knowledge in a deliberate fashion (though some have made allusions to the link between their ideas and management). Because of this, it is very likely that I have imported my own interests into the discussion of their ideas. My interpretation might make some of the original theorists' hair stand on end. But it is essential that we gain some idea of the importance of this tradition, even if it gets a little distorted in the process, in order to evaluate how far (if at all) management research is valid.

The third point is that language in this area is as subject to fashion as any other subject of intellectual enquiry. So different writers may be keen to squeeze their views into a currently fashionable category. Not all writers will therefore mean the same when using the same term, and hence one commentator may describe someone as a phenomenologist where another may describe the same person as a hermeneutician.

In similar fashion to the discussion in Chapter 5 relating to realism, we shall see that most of these approaches make an important point, but when they elevate this into an overall grand theory this takes the point beyond what it can sustain.

The views we shall consider here in some places overlap (most notably in their emphatic rejection of the natural science analogy) and in some places are quite clearly differentiated. By the time the reader has finished Chapters 6, 7 and 8, s/he will recognise both that the dividing line between their subject matter is somewhat arbitrary, but also that there is some rationale for dividing them as I have. In this chapter the accent is on approaches which depict research more or less entirely as an interpretation (hermeneutics and phenomenology, as well as some implications of feminism); in the following chapter the emphasis is on views which purport to represent a development or improvement on the main interpret- avist theories (the best examples being post-modernism and Deconstruction); whilst the chapter after that deals with a more multi-levelled approach which draws on interpretavism but tends to add a greater emphasis on the interactive nature of management research (Participatory and Action Research). It is important to bear in mind again that these are approaches which have a history, but also reflect current research activities.

There are two main strands of thinking reflected in this chapter:

1   interpretavism
2   situation specifism

Interpretavism is the group of approaches which spring out of the idea that we *construct* social reality, that social phenomena are prod- ucts of human thought and remain dependent on thought for their meaning and life. As mentioned in the introduction to Part II, this view of social research grew up in the early to middle twentieth century, but had antecedents in the work of writers such as Dilthey in the nineteenth. It reflected a recognition that social research which emulated natural science could establish regularities and patterns, but could not establish *meanings*. And meanings are uniquely entertained by cognitive beings such as humans. A rock bouncing down a mountain can be analysed by purely independent observers because there is no internal meaning which it has in the way a person jumping up and down would have.

According to this view, a social activity such as management, or a social 'object' such as an organisation, is only significant because someone sees it in certain terms. Any attempt to understand, say a manager's behaviour, makes little or no sense if that behaviour is investigated independently of other phenomena (for example, by defining a set of observable behaviours and then conducting the necessary observations). There are many factors which are all intrinsic to the kind of understanding required: most notably the perceptions of the various relevant parties, which in some versions of this tradition may include not only the manager, but also those whom s/he manages, other professional colleagues, and even the researcher her/himself. *To be* is quite literally to be *perceived and understood*, in contrast to the natural sciences where it is presumed that the phenomena studied are distinct from and independent of human perception.

Following the Lincoln and Guba questions of social research, this approach could be characterised as:

Ontology: what exists is what is the subject of general agreement
Epistemology: knowledge derives from what is agreed
Methodology: creating communities of subjects who can embark on
                        activities resulting in agreements about what exists

The main approaches which fall under this heading include the ideas of phenomenology and hermeneutics. They form the largest group of ideas in this chapter.[3]

By contrast, what I call situation specifism[4] is a much smaller corpus of writing, but represents a quite separate approach to the idea of management knowledge. The prime version of this is often called Feminist methodology, though for reasons which will become clearer in the discussion I prefer to regard the gender perspective as a version of the wider idea that forms of research activity are themselves rooted in specific features of the life histories of the researchers – an idea which for want of a better term we could call biographism (for readers who need to have an 'ism' for everything). In some ways this approach could have been placed in the previous chapter on naturalism, as it undercuts both approaches – almost arbitrarily, then, it sits here.

6.1   INTERPRETAVISM

There are so many different versions of this approach that any starting point is a bit indiscriminate. In starting with the idea of phenomenology I do not mean to imply any sense of logical priority of this over other versions of interpretavism – it is just a starting place.

6.1.1   Phenomenology

Finn Collin's quote from Max Weber is perhaps the best starting point for a discussion of phenomenology: 'Action is social in so far as, by virtue of the subjective meaning attached to it by the acting individual...it takes account of the behaviour of others...' The key term here is 'subjective meaning'.[5] What Weber is saying is that human behaviour only makes sense when the 'inner' interpretation is taken account of alongside the explicit observable behaviour. For example, industrial conflict is not simply a matter of the volume of disputes which occur. It is not enough to observe that an organisation has, say, more than the average number of stoppages, grievances, strikes, and so on. What is necessary is to get an idea of the significance of this for the participants. Are people trying to undermine the role of management? Are these events attempts to improve the overall reward package? Are they a cry for help? What matters, on this view, is how individuals perceive their behaviour. It is their individual intentions which define what kind of actions are being undertaken. The same outward behaviour may arise from many different underlying intentions – only the latter give meaning to action (or at least to social action, on this view).

The central idea of phenomenology, then, as applied to social knowledge, is this emphasis on the inner intention or interpretation of behaviour. This idea has been developed further by Alfred Schutz, who linked it with the views of the philosopher Edmund Husserl. Husserl was concerned with a general philosophical idea of how to discover the nature of what he called 'pure' understanding. His idea was that the inner essence of an object could be understood by means of a series of thought experiments – imagining various changes in something and seeing how far one still thought of the object under scrutiny as the same or different. The 'purity' here is that because the changes are all hypothetical mental ones, the mind is freed from the objective world and thus can investigate ideas uncontaminatedly.

Schutz was interested in the application of this idea to social phenomena.[6] He felt that the subjective meaning of people's behaviour could be grasped in an analogous way. Analysis of people's subjective intentions behind their acts can thus reveal what their acts really are – the same physical behaviour may represent a range of different actions. This point has been echoed by several Anglo-Saxon analytical philosophers.[7] But whilst the Anglo-Saxon approach has been to emphasise the difficulty of explaining exactly what an intentional action is, the phenomenological approach has been to emphasise the internal nature of such intentions.

There are two points which imply that phenomenology is of questionable relevance to the practising management researcher. Firstly, there is the problem that phenomenology depicts intention as a deeply personal, subjective, essence of someone's action. Collin quotes Schutz's example of the potential variation in what may underlie someone's behaviour: '...one and the same routine of native behaviour...may amount to entirely different actions...it may be a war dance, the ceremony surrounding a barter trade...or the reception of an ambassador.'[8] Although this is couched in anthropological terms, the application to organisations is clear.

But this point creates more difficulties than it solves. Suppose I always hold a monthly meeting at which someone receives a salesperson of the month award. Doubtless most people would see this as a motivational tool – as an attempt by me to maintain motivation and/or morale. I might deny this – I might, for example, claim that it was nothing to do with motivation, but rather my way of continuing to reassert my role as the leader of the team (it would be odd to ignore the motivational benefits of the action, but it is not implausible). Suppose, instead, though, that I said it was a way of maintaining financial control. One would hardly accept this as an explanation on its own – there are after all a lot of ways to control finances and giving people monthly sales rewards doesn't figure highly on the list. The link between the behaviour and such an intention is opaque to most people, and therefore needs a strong supplementary explanation (in a way that the intention to raise motivation does not). If my explanation is not convincing then someone would likely conclude that I was deliberately trying to mislead them (or maybe that I didn't know what I was doing). In other words, there is more to action than just having an intention and indulging in some activity.

Behaviour is not *just* linked with some intention – there is a range of appropriate explanations for someone's actions, a range with clear limits. Action after all is an attempt to achieve something, so even though we may find it difficult to see just *what* someone is attempting, we must be able to see that it is an *attempt of some kind*. Phenomenology seems to work on a model whereby we look at someone's behaviour, then try to find out what the inner significance is for them, and as a result we can understand the action in full. But sometimes what we find out about inner significance might make the behaviour *less*, not more, intelligible. There are limits to what is an intelligible way of, for example, controlling the finances of an organisation. If someone goes outside these limits then we simply don't understand what they are trying to do. The onus is on them to give an explanation of how that intention links with their behaviour. Intention and behaviour have a more intimate link than simply the former giving the latter its significance. Just as easily one could turn this around – if I say I have an intention to maintain financial control, then some types of behaviour fulfil this intention, and make this intelligible, just as others make it unintelligible. The link is two way.

Once one looks at the real world where people's intentions are often fuzzy, and can easily shift around in the course of one extended project, then the idea expressed in the quote from Weber with which we started this section becomes less useful as a guide to research in the social world. A manager states that they intend improving the working conditions of their staff. She may say this because the staff are pressing strongly on this point. She may really want at that moment to improve conditions, but *her underlying concerns and priorities may at that moment be unconscious*. Only later, as events unfold, may it become clear what the underlying intentions of the manager are.[9] When it becomes clear that there are severe pressures from the marketing department to increase sales activity, for example, then the manager might find herself looking for ways to *minimise* the extent to which working conditions are improved, in order to free up resources to improve sales performance. So, although the manager may have *wanted* to prioritise working conditions, and really thought that she would do this, at critical moments it becomes clear – to her as well as to others – that she in fact has other priorities.

Intentions in the real world compete, and are in a constant state of flux, so it is implausible to look to these to provide a stable basis for explaining people's acts. An expression of intent made at the time may well be superficially sincere, but at a deeper level self-deceptive. It may well reflect a strong desire on the manager's part, which then gets undermined when s/he links it with other needs, with available resources and what these have to cover, etc. This does not undermine the phenomenological idea in principle, but it makes it significantly less plausible as a guide for working researchers.

The second difficulty with phenomenology is that it seems to fix on something which can give an action meaning or significance, and then suggests that this is *all* that is really required to explain the behaviour. I may well have an intention that by stopping work I will draw attention to the poor reward package available to workers in my organisation, but I could easily have done this in a number of other ways as well. Just as the same behaviour may be motivated by any one of a number of different intentions, so the same intention could have been actualised in many different ways. I could have written to the CEO, I could have phoned the local paper, I could have thrown a tantrum. Why I choose one particular way is not simply down to a single, simply identified intention. A whole range of factors is also involved – beliefs about efficacy of behaviour certainly, but also supplementary wants and desires which may condition and qualify how I choose to pursue a certain end.[10] Yes, to understand someone's particular intention, it is necessary for a full understanding of their behaviour, but it is not at all enough on it's own. To adapt a point from the American philosopher Thomas Nagel: that I want something to drink may lead me to put a coin in a drinks machine, but on its own it could as easily lead me to kick the machine, or try to put something else in it.[11] There is more to action than just having an intention – a connecting thread of beliefs and expectations is also needed.

Phenomenology is therefore too strongly rooted in an idea of what gives the essence of a person's action to provide a full explanation of social behaviour. The insight that someone requires an idea of the inner significance of an action to fully understand it is important, but this cannot be construed as a simple subjective inner feeling. Hermeneutics became popular as an improvement over phenomenology because it provides an idea of the kind of process by which we come to understand other people's behaviour.

6.1.2 Hermeneutics

Originally coined to depict the work of German Biblical scholars interpreting religious texts, the term 'hermeneutics' evolved over the nineteenth and twentieth centuries, almost in parallel with the idea of phenomenology, to cover the interpretation of phenomena in general.

The crucial difference between hermeneutics and phenomenology is that the latter is an individualistic approach, whereas the former is rooted in the idea of language as a social phenomenon.

Central to hermeneutics in its modern form is the idea that social knowledge is derived from a complex of social events – rather as a translator, historian or interpreter would derive meaning from a written text produced in an unfamiliar language. Events, such as a conflict in the workplace, are treated by analogy with a text needing to be translated. There is a 'text' – the events themselves. Then there is a 'translation' – the interpretation in terms of what the researcher or observer makes of the intentions and expectations of the actors involved.

Drawing this analogy between an organisational event and a text implies that all perceived organisational phenomena need to be construed as texts, or as text-like, but also that the way of understanding these is more like understanding something we encounter in a foreign language. Understanding a text in a foreign language means linking it with a whole range of previously established interpretations, testing and retesting these in the light of the most illuminating general concept of the language. Similarly, understanding people's behaviour in an organisation means linking it with a history within and without that organisation, creating an account of what the events mean to different individuals (which in itself involves the highly speculative process of developing an interpretation of what their verbal responses really amount to), testing and retesting all this in the light of further events and perceptions of the affected individuals.

One key implication of this when applied to organisational knowledge is that there is no independent explanation of reality (which on a realist model we would gradually approach via systematic enquiry). Just as every fresh statement or text needs to be interpreted – even when it has itself been produced to interpret something else – so every new step in the chain of enquiry is itself an item which on its own requires interpretation. As one leading theorist in this area, Hans-Georg Gadamer says, 'Understanding is not reconstruction but mediation'.[12] In other words, the idea that a statement of applied social theory reconstructs, or reflects, the structure of the reality which it refers to is misleading. For the hermeneutician, a statement about social reality is a link between that reality and the person making the statement, and can only be understood in terms of the circumstances in which it is made. The idea of mediation here is the view that the reality is translated into a form which can be made intelligible by the person who makes the statement. It is modelled or phrased in such a way that the individual can make sense of it within their own conceptual framework. So if I say 'Meetings without agendas are always going to end in chaos' this is not to be taken as a literal prediction that every or most agenda-less meetings will be chaotic. It is a way of me making sense of my experience, and therefore is phrased in a way which links with my other perceptions and beliefs.

This is not, in the hands of hermeneutics, a subjective approach. Individuals' own perceptions cannot be completely taken on their own (this is a key difference of emphasis from phenomenology). A *circle of interpretation* is necessary, in which a range of linked 'texts' function as a mutually supporting network of ideas. Part of their contribution can be to supply the contextual circumstances within which the individual makes a statement about social reality. My statement about agenda-less meetings, then, gets located in a context in which, for example, it becomes clear why I am making a general statement, rather than simply stating that in cases I have observed there has been a tendency for absence of agendas to lead to a degree of disorganisation.[13]

An additional function of the 'hermeneutic circle' is that in coming to understand social phenomena we try to establish or hypothesise an underlying coherence which gives meaning to the variety of symptoms we see before us. We try to find an interpretation under which the various social events we observe are linked together as a meaningful network, a self-supporting circle of texts. Grasping the hermeneutic circle is akin to getting a feel for a group or community – coming to understand phenomena as that community does.[14] To do this requires synthesising and arranging a whole variety of texts and text-like objects. The potential sources of these texts (or text like phenomena) are diverse – they are not limited to one person, but can and do include the utterances of other people, other textual sources, artefacts even. But the hermeneutic circle is continually open to reinterpretation: as Gadamer argues, concepts are formed and re-formed through the manner in which their *universal meaning* is required to integrate with the *particular situations* in which they may be uttered.[15]

Concepts, on this approach, are not maps of reality. They do not determine their application to all possible future situations – there is an element of creativity in how a concept may apply to a new situation. This echoes the arguments of the Austrian twentieth century philosopher, Ludwig Wittgenstein, who pointed out that whilst a pattern must be evident for us to say that a concept or rule exists[16] it is open to creative innovation. The series 2, 4, 6, 8, ... may seem pretty obvious, until we find someone who follows that and then goes 10, 20, 30, 40, ... which in itself may seem clear until we get to 100, 102, 104, ... which remains puzzling even when we get to 1000, 2000, 3000, ...[17]

A rule cannot pre-determine exactly how it will be applied in all possible future applications. In other words, we cannot say that we have come to the definitive analysis of a concept, which sets out precisely how all conceivable future examples of, say strategic decision-making, may be construed. Fresh examples may present new aspects, may creatively diverge from existing practice, in ways which stretch our understanding of the idea. We cannot map these out in advance – concepts change as a matter of course in the real world.

Perhaps the most obvious kind of example of how this idea of a hermeneutic circle works is the concept of organisational culture. This notion embodies the idea that how an organisation functions – and how successful it may be – depends on something other than the formal official structures and processes consciously set up by managers. How does a newcomer come to perceive what kind of culture exists in the organisation they have just stepped in to? By trying to postulate – or read – some underlying factor which explains the behaviours of individuals in the organisation.

The hermeneutic metaphor depicts these behaviours as texts – bearers of some kind of meaning – and the task of the newcomer is to create a sense of what the meaning is which underlies these 'texts' and makes them intelligible. On day one the CEO walks in and everyone stops talking. The newcomer tries to read this 'text' – s/he speculates that there is a high level of tradition, or maybe fear, on the part of the workforce. On day two the CEO comes in again, and no one pays any attention – a new 'text', which the newcomer tries to understand in the light of their reading of the previous event. For example, they may read both events as expressions of deference, but see them as differentiated, maybe they postulate that on the first day it was early morning before anyone had gotten down to work and on the second it was a busy mid-morning. The newcomer sees similar things happen with some senior managers, and maybe not at all with others. Different colleagues speak with or without respect for specific members of the management team.

Other events are also slowly fitted into general patterns – such as what is regarded as acceptable behaviour when there is a major crisis in the organisation, or when customers complain, or what to do when there is serious conflict within the team. In each case there is a 'text' which the individual tries to fit coherently into their overall interpretation of the reality of that organisation. The newcomer thus starts to build up an idea of what has high value and what has low over a range of different kinds of event. This gets slowly more refined as these different events are fitted into an overall pattern – so that after some time the newcomer grasps that certain ritualised occasions require a formal response, that certain roles in the organisation have a higher than expected significance, that certain kinds of outcome are strongly approved of and others equally disapproved. It is not difficult to link this to a model such as the Handy–Harrison fourfold typology of organisational cultures.

What is important is that hermeneutics, as outlined above, not only affords an idea of some of the concrete methods of uncovering the 'inner' culture of an organisation, but also finds a clear role for the whole idea of organisational culture – for this is precisely the kind of concept which can lend an overall significance to the range of explicit phenomena to be seen in an organisation. The newcomer is reading the whole of the functioning of the organisation as an expression of the postulated culture.

So the idea of culture is what links together a range of apparently disconnected elements. The several different phenomena described above could be easily explained one by one in terms of a set of several separate hypotheses about the organisation. We would then end up with a range of discrete, independent, results about the organisation – one about the power of senior managers, another about, say conflict management, yet another about the importance of customers. What binds together a 'hermeneutic circle' of this (potentially vast) range of events of micro and macro proportions is that they exist *within* the specific culture. In other words the concept 'organisational culture' *binds* together events and processes which otherwise would be perceived separately – or at best as only dimly connected. It represents the glue which holds together a network of broad phenomena, and behind these the various events which themselves contribute to our recognition of each of those broad phenomena. In 'reading' the 'text' of the culture of an organisation the newcomer finds a way of pulling together a number of different aspects into a coherent whole.

Crucial to this is that the hermeneutic circle is an open one. It is an explicit part of this idea that the interpretation is not private, but is itself open to critique and discussion between individuals. In other words, it is open to *inter-subjective enquiry*. By this is meant that we can investigate issues (such as what is meant by a manager's behaviour) *jointly*, and take account of other people's views and beliefs, even though we could always be mistaken about anything which goes beyond our own thoughts.[18]

In trying to evaluate hermeneutics it is instructive to hearken back to realism, which we considered in Chapter 5. This approach acknowledges the basic difficulty of ever saying 'I know this for sure', but it retains an element that bit by bit, somehow, investigation gets us ever closer to the real truth, even though this may be never completely attainable. It shares with hermeneutics a sense of investigation as a process. But where it sharply differs from hermeneutics is in the idea of where such a process is going. For the realist the process of investigation is intended to be convergent – slowly we draw closer to an independent truth (even if we don't realise how gross are the howlers we still cling to). In the hands of some of the leading writers on hermeneutics, such as Gadamer, there is no such convergence in social research. 'Knowledge' is really just a link between individuals or groups and the 'texts' they are trying to make sense of. There is no independent truth to be had – at best the truth is to be found in which ideas fit together most coherently.

So the process of interpretation makes things more or less intelligible to the researcher, but cannot be said to approach closer to some independent social reality. In other words, the key test is not whether the interpretation reflects what is really out there, because there is no 'out there' to approach. Instead it is how far interpretations can make sense of the various pieces of evidence which the researcher has access to. Because the hermeneutic circle is open, this is not confined to one person or to one point in time. In this respect hermeneutics is a more extreme view than phenomenology. For the latter view still accepts that there is an internal 'real' meaning to people's actions – it's just that this is, by its internal nature, not really explicable. Hermeneutics, by contrast, denies this. There is only a 'text' and the interpretations which are made of it.

From a practical point of view, one might be tempted to conclude that if hermeneutics is the best account of management research then we may as well give up the attempt to gain generalisable results. For this view seems to imply that there is no room for saying what is the best available interpretation of event. If my interpretation diverges from some commonly accepted one which is to be preferred? One answer here is that the circle of interpretation is open, and therefore one person cannot insulate her- or himself from common enquiry and insist that their interpretation is the correct one. Other writers on hermeneutics have employed other arguments to ensure that this approach does not degenerate to some kind of subjectivism. The French philosopher Ricoeur, for example, has argued that social research methods must be accepted as having some kind of inter-subjective validity (and therefore social knowledge is not irretrievably subjective). In the course of a complex analysis of hermeneutic ideas in the context of structural linguistics, he emphasises the primacy of existing research methods in social research – philosophical hermeneutics (as he calls it) must not be used to undermine processes which are independently accepted.[19]

But there are two difficulties with the idea of hermeneutics as a dialectical process which uses a circle of evidence to create or generate interpretations of social reality.

The first of these is whether there is room for disconcerting results. It is a central feature of natural science that from time to time results are obtained which fly in the face of the current orthodoxy. Some examples of these were mentioned in Part I. Even the approach to natural science envisaged by Thomas Kuhn, which comes close to hermeneutics in its scepticism regarding the idea of intellectual progress in science, is founded on the idea of revolutions in knowledge. By contrast, it is not clear how such major turnabouts can come to pass on the hermeneutic approach.

Take as an example perhaps the best known piece of research in the history of organisation – the Hawthorne experiments. Here is a case where the process is well explained in terms of the analogy with natural science: a clearly defined experiment was designed, observations were taken and the results were not as expected. New questions were asked, and hence new kinds of data were collected. The explanation for this new data not only included an explanation of the unexpected results but also suggested a wide range of new ideas and possibilities for further research. This example is also well explained in phenomenological terms – the research was unsuccessful while physical behaviour was focused on, and was more successful when an idea was gained of what the workers' behaviour actually meant to them.

But the hermeneutic approach has surprising trouble here. At first one would think that the same kind of argument as phenomenology can be given. But there is a key difference – phenomenology insists that an *inner interpretation is necessary* for a complete understanding of behaviour. Hermeneutics does not have this insistence. Rather it states that *some interpretation* needs to be given which provides *a* coherent account of the phenomena involved. One gap here is where to draw the boundary – what data is relevant and what should be excluded? The other key gap here is what counts as a better more coherent explanation? In natural science there is a preference for ever more simple elegant explanations, but this is itself vague – what are our criteria of elegance? Mathematical simplicity? Smallest range of fundamental objects or kinds of law? When one considers the criteria for what might make one social explanation more coherent than another there are various complicating factors. Not the least of these is the irretrievably probabilistic nature of social concepts. Two interpretations may simply differ in which areas of probability to emphasise as important and which to downgrade. More critically the cavernous complexity of human perceptions, values and beliefs means that it is not at all clear when one has arrived at a more coherent account of these – there is always more to delve into.

The point here is that a hermeneutic approach to social research provides no guide as to when or where investigation should stop, because it gives no clear idea about what counts as a satisfactory explanation of behaviour. Going back to the Hawthorne studies – the explanations given by Mayo and Roethlisberger were provided some time after the initial puzzling results with factory lighting were encountered, and represented a significant step beyond the original problem. It was not so much that one explanation was more coherent than another, but rather that one explanation was *in itself* unsatisfactory. It is not clear how a hermeneutic approach deals with this. Positivism can. And for natural science, the near-hermeneutician Thomas Kuhn uses the idea of an anomaly, though that in itself needs a lot of explaining. When we look later on at Critical Theory, we shall see that in Jurgen Habermas' hands there is a clear advance on hermeneutics in this respect – for the critical theorist would say that the satisfactoriness or otherwise of the explanation is grounded in the kind of interest for which the explanation is sought. The Hawthorne studies clearly fell into what Habermas would call empirical-technological research, and thus they were found wanting in those terms.

This point leads us to the second main difficulty with hermeneutics: just what is the substance of the process of the hermeneutic circle? One approach is to try to link this with the existing range of social research methods. In other words, that the idea of a hermeneutic circle is not really more than a roundabout way of talking about what is currently done in the name of social science. For example, Ricoeur, as we have seen, wants to maintain the integrity of existing social research methods. But it is at least partially because some of these are themselves so questionable that social research is problematic. Freudianism, for example, is quoted with approval by Ricoeur, but this is hardly an uncontroversial approach to the science of the mind.

This stands in contrast with earlier hermeneuticians, such as Gadamer, who seemed to imply that the approach had its own way of approaching 'texts' and the range of items which could contribute to interpretation. But without a substantial account of how evidential items might combine hermeneutically there is a serious weakness in the theory. The devil is in the detail of how a circle of interpretation might operate. Suppose, for example, a community of researchers and others operated a principle of giving greater weight to 'interpretations' which came from older members of their group. Does this count as a valid method or not? One might think that biographical details, such as someone's age, are irrelevant to validity, though someone could argue that an older person has a greater wealth of experience of life to draw upon, and therefore their views should be given special attention. Hermeneutics (as a general theory of validity in applied social research) seems to be silent on what counts as a sound method of interpretation, but it is an important element of the approach, for it forms the basis on which methodology gets turned into method. As a matter of interest, the example of age given above will be relevant when we look at biographically based approaches to social research.

So hermeneutics tells us how we start the journey toward knowledge, but it doesn't tell us how to navigate between satisfactory and unsatisfactory waters, or what the destination looks like when we are there. It seems to presume that all extra material is relevant, which would make the whole activity degenerate very quickly – for if there is no criterion of relevance then literally any statement or 'text' could be included. How do we decide what to exclude? By consensus? Then we have the problem of whether the consensus is right or wrong. Realist/positivist approaches, as well as phenomenology, despite their own major flaws, give a better answer here.

In fact hermeneutics shares more with naturalism than would appear at first sight. It is still concerned with answering an ontological question via an epistemic one, and in turn an epistemic one in terms of methodology. The three elements are bound together functionally. In doing so, I would argue (though I am sure that many interpretavists would strongly disagree) that interpretavism remains committed to some sense of foundationalism. In other words that the key question for the interpretavist, as much as for the naturalist, is 'what are the foundations on which we can build our knowledge of the social world?' Whilst the naturalist bases the answer to this question on a relation between observation and inference about what is there, the interpretavist bases it on a relation between inter-subjective agreements and inference about what is there.

6.1.3   Whither Interpretavism

To sum up, hermeneutics seems to provide a substantial advance on phenomenology, in that it sketches out activities for constructing the meaning of social events. Where it falls down, however, as a complete account of social research methodology, is that it fails to capture the link between these activities and our basic sense of validity. The approach does not seem to give us an idea of why at times we have strong intuitive convictions (right or wrong) about some phenomena, and in other cases we do not. The insights about the process of investigation are not linked with the idea that this is an investigation *into reality*.

We have looked closely at two versions of interpretavism, but it is important to reemphasise that this field is fraught with difficulties of categorisation. I have deliberately construed these in a polarised form.

Some writers are called phenomenologists by one commentator, and hermeneuticians by others. For example, I quoted Weber earlier in relation to phenomenology, though he is generally seen as a precursor of the modern approach to hermeneutics.

Perhaps the most important aspect of this approach, however, is the emphasis on integrating and understanding different perspectives. While this may not provide a grand theory of the intimate connection with an independent reality which remains a feature of anything we would want to call knowledge, it remains a key element.

6.2   SITUATION SPECIFIC APPROACHES TO SOCIAL THEORY

The naturalist model of social knowledge is based on the idea that reality is independent of our expectations. By contrast, interpretavism bases the idea of social knowledge on the idea that a deliberate series of acts of understanding on the part of the researcher is necessary for knowledge to be generated. The category of approaches to management knowledge which I will discuss in this section is based on the idea that the specific biographical or demographic circumstances of researchers need to be taken into account as part of the evaluation of whether something counts as knowledge or not.

6.2.1   Biography and Knowledge

As mentioned above, this strand of thinking arises out of the feminist critique of social theory, although I want to try to generalise the idea. But it may make most sense to start with the feminist position.

The feminist argument regarding social theory is basically that in its current incarnations social 'knowledge' is a creation mainly of men and therefore reflects their limitations of perspective – men only see one side of the gender story, so to speak, and therefore they cannot help but construct social theories in male-oriented terms. This one-sidedness of perspective can operate at many levels – concept formation, interpretation of data and data collection methods. Hence a thoroughgoing feminist methodology needs to demonstrate at all these levels how the one-sidedness can be overcome. We have already mentioned the work of Janet Finch (who acknowledges Ann Oakley as a key influence) in Part I, amply demonstrating the differences that simply having female interviewers instead of male can make.

Organisations themselves are perhaps the best examples of gender imbalance. On a *supposedly* level playing field, it is undoubtedly the case that far fewer women reach senior managerial positions than men. Women on the whole earn less than their male counterparts, even in comparable posts (despite equal pay legislation in many countries). Equally, the language of management abounds in male-oriented metaphors and images. 'Strategy', for example, is a borrowing from military theory. 'Management' comes from the image of controlling teams of horses (in the ancient world almost exclusively a male activity). It has also been argued that the depiction of organisations in terms of a pyramid tree structure, at the apex of which stand the most powerful, controlling agents, is a reflection of a 'male' conception of work, in which status is emphasised as opposed to functional role.

Feminist discussions of social methodology have covered many areas, so that there is feminist positivism, feminist interpretavism and so on. Some commentators have noted that there is a parallelism between what might be said for the gender perspective and what might be said about other demographic groupings. Certainly similar arguments have been advanced for the racial imbalance in social research.[20] One aspect of this is a presumption in most management writing that western organisations and organisational norms are the prime source of examples of good practice, whilst another is the apparent assumption that management theory is primarily addressed to western organisations, and that organisations in other regions of the world do best by emulating western practice. Some of this has resulted in downright folly – witness the attempt to graft USA style free market economics on to the immediate post-communist Russian environment, which resulted in a form of robber baron economy unknown in Europe since the sixteenth century. It is easy to dismiss this as poor consultancy, rather than having any implication about the validity or otherwise of management research. One answer to this is that management research is rarely too far away from its associated technology, but more importantly this poor consultancy was provided by supposedly the best of the west – the IMF, the EU, and the major western accountancy/consultant firms. More was going on here than mere imperfection of advice – there was a conceptual myopia.

Another aspect of this is simply the great provincialism apparent in management research journals. UK journals have articles about how managers in British firms operate, at best how they have interacted in international contexts. US journals are similar. If you want to learn about how Malaysian management works – look at a Malaysian academic publication, for you find little to nothing in western publications.

The other side of this level of racial or national prejudice in management theory is the failure of management theorists in general to address the really major global organisational problems. Economic imbalance between the so-called Northern and Southern countries is a genuinely global issue, as it affects the whole relationship between nations, but it is virtually absent from any research into management. True, at the time of writing there is much attention in the UK and the USA to the global financial system, but this is only tenuously about the whole world – in practice it affects three regions: North America, the EU, and the Pacific Rim. Africa, South America and much of Asia are only peripherally involved in this – and when they are it is generally in a passive sense of being conceived of as a range of markets to be opened up and exploited. Environmental degradation is on the other hand a problem which affects every country's future, and is global by definition. Part of the problem here is that management as a discipline has mainly evolved out of microeconomics, and global issues such as those alluded to above are on a macro scale. Hence the temptation is for management theorists to insulate their work from such questions, which presumably are relegated to the study of government policy analysis. But there is a subtle and prejudicial assumption at work here. Where there is interest, such as in the operation of mature industries in western markets, then this grey area between macro and micro issues is happily explored. The theory of financial regulation is perhaps a case in point – a growing field which has attracted both organisational and economic and policy academics. But, as pointed out above, this is precisely the kind of global issue which interests the west. The point here is not to criticise or castigate, but rather to indicate that theory is not inert, but responds to social forces and interests.

6.2.2   The Limits to Biographism

So there is evidence of racial bias in management theory, just as there is of gender bias. How far can this be taken? The immediate instinct is to say that as well as gender and race, other demographic differences must have some impact on how management research questions are conceptualised and conceived, how they are investigated, and how the results are interpreted. So one might find an argument that religion and spiritual orientation creates its own perspective, that sexual identity, age, physical ability and mobility, all have a subtle influence on how researchers work. Despite my sympathies here, I must confess a degree of perplexity in the face of this argument, for it would seem to suggest that there are potential constraints on all attempts to understand organisations and management, for we all are members of discrete demographic groups (multiply so – we all have one particular gender, a specific racial origin, some kind of spiritual orientation and so on).

Perhaps a better way of thinking of this perspective is to regard it less as a substantive approach in its own right, but rather as a critique, or better still as a set of pointers of how to construct appropriate criteria of what counts as good management research. Reinharz, for example, has developed a view of feminist research as less a substantive method and more a perspective, a source of critique.[21] So soundness of management research could be evaluated partially by reference to a series of tests, amongst which perspectives drawn from biographical or demographic profiles of the researchers involved would form one category. This is in principle wholly praiseworthy. Unfortunately in practice it is difficult to see how far it can go. Some collections of articles and sets of conference papers often have brief biographies of their contributors, though this is usually included as much for reader interest than as a touchstone for testing validity. At the time of writing, a few academic journals do the same, but far more do not. Perhaps it would make some sense for all journals to adopt it as a standard practice.

The biographical approach, then, is an important perspective on management research, but it does not look as if it can furnish a substantive account of validity and methodology in its own right. It is more a source of critiques of research. As such it may represent an impossible ideal – that of the totally fair, totally unbiased, research study. But such an ideal may act as a regulatory mechanism on actual research projects and realisable methodologies, setting criteria which may never be entirely obtained, but which should never be ignored.

SUMMARY

In this chapter we have looked at the idea that management research is best understood as an interpretation of what the researcher collects, rather than as a claim to accessing an independent reality. The prime versions of this, hermeneutics and phenomenology, have specific philosophical difficulties, whilst the demographically based approach is more of an ideal than a substantive methodology. Each of these approaches, though, makes key points which need to be taken into account if we are to have a comprehensive idea of validity in management research. Their fault, as was the key fault with naturalism, is to try to generalise these points into a full theory of social research. We shall see fit to return to these points in Chapters 7 and 8, which explore other non-naturalistic approaches.

■ NOTES

1   The tendency to present these concepts as pairs of opposing terms is tempting, but as Andrew Sayer puts it '...although these dualisms are second nature to us and look quite harmless...every one of them is beset by misconceptions and generate problems in our understanding of the world and of ourselves.' Sayer (1984).

2   To be fair, texts such as Easterby-Smith et al. have acknowledged that this is a clustering which may not reflect precisely the view of any one theoretician of social science. Still, it's what most people learn on their MBA course (or the like).

3   This is not to deprioritise the importance of other interpretative approaches such as ethnomethodology; most of the points made about hermeneutics would also apply to this concept as well.

4   This category has not been independently identified previously to sufficient extent for a generally accepted tag to have evolved.

5   Weber (1947) quoted in Collin (1997) p. 109.

6   At an early stage of his career – he later dropped the idea.

7   Most notably Elizabeth Anscombe (1957).

8   Collin Chapter 7.

9   This is part (though only a part) of what Mintzberg is getting at with his concept of *emergent* strategy.

10 Indeed, in cases of individual choice in acute situations, motivation can resemble a problem solving exercise. See Chapter 1 of my 'Managing Values' for an illustration of this.

11 See Nagel (1969) Part Two.

12 Quoted by Blaikie (1993) p. 64.

13 For example, by identifying the context as highly blame-oriented, where failure to control a meeting may be severely disapproved of.

14 In other words, it is broader than simply getting inside an individual's head.

15 Gadamer (1960).

16 And for a rule to exist people must follow it in virtue of it being a rule – not simply do things which happen to fall into a pattern.

17 Wittgenstein (1953) – paras 172–99. For example, the sequence may be an instance of the rule – increase the right hand digit by 2 where there is an odd number of digits, and when an even number of digits is reached increase the left hand digit by 1. The point is that we will normally jump to an interpretation which is consistent with what we have seen so far, but may be an instance of a more complex series which only becomes apparent later. Incidentally, it should be noted that some commentators on the work of Wittgenstein from Anglo-Saxon philosophical traditions might deny any close link with hermeneutics.

18 We could be mistaken about those as well, but since the time of Descartes there has been a presumption that the conscious contents of our own mind are more likely to yield certainties than what lies beyond the mind. It is a running controversy how far we *can* be sure about our own thoughts – the classical exposition of the idea that we can be certain

can be found in Descartes (1637) and Wittgenstein (1953) provided the strongest modern rejection of the idea.

19 Though one would really need to establish the basis on which something is 'independently accepted'. See Aylesworth's article in the Silverman collection (1991) for an explanation of Ricoeur's views.

20 One good example is Ahmad and Sheldon's short but penetrating analysis of race and statistics (1991).

21 Reinharz (1992) quoted by S. Webb in Burton (2000).

A Postscript
(to Chapters 5 and 6)
which is also
a Preamble
(to Chapters 7 and 8)

In Chapters 5 and 6 we have looked at two contrasting approaches to the question of what justifies our belief that social research can provide us with knowledge (in particular knowledge about organisations and management). In both cases the answer has been in terms of a kind of foundation, a basis which is firm and stable – in one case (naturalism) enough for us to build structures of knowledge on its root, in another (interpretavism) enough to allow us to add fresh insights and incorporate them into an existing nexus of perceptions and texts. Obviously, phrased in this way this is naive. Not everyone who calls themselves a naturalist or hermeneutician is so innocent of the difficulties of establishing knowledge. But this is the aspiration, whatever its reality.

This kind of approach, which from here on I shall call foundationalism, makes two key assumptions. Firstly, it presumes that what has been identified as the root or foundation is, in one way or another, stable. In some ways this seems too obvious to challenge, but it is important to recognise that this is an article of faith. From the naturalist perspective this is especially problematic. No specific item of knowledge of the form which is generally accepted as 'scientific' in a natural or social sense has in fact remained that stable. If we look at the most fundamental of areas of knowledge (in the case of human beings the linkage between behaviour and biology, in the natural world the basic laws of physics) these are currently in crucial states of crisis: certainly not the kinds of foundation which we could rely on to remain as a fixed starting point for knowledge of things or of people. The kinds of beliefs which we share with, say, the people of six hundred years ago are *pre-scientific* – if you put a kettle of water on a hot fire for ten to fifteen minutes it is likely to boil; if I deliberately violate the key values of the most powerful people in the organisation for which I work (be they a corporate director or the Holy Roman Emperor), I am likely to suffer some form of rebuke or tribulation in return. The explanations of those phenomena in more systematic terms – in the past using ideas such as the 'fire substance', or 'vertu', in today's terminology talking about latent heat, or managing corporate power relationships, is changed out of all recognition.[1] This represents something of a paradox: science, which purports to provide a firm and unshakeable basis for all knowledge, turns out to be much more variable and unstable than unscientific localised knowledge rooted in practices, such as traditions of home cooking or carpentry.

So the naturalist approach, to try to make all knowledge of people and organisations as much like the forms of natural science as possible, rests on a fiction. But there is also another difficulty for the hermeneutician. For whilst this approach does not rely on the idea that all forms of knowledge can be reduced to a single set of basic elements, it does accept that there is some sense in which a consensus of interpretative items (texts, utterances, depictions and so on) provides a basis for, or a unification of, knowledge. The *process* of forming a consensus is not often discussed in detail by hermeneutics, but clearly some process there must be, and it must in some way be a social process, whereby people come to an agreement about what they will accept as 'fact' – and thus what is rejected as not 'fact'. Needless to say, this consensus changes (one aspect which seems to slip by many discussions of hermeneutics is why such a consensus would *always guarantee* knowledge), so where is the stability? Again this comes not from central abstract concepts, but from the concrete periphery – key beliefs and assumptions which people seem to adhere to irrespective of their underlying theoretical foundation, such as kettles boiling, or organisational leaders using power to control dissent.

The second key assumption which is common to the two examples of foundationalism we considered is the idea that analysis is a *finite* process which can lead us to the roots or foundations of our knowledge systems and structures.[2] This is the core of reductionism, which is a key aspect of the naturalist approach, and which we have already seen carries problems. Again, although at first sight the interpretative tradition seems less vulnerable to this kind of problem, it is subject in a different way. For the hermeneutician, the foundation of knowledge is provided by a circle of interpretation. Now this has to be – at any one time – a finite circle, otherwise how could there be any principle by which we accept some ideas and reject others? If the circle were infinite, then someone could always claim that their idea, however batty, however improbable, fits into the circle somewhere, but not quite here. So the circle must have an identifiable size (to prolong the metaphor). Indeed (to prolong the metaphor even further) if the circle were infinite, could we tell that it was a circle at all? There has to be some manageable way in which the judgements are combined – hence hermeneutics involves an assumption that it comes to a definitive and (relatively) stable network of connections: not a foundation in the same sense as naturalism, but nevertheless a basis on which knowledge is *founded*. Of course the hermeneutician will say that it is always possible that new perceptions will crop up and that keeps the circle open – but that is in fact no different to the natural scientist saying that tomorrow we may discover some new result in quantum theory that turns everything upside down. It does not mark any special characteristic of interpretavism at all.

It is this assumption which provides the starting point for the arguments of the following two chapters. In the later decades of the twentieth century the optimism that characterised previous research began to fade. Not only did natural science seem to bring as many new problems as it solved, but social explanation also seemed to solve some problems only to create or uncover fresh ones. The belief that was shared by naturalism and interpretavism was that social research could lead to a commonly investigable and generally applicable kind of knowledge. We still see that optimistic belief in many research papers and reports. But the two approaches we shall now look at start from the perspective that this is not the ideal to aim for. In their different ways they abandon the idea of foundations or of an ideal of accreting knowledge – in one case (deconstructionism) in favour of a more dynamic view of knowledge and practices, and in the other (participatory/action research) in terms of localised problem solving.

In Chapter 7, then, we shall look at ideas of two French theorists of the mid-to-late twentieth century, Jacques Derrida and Michel Foucault, both of whom are very clearly anti-foundationalist. Their two different approaches share the conviction that any attempt at analysing ideas down to their essentials is misguided. Perhaps Derrida is more thoroughgoing in this, but it is also a key point of Foucault's position (which is more difficult to pin down than that of the superficially more difficult Derrida). Rather than try to recreate a structure of management knowledge by specifying a foundation and the building bricks of different parts of the overall edifice, until the whole temple of knowledge is mapped out, the anti-foundational approach attempts to show the different tracks which analysis can take. If there are different ways we can analyse ideas and knowledge, then there cannot be a single structure of knowledge, but alternatives which serve different purposes. There is a political agenda here as well. Both Derrida and Foucault come from that radical French post-war tradition we mentioned earlier, that leant heavily on Marxism, and was therefore far more critical of the establishment bias in all social knowledge, let alone the managerial bias in organisation theory, than either the interpretative or naturalist traditions.

Perhaps the main difficulty with both of these writers is their obvious pessimism about the possibility of knowledge of people and groups (and by implication, organisations and how these are managed). In Chapter 8, we shall see an attempt to work positively without subscribing to naturalist or interpretavist assumptions. Approaches such as action science and participative inquiry, are intended to start from what we are familiar with – the organisation as a place where people work and bring their own views to bear not only in planning and executing operational change but also in the construction of organisation 'truths'. These can be made sense of within the context in which they were developed (that is, as part of organisational practice) and indeed are developed partly to create some kind of understanding *of* that context. But they are not designed to create a knowledge which is transferable to other contexts.[3]

In some respects, although we shall also note some weaknesses in the ideas of action research and participative inquiry, the more positive view they suggest hearkens forward to the account we shall try to develop toward the end of Part III of this book.

NOTES

1 The idea of a fire substance or phlogiston, as it was then called, was only decisively refuted by Lavoisier when he measured oxygen. 'Vertu' is an early piece of occupational psychology, being Macchiavelli's term for one of the key qualities of a successful prince.
2 We could add a third assumption – that knowledge can be put into a systematic structure or order.
3 Which is not to say that cannot ever be transferred, but that this is not the intention behind their development.

Chapter 7

Deconstructing Management

In Chapter 6 we looked at some versions of the idea that knowledge about management (in fact about social matters in general) is really a form of interpretation. This chapter picks up where that left off. As we saw, the optimism which informed both naturalism and interpretavism in social explanation gradually gave way in the later part of the twentieth century to a more cautious view, that maybe human behaviour is not so easily grasped as that of rocks and plants (though even in the natural sciences there was a falling of optimism about its successes). Beyond the idea that knowledge in a social sphere such as management is best considered as an interpretation or construction, grew up the view that the *interpretation itself* needs to be explored as a phenomenon meriting investigation. In other words, that the interpretation needs to be analysed, or to use a term often employed in this area, *deconstructed*.

This appears to accept the key first premise common to the hermeneutic argument – that interpretation is a central part of social knowledge. But while hermeneutics takes this as a basis for creating a circle of interpretations which are synthesised into an understanding of the 'texts' of management events, the deconstructionist approach regards the interpretative event as *itself problematic*, and in need of analysis and explanation. In some cases, such as the post-structuralism of Michel Foucault, the analysis is rooted in the historical circumstances of the interpretation, whilst in others, such as the even more radical approach of Jacques Derrida, it needs to be deconstructed into component sub-texts. As mentioned in Chapter 6, it is something of a grey area where hermeneutics stops and deconstruction begins, though as I have argued above part of the difference is the belief in foundations.[1]

In many ways it does less than justice to the ideas of Derrida and Foucault to lump them together, but for the sake of completeness we ought to give a rough location on the Lincoln and Guba questions:

Ontological question:	what is, is always a step away from what we can directly identify in our current historical circumstances
Epistemological question:	we can know the results of our analytical (or, in Derridan terminology) linguistically playful activities
Methodological question:	As with interpretavism, we look at texts, statements and human perceptions, but we treat them to a wider range of techniques – in one case comparing and arranging them, in another examining the linguistic avenues of semantic connection

A much longer set of answers, couched in more specific terminology. Hopefully some of this will become clear during this chapter. But the main thing is to note a severance between ontology (that is, the reality of, for example, management) and epistemology and methodology. Put non-jargonistically, what these two writers are doing is abandoning the comfortable presumption that there is a neat relationship between what management really is and how we could discover this. In contrast, this approach suggests above all that we can only analyse and depict, we cannot reach a point where we have a clear statement of management reality. It shifts – either because of our own essentially parochial historical position, or because the language we use to try to pin things down refuses to be pinned down, and always leaves something just out of our reach.

The caveats given earlier regarding the original material apply even more strongly – this material is all drawn from (in some cases) very obscurely expressed sources; neither of the two main writers considered directly discuss management knowledge, so I am interpreting their writings in a manner which may not find favour with the principal adherents of these views; and finally the language is in some places very 'stretchy' and subject to the whims of fashion.

7.1 MICHEL FOUCAULT AND MANAGEMENT KNOWLEDGE

Michel Foucault was a French social philosopher-historian who wrote in the latter part of the twentieth century. His wide ranging work was firmly rooted in a French intellectual tradition, which made little direct reference to organisations and management, but much of 'big' theories of human nature such as those of Freud or (maybe especially) Marx. Foucault's ideas clearly changed during his career, although the work of later commentators suggests that they can see a connecting thread over time.[2]

The key ideas of Foucault which have a bearing on the possibility and validity of management knowledge are as follows:

1 *Ideas, knowledge and power*:

- ideas (or, in Foucault's terms, *discourses*) need to be understood in historical terms
- knowledge and power are inextricable
- the power/knowledge axis is itself closely bound up with social practices

2 *The meaning of ideas*:

- the intellectual bases of ideas cannot normally be articulated in their own time
- these unarticulated foundations – *epistemes*, as Foucault originally called them – define what can and cannot be said at a particular time
- Foucault talked at different times about two distinct but complementary methods of analysis of ideas in their historical aspect: genealogy,[3] and archaeology[4]

3 *Subjectivity, materiality, and discontinuity*:

- there are no pre-existing, independent ideas or aspects of human nature which stand outside of any discourse

- the historical analysis of discourses is not always (or even often) a search for continuities or causal links
- the individuality of a person (and their own self-understanding) is itself profoundly influenced by the power/knowledge axis, and its associated social practices

These have been stated above in a list form, because they are key themes which can be seen in much of Foucault's writings. But they were never set down by him in that way. In some ways they probably cannot all coexist together simultaneously. Be that as it may, much of the interest in Michel Foucault is related to one or more of these themes. The following discussion will hopefully put these into a context in which his relevance for the question of whether management knowledge is valid becomes clear.

7.1.1 History, Knowledge and Power

The central kernel of Foucault's approach is that knowledge about society, about institutions, and about the self, has to be seen as a historical event. There is no basis for identifying an independent reality which persists from one time to another. Our ideas about social issues and institutions – and the nature of management – have to be seen in the context of the time in which we make them, if they are to be properly understood. But that context does more than just give them a flavour. The historical context in which an idea about society is expressed is, for Foucault, *central to its very meaning*.

The second key point is that more than almost any other writer, Foucault believed that *knowledge is intimately linked to social power*. The two are quite indistinguishable, for him. His own researches were in fields such as the evolution of practices and theories of legal punishment, social attitudes towards sexuality, and the treatment of madness, but they can readily be applied to the management context.[5] I shall try to construct an analysis of a management phenomenon in the style of Foucault's approach. Doubtless some will find this a travesty of his real views, but it is essential that we gain *some* kind of idea of what the approach has to say about management theory, however imperfect.

As mentioned before, Foucault's ideas clearly developed significantly over his career, so an additional caveat is the extent to which I have been selective in what I make use of. I have therefore leant heavily on the commentary of Paul Rabinow, as he provides a fairly comprehensive review of the whole of Foucault's career.[6]

Take an idea such as Total Quality Management (TQM). This is generally perceived as a framework for pulling together a cluster of techniques for making quality a central feature of the way an organisation works. Although the ideas were originated in the USA in the immediate post-Second World War period, they were really developed in Japan, and tend to be seen as a Japanese export to the West.

The Foucault style approach to this phenomenon would be to focus, not solely on an impersonal and 'timeless' *intellectual* structure of this idea, but also on its *social* origins – the prevailing power relationships within which the idea acquired force, and the economic and social circumstances in which it has developed both in Japan and, more importantly, as it has been exported to other countries. We can see here that for Foucault a concept is not simply an event in someone's mind. It exists through its public expression – the variety of ways in which it appears in public debate and discussion. One implication here is that this public aspect of expression is not a neutral aspect. It is not as if the linguistic expression of an idea is simply a window through which the light of argument shines. A more appropriate image is that the language – the discourse – is a raw material, something which has to exist before anything can get transmitted at all, and which has a definite nature which rules in certain forms and rules out others. *What gets publicly expressed is a product of social forces.* So an idea about a management technique is disseminated and developed in virtue of its role in a power complex.

Furthermore ideas and practice are inextricably inter-related. An idea, once expressed, is immediately linked by its audience (explicitly or implicitly) with the current state of relevant practices, the current level of debate and uncertainty regarding those practices and the current perception of the limits of debate in this area.[7] In other words, one cannot completely separate out an idea (as a 'pure' thought) from how it links with current practices and technology (construed in the broadest sense of the word). The concept exists as a part of the overall social structure.

One of Foucault's best examples of this linkage is the way that madness was treated in different eras (at least in France and by implication other parts of Western Europe). The idea of madness as an illness evolved alongside the development of institutions for the mad being designated mental hospitals – before that time it was seen differently: as possession, as a special gift, sometimes as a form of magical power. A whole range of approaches to madness, including incarceration, treatment, nursing, and the possibility of 'cure' are brought into the arena once the image of illness is raised.[8] And it is impossible to separate out practice from concept and say which came first – they coevolved.

Similarly, the idea that quality could be managed in terms of an over-arching philosophy emerged alongside the growth and extent of a range of different practices. Implicit in the idea of a quality circle, for example, is the idea that quality can be managed effectively by involving workers from all levels of an organisation in the problem solving process. It is probably impossible and certainly misleading to say precisely which came first. In some ways early examples where a quality circle was set up created the idea of group problem solving as a practice, which later became recognised as an early form of a key element of TQM. Practice and thought coevolved. Equally, some ideas which pre-existed the concept gained a new relevance once the idea of TQM had become current. Statistical Process Control, for example, pre-dated TQM but became subsumed by it.

7.1.2   The Limits of Sense

Another aspect of Foucault's historically based approach to knowledge is that ideas survive in virtue of their social tolerability. Ideas which fall outside the current social orthodoxy[9] are excluded. But this is not deliberate censorship – the ideas are not necessarily excluded as a conscious choice by some kind of elite or dominant consensus which holds the reins of power. The influence is more subtle. The unorthodox is perceived as beyond the bounds of what is accepted as making sense. What defines the boundary is what Foucault in his early writing called an *episteme* – a primitive conception or model of rationality which cannot be articulated by people under its influence. An episteme operates in a particular point in history. Like all other ideas, probably even more so, it needs to be construed in its historical circumstances, both for it to have sense in its historical setting and for it to make sense of that setting. If an individual tries to express an idea which conflicts with the episteme – that is, it transgresses the bounds of rationality – then there is no linkage, no point at which it is allowed to connect with the range of allowable ideas.[10]

So what is the *episteme* which underlies TQM? In this case one of the main questions is why this particular idea out of many Japanese concepts of managerial practice has been received positively in the West. Why has TQM made sense for the West when other ideas have not? The Foucault style answer is to locate the idea within the power relations of individuals, particular companies (with their own idiosyncratic management–worker relationships), industries and their dominant global players, and competing governments and continental regions.

One aspect of this is that TQM primarily looks at changing worker behaviour, and is easily compatible with the focus in the post-war period on productivity improvements through improved internal efficiencies and enhanced worker motivation (and hence performance).

Because of this the idea is not especially challenging to the central power structure of Western companies.

Compare this with the possibility of Western companies emulating the Japanese way of corporate governance.[11] This cuts to the heart of modern Western business (especially in its Anglo-Saxon versions), which is heavily dominated by corporate level activity, much of it driven by the personal interests of wealthy individual entrepreneurs and the enormous weight of the institutional investment funds. Each of these two groups has an agenda, and although these do not coincide, they do collectively exercise a significant degree of influence over commercial behaviour, sometimes leading to a continual round of corporate activity, including acts such as merger and acquisition, downsizing and asset stripping, consolidation and rightsizing, and then reentry into the mergers/acquisitions market.

TQM fits very neatly into this framework. It deflects attention from the effectiveness or wisdom of the behaviour of senior managers and directors, and focuses instead on the behaviour of employees. This kind of focus tends to present the vicissitudes of Western corporate performance over the last twenty years as a result of failures of the workforce, rather than of the directors.[12] Arguably, this explanation reflects the power differential between managers and workers. The definition of Total Quality and its prominence as a key component of management theory and practice in the late 1980s and early 1990s reflects the imbalance between managers and employees both in the *practice* of organisational evaluation and in the construction of a *theory* of organisations. Put crudely, managers can tell employees that they need to work harder, but employees can't reciprocate the gesture.

This power imbalance is central in defining what makes sense in discussions of organisational performance and enhancement.[13] It is also enshrined in practice – legal as well as social and economic. It is in the context of this imbalance that the intelligibility of a whole variety of organisational phenomena needs to be understood. Amongst these, components of TQM, such as continuous improvement or quality circles, draw their intelligibility from this idea of imbalance (n.b. as it manifests itself in the late twentieth century – one must never forget the historical perspective when considering Foucault's ideas). The idea of, say, continuous improvement of *directors'* performance as measured by *employee* criteria, is not only ruled out by this basic imbalance – it is difficult to see how organisations as currently structured (as opposed to individuals) could even recognise what this could achieve, how it could work, or what impact it could have on organisational quality.[14]

Implicit in this is that what counts as acceptable social behaviour defines groups in general, not just the 'deviant' groups Foucault studied. Power relationships – for example, the ability to influence public opinion, the psychological contract between employer and employee, or the possession of legal rights in relation to the corporate entity – these define those social groups which are relevant to the operation of organisations and what knowledge is used to inform practice. Rabinow uses the term 'dividing practices', which is fair enough, because the social structures and behaviours Foucault refers to do in fact divide, but such practices *define* as much as they divide. 'Manager' is not a job title (or not just that): it is a position in the chain of human interactions which has the customer or client at one end and the ultimate owner at the other. Any one group (trustee, employee, etc.) is divided from others by this power nexus, but by the same token they are also united with them – without such a chain there would be no such roles at all.

Hence the late twentieth century focus on employee behaviour stems not only from a power imbalance, but also from an associated conception of what organisations are and what counts as their effective performance. This is a key aspect of Foucault's approach – theory and practice are interlinked. In the modern era, a successful company is measured primarily in shareholder value. This is generally taken as the benchmark of organisational performance.

This locates the central example of the organisation as a commercial company (the most recent form of organised activity in history). Corporate theory in the post-war era has thus been developed in the main to enable limited companies to gain greater market share or make greater profits. Other forms of organised activity have been depicted as deviating to a larger or smaller extent, and thus the theory of how they work is depicted as derivative from the primary type of organisations. Thus the theory of public organisations is generally conceived as *rather like company theory but without the profit motive* – that of voluntary organisations often quite misleadingly being lumped together with the public sector on the basis of the 'not-for-profit' aspect. Similarly, the theory of partnerships is conceived as *rather like company theory but with a more direct owner/director role* in management. The theory of small businesses is seen as *rather like that of large corporations but scaled down in size.*

This primacy of the limited company places the idea of TQM in a specific context, one in which the primary kind of organisational activity is creating value for shareholders. This is a reflection in intellectual terms of the actual economic imbalance we discussed in the previous paragraph, which itself has coevolved with the underlying core conception of an imbalance between owners (or managers) and employees. Management as a set of ideas and forms of enquiry is therefore inextricable from the power nexus which exists at the time and place where those ideas and enquiries are activated. It cannot but reflect the economic structures within which it operates.

This is the heart of Foucault's relevance for the question of the validity of management knowledge. For it implies that there is no long term, persisting knowledge about how to manage at all, but only immediate current 'truths' which depend on their historical circumstances for any sense to be made of them, and which will fade as those circumstances change.

This has resonances with Marxist approaches to the connection between economic structures and cultural ideas. It also has links with the related view that management theory is ideology in disguise, which we discussed in Part I. But there are also clear differences between the Foucault type of approach and the Marxist. For one thing, Marxism lays claim to a special authority to knowledge derived from historical analysis.[15] On the Marxist view, the enlightened theorist who perceives their position in the class struggle is able to produce a clear view of social relations, one which goes beyond the contamination of ideology. For Foucault, on the other hand, the historical underpinning of knowledge affects all social theory, however and whenever produced. There is no place where a more enlightened theory is possible. All theories exist in their social power structure, and have an intimate connection with the accepted range of practices. Another point is that the Marxist approach takes the link between economic structure and intellectual ideas as an assumed fact, whilst Foucault's approach is more of a methodology. Yet a third difference is that the Marxist view holds that social knowledge, as with other cultural phenomena, is ultimately determined by economic relationships. For Foucault the relationship is more two-way. Power relations and social practices are as much *caused by* social conceptions and ideas as *causes* of them.

7.1.3 Probing the Past of Contemporary Theory

The above is an attempt at a Foucault-style analysis of one idea in management. We quickly moved away from the specifics of this to the underlying context. This is closely in line with the trend in Foucault's approach to social phenomena. But in any case the link between social forces on the one hand and social ideas on the other is only a part of Foucault's position. He also takes a wider perspective, looking at the context in which thinking about social phenomena operates – what makes it possible – and also how this links with individuals' own beliefs about themselves and their own social position. As mentioned earlier, the terms he used (at different times) for this aspect of his analysis were genealogy and archaeology. The way that

Foucault uses these related ideas provides the clearest point of contrast with other approaches to the idea of social knowledge.

Both of these terms were meant to reflect the need to get behind the language in which we discuss and conceptualise issues such as madness or sexuality (or, in my example above, quality in management). Foucault explained genealogy as the presentation of 'historical ontology' – roughly speaking the manner in which ideas and social practices and structures can be said to exist and operate inter-dependently in a specific set of historical circumstances. Just as a family tree traces back the linkages between individuals in history, so the analysis of social ideas traces the linkages between those ideas and the historical circumstances and organisational activities in relation to which they are conceived. It displays without raising any underlying explanations. Foucault also, by means of the idea of genealogy, introduced a further element into social knowledge: the manner in which individuals accept and adopt both social practice and social ideas as part of the way in which *they understand themselves*. This has several different aspects. 'Three domains of genealogy are possible. Firstly a historical ontology of ourselves ... in relation to truth ..., second a historical ontology of ourselves in relation to a field of power ..., third a historical ontology of ourselves in relation to ethics ...'.[16] Paraphrasing, Foucault is suggesting that the manager creates his/her own self-image in terms of ideas, practices and morals. Thus Foucault rejects emphatically one of the central tenets of the naturalistic approach – that of intellectual value-freedom. TQM is not *just* a practice of many managers. It is considered as a potential *technology*. The power of this term is that it implies that the idea, if applicable, is itself inherently valuable – it is intended to make work and organisational performance better. Investigation into practice cannot ignore this aspect, it cannot be value-free in the way that an investigation into, say, the ability of the Black–Scholes model to predict actual financial results can be, still less an investigation into the life history of the slow worm.

The other aspect to this is that TQM is conceived of as a philosophy of practice – in other words it creates self images. For example, team workers are not just people who work well together; problem solvers are not merely people who are able to work effectively through unexpected circumstances. People acquire a self-conscious mantle through such epithets. The label changes how people see themselves and their interactions with others. This is part of what Foucault means by talking of historical ontology *of ourselves*. We do not only accept practices, we do not only take on the ideas which go hand on hand with those practices, we also *locate* ourselves on that conceptual map – we take on the roles created and defined by those concepts, and think of ourselves in those terms.

The idea of genealogy concerns the structural features of social relationships and how these affect social thinking – Foucault at times talked of it as a method dealing with the *surface* of phenomena. Archaeology, on the other hand, aims at the underlying conceptual context within which social ideas are expressed, and seeks to relate this to historical and social factors. 'Archaeology tries to define, not the thoughts, representations, images, themes, pre-occupations that are concealed or revealed in discourses, but those discourses themselves, those discourses as practices obeying certain rules.'[17] In other words, archaeology (in Foucault's sense) is not concerned with the detailed content of, for example, how concepts of quality management are influenced by the power structures of organisations – this kind of linkage is genealogical. Rather it is concerned with how that kind of idea is able to exist as a social phenomenon at all. Thus Foucault goes beyond the interpretative approach, which remains firmly fixed at the level of how individuals put together the various 'texts' which they collect and synthesise them into knowledge. In contrast the Foucault approach asks the question what makes such 'texts' possible – what social conditions need to prevail if there is even to be a dialogue or debate about knowledge at all.

Following this analysis, what kinds of things need to happen in order for quality management, as an issue, to be an acceptable kind of subject? It certainly did not have an opportunity for expression several decades ago – the era of Taylorism focused on management as an extension of technology. The idea of team-based problem solving, for example, a central idea of most approaches to TQM, simply was not accepted as part of this kind of dialogue. Mary Parker Follet talked about it in the 1920s and, although her work was published and achieved great prominence for a short time, it was more or less ignored after her death, excluded from the orthodox debate.[18]

Clearly there are several factors affecting whether or not a certain kind of management topic is a legitimate area for discussion: the existence of a willing audience, the opportunity for an idea to be tested in practice, the existence of practices which have some kind of congruity with the idea, and champions who will take the risk of advancing such an idea, are all important. But above all these is necessary some sense in which people – managers particularly – take this as a legitimate part of their role and responsibility.

So what we have seen here is that the genealogical approach identifies linkages between one idea/practice and others, whilst the archaeological approach looks to the deeper meanings which make possible the idea/practice at all, those meanings which create a field of thought, experiment and discussion. In the example of TQM the genealogical links were identified through the comparison of this idea with practices of corporate governance. Its archaeological root lies in a particular conception of the psychological contract – one which has firm limits, even at the cost of organisational effectiveness.

We have spent a significant amount of time on exposition of Foucault's ideas. This is principally because outside of a small group of research theorists his name is rarely encountered, though hopefully this exposition has shown that his ideas have a major implication for the validity of management knowledge. We shall turn to this now.

7.1.4   Foucault's Legacy for Management Knowledge and Potential Criticisms

The key legacies which Foucault has left for management knowledge are:

(a)   the idea of linking ideas to practices and power relationships
(b)   the view that ideas only make sense in their historical context

As was briefly noted earlier, these two ideas, when put together, provide a striking rebuttal of both the naturalist and the interpretavist approaches to social knowledge. For the key assumption of naturalism is that researchers can reach an independent view of reality, something which cannot make sense if ideas are tied to their concrete historical circumstances, where this includes practice as well as theory. And the interpretavist approach rests on the view that ideas can be synthesised to form an overall coherent picture of the world, something which cannot be the case if thoughts and perceptions are forever changing as their historical context changes. Both these approaches are attempts to find a stable foundation for knowledge of management. But Foucault's historical orientation implies not only development through time but also *decay*. Neither positivism nor interpretavism can deal with the decay of their foundations.

So the approach of Michel Foucault is profoundly sceptical of any lasting inter-subjective knowledge of general theories of human behaviour. This is not to say that he denied that any knowledge at all was possible – rather he was saying that what we regard as knowledge is inextricable from our social life and our historical times. Paradoxically this may not be so damaging for an applied study such as management as it would be for a pure subject such as psychology. For management, as an applied study, is closely tied to its times. In contrast, the theories of the past are still important areas for discussion even in a discipline as (relatively) young as Psychology, so that Freud is still a major and highly controversial figure, a century after he had started writing on the mind and its normal and abnormal development. Psychology is seeking *timeless* truths about the mind. But the nearest equivalent in management is the work of Frederick Taylor, whose ideas are certainly not advocated (at least by serious management writers) as valid for today – though they may be important as historical documents. There is, it is true, a slow but growing trend to seek inspiration from beyond the Western twentieth century traditions in managerial thinking. Such a search still, however, remains within an expanded orthodoxy – so that we have a number of books about the relevance of relatively safe sets of ideas such as Zen, but almost nothing about the far more radical challenge to western thinking provided by the Dreamtime of native Australians.[19] History is not a central discipline for management theory currently.

But how valid is Foucault's own approach? There have been several areas of controversy even in the consideration of his own chosen fields. For example, his detailed researches into the treatment of the mad in Enlightenment France have been criticised as not comprehensive, though this is probably not of much relevance to our purposes. More important is the critique of Foucault's view of how people take on a self-image through participating in certain practices.[20] But perhaps the key issue is whether Foucault's approach could ever generate broadly based statements about organisations that said anything about the future. As tools of historical analysis, the ideas of genealogy and archaeology are capable of providing fresh insights into the past. They are, after all, looking at the past. But how can they be used for the future? By Foucauldian definition, the ideas which people will have at some time in the future will be rooted in the power relations and practices of that time. All we can do now is reflect our own times in our analyses of future events. Current theories about issues, such as e-commerce changing the face of business world-wide, tell us a lot about what people are thinking about at the end of the twentieth century. They tell us less about what will actually be happening in 2050, though, and still less about how events happening then will be perceived at the time.

This is a crucial issue for a subject matter which represents, in part at least, an attempt at soft technology. Management studies would be of an entirely different nature if there were no interest in making organisations more effective. The technological aspect is central. A theoretical perspective which does not help us project into the future is unable to provide a basis for devising technologies or new practices. Given Foucault's own view of how practices and ideas coevolve, it is difficult to see how he could include an element in his theories of managers and professionals deliberately reinventing approaches or practices. The Foucault approach cannot therefore provide a basis for projecting how the tools for constructing new practices and techniques to help organisations run better can be consciously created. Of course, Foucault can explain what kind of process, in the abstract, will lead to new managerial practices, and once they have happened he can provide a framework for explaining how they came about (at least in terms of how ideas, power, practices and self-consciousness codetermined the new practices). But there is no framework for making statements about what the future will look like or how organisations be best managed in the future.

This points up one advantage of a naturalist approach – that the idea of capturing an independent and stable view of organisations means that new practices and techniques can be developed and applied, in the belief that they will not lose their applicability once circumstances change. Whether or not this is *possible* is of course a different matter, but crucially the Foucauldian approach rules it out before any attempt is made. Perhaps Foucault himself would say that he is happy with this conclusion, but if we are looking to his ideas to help understand what management knowledge is and how it might be valid *we* have to take the problem seriously, even if Foucault does not.

Another less damaging problem is that the Foucault approach has an element of anarchism about it. It takes the past and then delves into it, without a systematic algorithmic basis for when a particular approach such as genealogy should be used, and how far should the analysis go. It could be argued that this simply puts it in the same position as other approaches to knowledge. For there has to be a degree of open-endedness in all investigation. Fresh evidence may always come to light, so the naturalist approach has to allow that probabilities and degrees of confirmation may shift as new evidence is acquired, and the interpretavist approach has to accept that there is no such thing as a closed hermeneutic circle (because it can always be widened). But the Foucault approach includes uncertainty at a different level. It is not just that the result of the analysis may be revised as new material appears, it is that it is unclear where an analysis should start, or what scale of investigation is involved.

This, supported by the previous point, suggests that here we have an excellent framework for post hoc explanations, but not a *methodology* at all. Perhaps Foucault would be pleased that his views are not viewed as a system. But it means that we are no further forward with understanding whether or how management research might be considered as valid. Foucault's views have provided added critique to positivism and interpretavism, but they do not seem to furnish a basis themselves to management knowledge.

7.2   DERRIDA – THE ARCHDUKE OF POST-EVERYTHING

We shall discuss the views of Derrida in much less detail than Foucault. This is not meant as an indication of respective importance, but more a reflection of the difficulty of their views. At first sight the work of Jacques Derrida is profoundly dense. His writings are epigrammatic, full of asides and tangents, and deliberately mischievous – packed full of wordplay (and for all these reasons he has attracted a hothouse of passionate adherents and violent detractors – neither much help if we are to extract material to help us understand how far management knowledge is valid). But on a deeper level he is remarkably consistent. This contrasts with Foucault, who seemed to have several ideas working in almost different directions at times, and whose ideas changed as his career progressed.

Derrida seems more motivated by an attitude than by a specific set of precise beliefs. At various times he has been described as a post-modernist or a post-structuralist, but whilst he may have said things which others are keen to shovel into one or other of these highly abstract bins, it is unlikely that he would want to be identified with either, or with other late twentieth-century movements. He is above all an anti-foundationalist, who focused his attention primarily on the nature of language. From our point of view his relevance is that his comments on language implicitly reflect on the idea of knowledge in general, and especially for an area of applied social knowledge such as management (given Derrida's more recently expressed sympathies with some of the ideas of Marx maybe *especially* management).

There seem to be three related strands in Derrida's work which are relevant to our basic question of how far is management knowledge valid:

(i)   his scepticism with regard to the idea of a simple structure of language which can be revealed through an unproblematic process of analysis

(ii)   an opposition to what he calls logocentrism – the idea that when we use language we have a clear idea of what we are expressing, and that this is neatly captured by our words – which is part of what he means when we say that writing preceded speech[21] and also partly what he means by talking of 'différance'[22]

(iii)   consequent on the first two points, a focus on the idea of *deconstructing* language and linguistic forms, which has led Derrida to be enthusiastic about multiple methods of exploring links between ideas, especially those prompted by word associations and verbal similarities

On this view, we cannot look for a single stable configuration, framework or composition which will lay out clearly and unambiguously what we know about organisations and management. When someone uses terms such as 'leadership' or 'strategy', for example, they cannot capture an entire sense just by using those words – for these have meaning just as much in terms of their contrasts with other terms as they do on their own. Leaders are contrasted with followers, sometimes with (mere) managers. Strategy gains its meaning partly through its contrast with operations. It is in virtue of these contrasts that we gain an idea of where someone is trying (and this is the operative word here) to direct our attention. 'Effectiveness' not only contrasts at different times with 'ineffectiveness', 'ability', and 'efficiency' but also continually defers a complete explanation – for it implies a kind of success in management which is only ever measured in retrospect, and then often only fleetingly. It is far easier to identify the moments of effectiveness of past managers than it is to identify those of today. Is Microsoft a reflection in the 1990s of the IBM of the 1960s – a leviathan waiting for its comeuppance? Was Michael Gorbachev an effective manager of the Soviet Union? Depends who you ask – he certainly made an effect, but whether he effected his own aims is another question. The point is that we cannot ever answer one question without relying on the answers to other questions and the meaning of other terms – the dispute about Gorbachev's effectiveness will naturally lead us into discussions of other words, with the result that the resolution of the debate is continually deferred.

It is inappropriate to rely solely on the utterances of an individual to try to understand the full meaning of their statements (if indeed there is such as thing as *the* full meaning at all). Just as useful is to *deconstruct* the terminology. This goes beyond the idea of analysis. The latter idea suggests a single process which gradually reveals the true structure or nature of the statement. But Derrida's concept of deconstructing is without a definitive end point. For Derrida, there is no single structure of someone's ideas – the process (which it is worth emphasising is only *like* analysis, not analytical in itself[23]) is as much like playing with words as investigating. Deconstruction is, as Derrida might say, a search for the roots/routes of the utterances considered. In other words, in following down a trail hoping to find the final roots of meaning, we find that, as with real roots, they taper off, and we find we have simply followed one amongst many routes, learning something, but not everything, about what has been said.

This represents an even more pessimistic approach than that of Foucault. For he was at least prepared to acknowledge some kind of role for statements in their historical context. Derrida, on the other hand, is almost striking at the heart of the use of language as a vehicle for establishing contact between different human beings – it is as if he is suggesting that whatever someone says or writes, the link with other people always fails to capture something entirely and captures a bit of something else instead.

It is likely that we make best sense of this as a critique of the assumptions which we have to make in order to survive as communicating beings, rather than as an attempt to rewrite the way we think and speak. So deconstruction should not paralyse normal processes of researching, investigating and acting. Rather it is best seen as a corrective, a reminder not to place more weight on our ideas than they can bear, and a reminder too that those ideas may indicate many more directions than we realise.

We again find here the same problem we had with Foucault's views. Deconstruction is fine, but it needs something to deconstruct. So by definition it can only help us understand what we have already thought and investigated. It serves as no guide to the future. Deconstruction can only interpret. It's role as a creator is severely limited to extraction from what is already established.

This involves several serious weaknesses. For example, is this kind of wordplay open to all? Can it be done better or worse by some people? In which case what are the standards of deconstruction? I suspect that, as with Foucault, these issues would worry Derrida not too much, but they emphasise the limitation of this as a basis for management knowledge.

Nevertheless, although Derrida's approach does not look as if it can generate new knowledge on its own, it does have the potential to generate new understandings of ideas which are already current. The exploration of the multiple associations and inter-connections between ideas is itself a significant gain in knowledge, if only in the sense that someone gains a better idea of the complexities involved. For a field such as management, this is a major issue. As we have seen, management involves a wide range of different subjects, the combination of which is as much up to the individual manager as any over-arching theoretical perspective. Hence a technique which helps people recognise this has a value in virtue of this alone.

SUMMARY

In conclusion, then, we have seen that the principled anti-foundational approaches of Derrida and Foucault, whilst extremely challenging as critiques for foundational approaches such as positivism or phenomenology, are unable themselves to present substantial answers to our question of how valid is management knowledge. Their key importance is in the task which they set for any account of management knowledge which purports to establishing any sense of validity. In the next chapter we shall see a range of less systematic but equally non-foundational approaches to management knowledge.

NOTES

1   I doubt that that many hermeneuticians consciously think of their work in foundational terms – as I have argued above, though, they are committed to an element of foundationalism, which distinguishes their approach from those considered in this and the following chapter, where there is no such suggestion at all.

2   Though it is likely that if he were consistent Foucault would have played down any suggestion of long-term continuities in his work.

3   The object of which is (very roughly) to identify an idea (discourse) in its own historical terms, without trying to explain it in terms of historical continuities or in terms of an underlying independent idea of human nature.

4   The object of this is (again very roughly) to identify the underlying and inarticulable thoughts and beliefs which define what is acceptable or makes sense for a range of discourses in their historical setting.

5   Regrettably Foucault's ideas have spawned an academic industry. A collection of 'Foucauldian' management theory can be found in McKinley and Starkey (1998), and a good critique of 'Foucauldian' studies can be found in Newton (1998).

6   Rabinow (ed.) (1991) though the reader should realise that the 'archaeological' side of Foucault's work is less fully explored by Rabinow than the 'genealogical'. However, Merquior (1985) does better justice to Foucault's concept(s) of 'archaeology'.

7   That is the limits of which ideas are seen as relevant to the field and which ones are not.

8   All this and much more is discussed in Foucault (1979).

9   The current orthodoxy of what is the appropriate range of relevant ideas. 'Orthodoxy' here is not meant to indicate a single set of established *beliefs*, but an established range of *debate*.

10   This is the dark side of a hermeneutic circle. It creates a dispossessed class – those who feel they have something to say but for whom the means of expression is denied.

11   Which emphasises maintenance of good face to face relationships and consensus in decision making, and often involves cross-shareholding between networks of related companies, so that they are closely networked without there being the traditional western holding company to subsidiary style approach.

12   When in fact both groups have contributed to such vicissitudes.

13   Whilst it would go beyond the letter of anything that Foucault said to call this an episteme, it is consistent with the spirit of his thought.

14   The practice of Semco, as described in Semler (1995) provides the best known exception – though of course it is well known precisely because it *is* an exception.

15   In the special Marxist sense in which history is the development of the conflicts between different socioeconomic classes.

16   Quote of Foucault by Dreyfus and Rabinow (1984).

17   Foucault (1972).

18   See Follett (1920). Maybe one of the greatest hindrances to economic progress in the middle twentieth century was the failure of the west to pick up early enough on Follett's ideas.

19   Though one striking exception is Rigsby's examination of one key cluster of concepts relating to land and ownership. Rigsby (1999).

20   For a difficult but insightful discussion of this issue, as it applies mainly to followers of Foucault rather than to himself, it is worth consulting Newton (1998).

21   Not in a historical sense but in the sense that when we speak what we say cannot be interpreted solely as sound, but has to be taken as if it were written. Languages – especially those such as French or English – have sounds which can only be distinguished for certain on the page – 'on' and 'en' in French, 'piece' and 'peace' in English.

22   A typical but central example of Derrida's wordplay – the word is a deliberate mixing of two French words, one of which means *difference* and the other means *deferral*. So 'différance' means both the idea that words always have a difference of meaning between users and over time, as well as the implication that they can never furnish a complete mapping of a set of ideas, this being in effect continuously deferred from any one time. I owe much here to Stuart Sim's discussion on Derrida's response to the idea of the end of history. Sim (1999).

23   Though in Part III we shall see the analytical element as one of the key benefits to be carried forward from this discussion.

Chapter 8

Research as Practice

In Chapters 5 and 6 we saw two different versions of the idea that management knowledge can be given a clear foundation, and that this foundation is what gives it status as knowledge. What we saw was that in each case there was an emphasis on one key element of the research process which, though important and indeed very fruitful in helping us understand that process, did not capture entirely what is involved in the idea that management (and more generally applied social) knowledge can be valid. The previous chapter looked at anti-foundational approaches which circle around the idea of deconstruction and historical context. As these arose principally from a critical radical perspective, it is not surprising that their strength as critique is matched by a corresponding lack of pragmatic application to research as an activity.

Not surprisingly, the critique embedded in the deconstructionist and post-structuralist traditions did not find much favour in the Anglo-Saxon world. The assumption – accepted as standard in mainland Europe in the late twentieth century – that social theory should embrace social criticism was not so prevalent in the UK and markedly less so in the USA. Consequently, management research, which really began to get going as a distinct subject in this period, was insulated from that political stance. But although this meant that management research did not encounter the debate which general social theory did, there were still criticisms which surfaced at that time. One important strand of these centred on the idea that research as traditionally conducted was as much a process of social exclusion as one of discovery. This perception underlay the development of the approach we shall consider in this chapter – a different kind of non-foundational approach, which I shall dub practice based research. What characterises this approach is an emphasis on some of the key physical features of the social research process, namely that it involves interactions between human beings, and in doing so it inevitably creates dynamics which go beyond the simple measurement of human events.

Two aspects of this interaction are primary – in a way they characterise two different versions of this pragmatic paradigm.[1] The first of these focuses mainly on the group dynamics of the social research process – we have people working together who in some way or another have to collaborate in order for the research to be done, and therefore investigation in fields such as management need to be treated as a collaborative inquiry. An implication of this is that the boundary between researcher and subject begins to blur – at times even disappears altogether. This version makes copious use of ideas and practices drawn from humanistic social psychology, and some of its main exponents – such as John Heron – are well known in that field.

The second version is closely associated with Chris Argyris, who has drawn important connections and contrasts between what he calls Action Science and participative or collaborative inquiry.[2] This version focuses on the link between the human interaction (essential to any practice based research) and the content of the research investigation. Hence there is an attention to: (a) the degree of localisation of practice based research; (b) the degree to which the research process intervenes in the situation (and thus cannot help but modify or change the data it observes); and (c) the level of generalisability to which such investigations can claim.

On the Lincoln and Guba questions, the position here is rather more consistent between the two main versions than in Chapter 7.

ontological question: management problems and interested
                            parties

> *epistemological question*: the results of organisationally located problem-solving activities
>
> *methodological question*: collaborative problem solving

What this approach therefore does is take further the abandonment of attempts to find broadly based generalisable conclusions. Rather it focuses in on what is generally the day-to-day experience of management – solving local problems. In common with deconstruction there is no stable overall picture of the world of management built up, but whereas that approach left us with a fluid and slippery sense of what organisational reality is, this one fixes on a familiar set of phenomena for which we can readily identify meaningful actions.

In the discussion which follows we shall see that this approach comes closest to grasping what is distinctive about management research (as well as other practice-based fields of inquiry). What we will end up left with, though, is the nagging question: how true is it all? Will link us forward to Part III of the book.

8.1 PARTICIPATIVE OR COLLABORATIVE INQUIRY

'Cooperative inquiry involves two or more people researching a topic through their own experience of it, using a series of cycles in which they move between this experience and reflecting together on it. Each person is cosubject in the experience phases and coresearcher in the reflection phases.'[3]

Thus writes John Heron, one to the key representatives of the collaborative inquiry approach to practice based/applied research. It is important to realise that Heron is not here trying to describe or explain all examples of applied social research. Rather he is taking to (what he sees as) a logical conclusion the influence of key aspects of the research process (as mentioned above – the necessity of collaboration and the interactive, group nature of the research process). So this is not a theory of what makes all practice based research valid, but rather a proposal that this is the most suitable way of ensuring the success of such research. Prescription, not elucidation.

8.1.1   The Democratic Ideal

This prescriptive aspect means some features of the above definition are not straightforward descriptions of the research process. One aspect is that Heron talks in an explicitly democratic way – each party has precisely the same role in each phase in the process. It is difficult to see exactly how this could happen, but I suspect that Heron knows that this is idealism.[4] Peter Reason, another proponent of this approach, is more realistic on this subject. He acknowledges that research projects do not appear out of nowhere. Someone has found the time or money to investigate something, and in some way tries to get other people on board. He suggests that this asymmetry can be gradually modified as the collaborative process progresses. Doubtless this is the case, though the question remains how far it remains as a key feature in the activity.

Suppose I am a professional academic, working in the area of human relations at work. I secure a research grant, having submitted a proposal to conduct research into how groups of workers in say, community health centres evaluate their interactions with customers. I then contact potential research partners – mostly such centres where I could collect data from their staff. I start meeting several groups and begin initiating a collaborative research process. Immediately the aims, purposes and potential significance of the research are likely to change, as the health centre staff begin to connect the research project with their own needs hopes and agendas. In itself this is not surprising, and people such as Peter Reason and John Heron are very clear about how this happens. Now a good collaborative researcher will work within this dynamic situation, with the result that what comes out at the other end may well be quite different from what was originally proposed. Fine if I can 'sell' the result to the people who funded me, but not so good if they do not see the connection with what I originally proposed.

Maybe collaborative researchers would say that my mistake was to develop a research proposal on my own and then try to involve others. What I should have done was to involve the proposed research community in the development of a proposal in the first place, so that we work together for some time in advance of seeking financial or organisational support. This too is fine, except that sometimes it is not so easy to find potential partners without the institutional support already in place.

These sound like objections that miss the point, for in principle the idea of research as collaboration is clear and illuminating. But the issue is how far that idea is realisable. The idea of collaboration used by Reason and Heron is rooted in that of equality. The image is one of participants progressively approaching a common understanding of the research subject. But there is a fundamental asymmetry here. Somehow, someone started the whole thing off – unless several people simultaneously initiated a research project together.[5] One person's role in the process, then, remains irretrievably different from the rest of the researching community, for it is 'their' project. This does not mean that they control the progress of the research – a true collaborative researcher will certainly make every effort not to do this. But it does imply that the route the project takes is different. The perspective of the majority of the researchers is that the project has *come to them* and they have worked together on it. The initiator has a different view: they have *created the starting point* and then relinquished this as they work with others.

The advocate of this approach can with justification point out that *every* participant comes to a research process in their own individual way, and therefore the idea that being the original instigator of the process marks someone off from others all of whom have a clear and identical view of the research is misleading. Every researcher comes at it from their own individual perspective.

But once we recognise the depth of variability in people's personal perspectives, perceptions and beliefs relating to a research project then we move into a much more dynamic and uncertain environment. As I have argued previously,[6] the idea of sharing other people's values and beliefs is riddled with difficulties, some practical some theoretical.

The reader should not think that proponents of cooperative or collaborative enquiry (I am using these two terms inter-changeably) are unaware of this aspect of their work. Peter Reason emphasises that cooperation is not the same as equality.[7] Different individuals can take differing roles in the research process. He might well also take issue with my claim that it is necessarily linked with an ideal of equality. As he points out there are diverse purposes of cooperative research, as indicated in Figure 8.1. Each of these raises different roles of participants, so that participants are best understood as making various complementary contributions than there being an undifferentiated sameness of everyone being equal and identical in their position in the process of cooperative research.

So, for example, a research project devoted to the development of new theoretical approaches to how customers react to the levels of service they receive in supermarkets, would require the participants to adopt different roles compared to a project intended to enable vulnerable customers (for example, differently abled groups) to have more influence over how supermarkets provide them with service. Whilst in both cases all may be involved in processes such as collecting and interpreting information, in the former case the initiating researchers

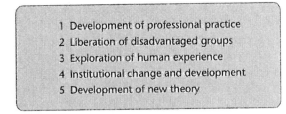

1 Development of professional practice
2 Liberation of disadvantaged groups
3 Exploration of human experience
4 Institutional change and development
5 Development of new theory

Figure 8.1   Five purposes of cooperative enquiry (Reason, 1988: 221–2).

may well be professional academics who would exercise a determin-ing role in setting criteria for what is a good new theory, whilst in the latter the vulnerable customer groups may well be the determining agents in setting evaluation criteria for new practices identified by the research.

We see how far this view goes beyond not only the realist/positivist views of writers such as Pugh, but also from the classical statement of hermeneutics. In each of those views, the issue is solely one of what is the case. Participative enquiry, though, as the items in Figure 8.1 demonstrate, can be as much about ways to change managerial and business practices as to make sense of them. In this respect it could be said to represent the true embodiment of Marx's final thesis on Feuerbach.[8]

8.1.2   Valid Collaborative Research

What does this say about whether the products of management research projects are *true* or not? One problem here is what adherents of the collaborative paradigm mean by talking in terms of research and discovery. John Heron has recognised[9] that there is an issue about how we can regard the products of collaborative enquiry as valid. He claims that he is adopting what philosophers call a coherence approach to truth and validity – namely that what is true is what coheres, or fits in, with all the other things we believe in,[10] but in discussing this he makes some revealing statements which suggest that he is adopting a strongly realist position.

For example, in discussing the degree of agreement required between researchers, he states that:

it is a matter of judgment when the degree of agreement is so low that it constitutes a criterion of inadmissible disagreement. When it is this low, the inquirers must face the fact that *distortions* at the subjective pole of their reality have obscured *their grasp of the object-ive pole*.[11]

In other words, a low level of agreement between coresearchers is to be explained by saying that people have an unclear understanding of what they are researching into. Which implies that there is an independent reality quite apart from how far people do or do not agree with each other.

Similarly, in talking about convergence of researchers, he says 'The weakness of such total convergence is that...it may become *falsely revised*...' Again, the ground for saying that a revision is false or not must lie in something beyond the statements themselves. In other places Heron talks of '...*distorting* rather than disclosing...' experiential content, of diverse conceptual views which '...illuminate a *common content area*', of *ideas which are independent* of their being thought by researchers, and of researchers who *collude in false aspects* of their research process.

In all these cases the words or phrases I have emphasised in the above refer to a concept of truth or independence which Heron has not explained. Indeed the easiest way to explain some of these would be to take a simple realist view that the world is out there waiting to be discovered. For example, what makes one example of researcher consensus a contact with a common reality, and another a collusion in falsity? Which cases are ones of distortion rather than illumination? When is a revision a false one?

Doubtless there may be specific answers to each, maybe to all, of these questions, but it is difficult to avoid concluding that this is realist based. If so, then Heron is not consistent in adopting an approach to validity based on the coherence of people's perceptions and beliefs, for these do not refer outside themselves. Early on he argues clearly for a hermeneutic style view of truth, but then seems to fall back on a realist approach to agreement.

Maybe this is not a damning problem – it does not mean that the paradigm is wrong. But the next section brings an altogether more difficult problem.

8.1.3   Practice Change and Knowledge Change

A second issue with the collaborative paradigm is that however socially valuable may be the inquiry processes which lead to outcomes such as liberation of disadvantaged groups, or institutional change, they do not seem to be directed toward *knowledge*, but toward *practice*. A change in behaviour of groups of individuals, though, is not in itself an addition to knowledge. It *might* lead to knowledge, and there might be knowledge developed about it, but that is a different – albeit maybe related – purpose. For participant or collaborative inquiry to be a form of knowledge, the purposes identified in Figure 8.1 need to be put into context. Purposes such as exploration of human experience or development of new theory must be accompanied by other purposes. For knowledge to happen, it is not enough that change occurs, it is also necessary that this be *recognised*. It is not simply that people change their mental state – this happens whenever any kind of change in a social practice happens. It is that in some way the change involves reflection or *understanding*. This hearkens back to Foucault's points about how social practices are often intertwined with theories. A change in practice is often thereby a change in the underpinning theory, but this is not to say that a process which changes practice is thereby a *research* process. Practices do not define theories, they create a context within which some are more acceptable than others.

One way out of this is simply to say that some cooperative or participative *inquiry* is not necessarily collaborative *research* at all. But this would seem to give away much of what is interesting in this approach. For the intimate link between theory and practice is a core defining feature of applied social investigation.

A more useful tack is to say that participant inquiry can indeed lead to a variety of outcomes, and some of these are clearly research related – such as development of new theories and creation of deeper understandings of practices and people's experiences of them. But even those inquiries which do not directly yield these outcomes are still research driven, for they depend on research activities (particularly data collection), establish certain items of knowledge along the way, and create outcomes which themselves are determinants or key influences on how we conceive of the practices under scrutiny. So all participant inquiry involves research, though traditional research outcomes – that is, changes in knowledge – may not be the prime focus of the process.

But whether these apparent changes in knowledge are the prime focus of the work or not, what is their status? A collaborative inquiry is work which is closely tied to its concrete circumstances – how can it say something about other organisations? It is tempting to say that the research can and should be transferable, but this is ambiguous. On the one hand it can mean that changes in knowledge ought to be capable, as a logical limit, of being applied in other situations. On the other, it can mean that the results are already transferable – that they are already of sufficiently general form to be useful for other situations. At first sight one might be surprised that a concept or result which has been carefully worked out to fit one set of particular circumstances would also fit a completely different situation, but this is not necessarily so odd – if the new knowledge is of the right level of generality then the close tie to one particular situation drops out.

But this answer only works at first sight. A key question is how much generality is enough to justify the attempt to apply the new knowledge to other cases? How similar does something have to be to justify saying it comes under the same category as the case we have investigated? There is no simple answer to this. Different kinds of case present different degrees of variation – even in the field of natural science. It is reasonable to presume that waves on the sea are following regularities – they look regular (at least from our point of view), and their overall behaviour appears to be predictable on the basis of general levels of knowledge: we have yet to see major surprises with waves.[12] By contrast cloud formations are much less easy to predict, and can fluctuate wildly on the basis of quite minor changes in base conditions. So even in non-animate, apparently deterministic contexts, it is difficult to say that there is a set level of generality which allows transferability of knowledge from one context to another: for waves that level may be much easier to assess than for clouds.

John Heron appears to take a different view on transferability, however. He suggests that replication is not to be construed in terms of simple repeat, but in terms of 'creative metamorphosis'. As he puts it 'If the present inquirers are truly going to construe the researched world of the previous inquirers, then they must do so...in their own autonomous...way.'[13] This view, then, depicts the transferability of new practice-based knowledge not as snapshot reproducible, but as a raw material for new researchers to work on afresh.

But this is not as helpful as it looks at first sight. Research is intended to establish what is the case, and activities which are intended to change behaviour rather than interpret it are *replacing* one practice with another, not *establishing* exactly what the first practice really is or was. The idea that there is a kind of knowledge which has to be revisited anew each time a new set of researchers come to it is good reason to say it was not transferable at all. One of the key underlying benefits of knowing what some phenomenon is like underneath its surface is to eliminate the need to carry out a full scale investigation every time we encounter an example of it. Which is exactly what John Heron's suggestion seems to require we *would* have to do.

The key points here would seem to be:

(a) that all collaborative inquiry involves some research activity
(b) collaborative inquiry results in changes to practices as well as potential changes to knowledge
(c) where practices change it cannot be assumed that there is clarity about what the practices actually were beforehand

(d) where understanding changes it cannot be assumed that this is context independent or transferable to other organisations or situations

We shall return to this issue a little later. Let us now consider the related view of Chris Argyris, that of action science.

8.2   ACTION RESEARCH AND ACTION SCIENCE

Though Chris Argyris has elaborated an approach to organisation based research which has close similarities with participatory inquiry (as we noted above, he has explicitly drawn the connections) he has a different emphasis. Theorists of practice-based research such as Peter Reason and John Heron focus on the fact that the research involves a group of individuals who at times may be coresearchers. Argyris, however, keeps very much a joint focus – on validity as well as on participation.

There are three key elements of Argyris' position:

(a) Typically, standard research depicts the process as controlled by the researcher, and thus those who participate in the process as subjects are part of the controlled; this is an analogue of some more traditional approaches to management – the less competent and less powerful employee (subject of research) is subordinate to the knowing and controlling manager (lead researcher). Traditional approaches to research, then, can easily lead to behaviours which have a similarity to traditional organisational phenomena, such as covert attempts by resentful subjects to frustrate the purpose of the research (industrial strife), or by deferential subjects to supply what is believed to be the controller's desired outcome (using assent as a means of creating managerial approval).

(b) Action science attempts to forestall this by using similar elements to Organisation Development (OD).

- collaboration between researcher and subjects
- a range of 'interventions' – interactions between researcher and subject which have an organisational justification in their own right but also serve as vehicles for study, reflection and analysis
- cultivation of a climate of openness, and behaviour which conforms to what Argyris calls 'Model II' – that is, valid information (as opposed to Model I: 'information' which is covertly the result of organisational defence mechanisms – the latter being merely devices to prevent the discussion of difficult areas)
- free and informed choices by participants

- commitment to choices made, so that these can be monitored as they are implemented

(c) Action science is still subject to the same requirements of validity as other forms of knowledge development; in particular conclusions drawn from the research should be testable, and alternative explanations should be evaluated – so conclusions should be seen as hypotheses or tentative conjectures in the first instance.

It is (c) which marks the clearest point of difference between Argyris' position and that of participatory research theorists such as Heron. For Argyris explicitly uses validity as measured in classical terms, alluding to a Popperian type of approach. Heron, as we have seen above, is ambiguous in this respect, espousing an approach which measures validity in terms of participant consensus, but talking in a way which seems more consistent with an externally defined 'detached' idea of validity. Paradoxically, however, Argyris seems to regard (a) as the prime point of differentiation. In distinguishing action science from participatory action research, he states '... it emphasises certain tacit theories-in-use that participants spontaneously bring to situations of practice or research ...'.[14]

We have already looked at the potential imbalances and discrepancies of role which can be involved in participatory research: it is not a meeting of identicals. One person or group is research initiator, others are later subscribers. There is a significant question here as to what exactly creates the epistemological equality between parties possessing clearly different positions with regard to the research project. How can the roles of various researchers be different yet equivalent?

This is a difficult but certainly not impossible question. But it is one which neither Chris Argyris nor Peter Reason and co. have sought to answer. The latter acknowledge that there may be an issue here, and make statements which imply that there is an equivalence. But Argyris seems not to see this as a problem. For him, the adoption of action research principles – if followed through systematically – seems to guarantee that the problems of 'Model I' are circumvented. When that occurs, just as organisational dysfunction is thereby eliminated, so (apparently) will be researcher distorted investigation.

Put in these terms the argument's optimism is laid bare – though it is so well argued and elaborated that this naivete is not apparent in Argyris' own writing. It is, though, latent in presumptions such as the point behind claim (b) above – that there is a clear and easily adopted way of identifying examples of Model II behaviour as opposed to Model I. In the light of that assumption, we can see Argyris' optimism as, firstly the idea that one can straightforwardly distinguish Model I from Model II behaviour, and secondly that appropriate interventions can transform the former into the latter – further confirming that we can see distinct examples of the changed, healthy behaviour.

But there is a problem. It is feasible that someone tightly bound into defensive behavioural routines will be able to 'learn' Model II behaviour, so that they look like changed people, but underneath retain the old attitudes of self preservation and self-deception. So perhaps Argyris is mistaken in assuming that Model I and Model II behaviour can be easily told apart.

A clear *definition* of the difference between Models I and II can be given – Model I behaviour is conditioned by organisation defence mechanisms, so that information is not openly given or offered on a trust basis, whilst Model II behaviour escapes that conditioning, presumably to emerge into the light of open and trusting communication. This is illuminating as an elucidation, but the key question is whether this can be seen by anyone – is it clearly *recognisable*?

Argyris relies heavily on 'before' and 'after' descriptions of his own research to explain and work out his overall view of organisational communication and defence mechanisms. These certainly indicate that the use of action research interventions can work as ways of pulling out organisational defence routines. But there are two difficulties here. Firstly, as mentioned above, the definitions of Model I and Model II behaviours are such as to allow the chance that someone can – whilst still in fact remaining firmly in a Model I mindset – mimic Model II behaviour, possibly as a means of enhancing their own position. Secondly, what if no 'after' effect happens? Does this mean that there is no defence mechanism at work? Hardly – more likely that the defence mechanisms are too strongly ingrained to be eliminated by OD intervention. But if we have no after effect we have no ways of showing that the behaviour of managers in the organisation are indeed following Model I – we have no change to measure them by. This hearkens back to Derrida's idea that one idea draws meaning from its contrasts – in this case that the two Models exist in virtue of each other, and can only find a clear and useful application when both are easily distinguishable.

Doubtless, Argyris would say that the presence of an external observer (who can observe the behaviour and draw out the internal contradictions between what people say and what they do) is the prime means of demonstrating that Model I is at work. This may be effective as a method of conducting OD interventions, and probably is satisfactory in most cases in ensuring that Model I behaviour can usually be flushed out, but it does create more of a problem for action science as a methodology. For it emphasises that one party of the research – the external party – retains a crucially different role to the internal parties, a role which means that their say-so is of greater epistemic value than the say-so of the internals. So while there may be participation, it is not of equivalent value. In terms of creating knowledge, the external is the more important participant (whereas in terms of solving organ-isational issues, the internal is doubtless of greater value). But in the land of the blind, the one-eyed man is a deviant, and therefore what they say is liable to be marginalised. What price the facilitator who feels that there is a significant degree of Model I behaviour, but is unable to persuade any of the other participants in the research pro-ject that this is the case?

Maybe Argyris would be happy with this consequence – but it makes action science rather more different from participatory research than he would seem to believe. However, both approaches, as we have discussed them (as with all the discussions in Part Two of this book, there is a great element of selectivity in the choice of source) share one key feature. Despite the appearance of an open method-ology, both approaches seem to contain a hidden element of realism. Both presume that there is a potential falsity of perception on the part of participants which can be independently identified. In other words, action science and participatory inquiry assume that people working in organisations may be wrong in their perceptions, beliefs, and judgments about their working experiences in ways which can be picked up and examined and potentially even resolved by the external participants to the research. We shall discuss the problems this creates for the participatory paradigm in the following and final section of this chapter.

8.3 VALIDITY AND DEMOCRACY

The core of both approaches is the democratic ideal. As we mentioned earlier, this implies, not that any actual research programmes achieve such an ideal, but that it is the guiding force behind the kind of research activity undertaken. There are key arguments relating to validity and the involvement of research subjects as participants in both the action science and participatory inquiry approaches.

As noted above, action science involves the recognition that most research follows a similar pattern in the way people are managed to that of organisational management. One party sets the direction, con-trols the implementation of the plan and is the source of any criteria of success. Eventually just that one party also decides on the outcomes and is identified with these. The consequence of this is that the other people involved in such a process become disengaged from it – they lose a sense of its value (they may not even develop such a sense in the first place). Because of this sense of alienation they may adopt tactics which are counterproductive to the research (though these might serve their own agendas and plans). Some of these might involve excessively compliant behaviour – giving the answers which the subject believes are expected. Others may result in non-compliant behaviour – sabotaging research which they see as potentially damaging, perhaps by filling in questionnaires perfunctorily, or by stirring up difficulties so that a researcher fails to control the direction of discussion which a focus group follows. The assumption is that therefore the material which is generated in such a research project is not a true reflection of what actually is the case. Involvement of subjects as coresearchers reduces this possibility.

Participatory inquiry approaches the issue from a different direction. If a research field is relevant to people's lives, then who better to demonstrate that relevance? Who is most likely to understand the impact of, say, lifelong learning policies on older people, than those older people themselves? If someone else tries to speak for them, then they may well fall into a number of well known traps. One of these is where the researcher repeats fallacies which have been written up in the literature and acquired a spurious authority.[15] Another is where the researcher speaks on the behalf of the subject group, defining that group's interests for them. Usually this involves a degree of projection of the researcher's own prejudices and stereotypes: in a way this is a sophisticated form of the 'does he take sugar?' fallacy. It should be noted that this is generally seen as a problem with researching disadvantaged groups,[16] but it is just as likely to happen with stereotypically perceived powerful groups such as yuppie financiers – if the researcher defines what is regarded as their key interests, then the research is unlikely to pick up contra-indications.

Put it this way it would seem that the subject is the source of validity. This is not a naive version of phenomenology, whereby each individual's statements are necessarily true as expressions of their own viewpoint. On the contrary it is clear from the work of both John Heron and Chris Argyris that a considerable amount of group processing needs to go on, and the result is not an individual's perception but a construction which ideally bears the hallmarks of all the participants.

But the statements of John Heron we highlighted earlier, which included crucial clues of an underpinning realist approach, and Argyris' overall conception of Model I and Model II behaviours, shifts the focus from what is defined by the subjects to what is presumed by the researcher to be present in collaborative research or action science. The key criterion of truth, then, on these approaches, is not what a group produces when it goes through some kind of collaborative process, but whether the experience of the group fits a pre-defined model of the process, and whether the results fit a pre-defined model of group dynamics.

To illustrate this, imagine a group which goes through the structure of a participative enquiry. Suppose this group does not reach agreement on key preliminary aspects of the investigation – for example, that they do not manage to agree on the key purposes of the investigation. Is this a failure? The implication of the participative and action science models is that it is. But there is a possibility that the individuals within the group *simply do not agree.* It has to remain open that the group dynamics do not work. But if this is so, then the participative paradigm is revealed as a *platform* for investigation, but is not the investigation itself. In other words, participation is a way of organising the means of investigation, rather as experiment is. But just as an experiment is not, of itself valid or invalid, so too the participative inquiry cannot be valid or invalid. It is what is drawn out of the experiment, or the collaborative inquiry, which can be valid or not.

This is not to deny the great value of participative inquiry or action science. But rather it is to point up certain inconsistencies in the way it is presented, and to suggest that the basic model is less radical than it might seem at first sight. The ideal participative inquiry allows a group to develop a set of concepts and practices which reveal or construct a reality about the situation investigated. 'Allows to develop' is important, as we saw in the previous paragraph – the process does not necessitate the development of new knowledge. The 'reveal or construct' is also important – this is not a simple realist position that the world is just out there waiting to be discovered. But equally it is not that what a group produces is intrinsically valid in its own right – it has to fit the rules of a certain kind of world, one in which openness and trust are paramount.

The simple objection to this, regrettably, is that such a world is not ours. Trust and openness are severely constrained by levels of self-defence, resulting in a degree of control in how far and how fast people open up. Lenin said in a different context that truth is so precious it has to be rationed. The same could be said about our own souls – we want them to be laid out to the world, but not to be destroyed by it, so we do it slowly, gradually, and with a view to self-preservation above all.

SUMMARY

In this chapter we have looked at two closely related approaches. Each is built around the idea that organisational research needs to involve a close relationship between those who carry out research and those who are part of the research. In both cases there is a degree of focus on what the research process does for an organisation. In other words management research is seen on this approach as essentially a form of technology, of a process of changing an organisation. The ideal that research can depict an independently subsisting nature of an organisation is now abandoned altogether in favour of the reality that all investigative activities are more in the way of interventions than they are observations.

This is a powerful view which will strongly influence the discussion in Part III. It does, though, rest on a presumption of what counts as effective participation. This constitutes the main weakness here – just what kind of activity is a genuine or productive kind of participation and what is unproductive or unhealthy? It appears that the main theorists in this area make a realist assumption as to what 'true' participation is.

NOTES

1   Though there is less clear water between these two versions than the differences between ideas we have seen in previous chapters – such as that between Foucauldian historicism and Derridan deconstruction, or between positivism and realism.
2   He especially points out the closeness between the two versions. See Argyris (1994) Chapter 20 – on which I have drawn heavily in this chapter.
3   Heron (1999). Opening of Chapter 7 (p. 117).
4   Elsewhere in the same text Heron does acknowledge that someone has to act as the initiator of such research (p. 110).
5   Actually, this is not so remote a suggestion as it might sound, so far as the coresearchers with whom Heron and Reason have worked is concerned, for once someone has been through a successful coresearch process then they are likely to be open to spontaneously interacting with other like-minded individuals. But of course, there are only so many people with that kind of sensibility around. For the most part, people need to be introduced to a research project, and have the benefits spelt out before they will engage in it.
6   Griseri (1998) especially Part 2.
7   Reason (1988) Chapter 1 and concluding section.
8   'The philosophers have only interpreted the world in different ways. The point is to *change* it.'
9   Heron, Chapter 2 in Reason (1988).

10   So the claim that the world is flat, for example, is false because it does not fit in with all the other things we believe in, such as the idea we can fly in a straight line and eventually we would get back to where we started.

11   These and the following quotes may be found in Heron op cit. pp. 44 ff. The emphases are mine.

12   But recall a point from Part 1 – major surprises with waves *from our point of view*. It may be that even waves are significantly less predictable in some respects than we presume, but because those respects are of little interest to human beings, they have not been researched.

13   Op cit. p. 58.

14   Argyris Chapter 20, p. 415 (1994).

15   It is easy to dismiss this as sloppy literature reviewing, but in practice it is rarely possible to investigate all one's written sources fully.

16   Easterby-Smith et al. (1991) emphasise in several places the potential power imbalances between researcher and researched.

Conclusion

In Part I we encountered a number of general questions relating to the question of how far management research is valid, including the issues of complexity, of contextualisation, and the inter-disciplinary nature of management.

In Part II we looked to some of the classical approaches to research and knowledge, in order to see whether any of these could establish, how far management research is valid.

Four overall focuses were identified (see Figure II.2):

naturalism:	a focus on the independence of what is studied
interpretavism:	a focus on the manner in which agreement is reached through discourse
deconstructionism:	a focus on the way that concepts are buried inside practices
participant/inquiry:	a focus on the interactive nature of applied social research

Each of these approaches represents an answer to two questions: (1) is the social world external to our perceptions or dependent on them? and (2) is the role of research to present the social world in structural terms or is it to reveal the fluidity of investigations? In each case there is a valuable and important contribution to the debate, but what we have seen is that none can provide a complete basis for stating that management research is valid. This is not surprising. We have seen that each approach represents a distinct stage in the development of the theory of social research. As usually happens with academic movements, one idea gains credibility because it deals well with a problem that the last approach did not resolve. Only after a time do its own difficulties become apparent.

Realism is the view that applied social research should depict an external world of human behaviour. But it fails to take account of the complexity of human events, nor can it satisfactorily deal with the looping mechanism – if I become aware of a concept or idea I may choose to amend my behaviour in the light of my knowledge.

Realism also fails to deal with the variety of different approaches and perspectives which may be brought to bear on a subject such as management. How all the results from so many different disciplines – such as psychology, economics, sociology, information technology – can be integrated into one overall truth about management is not clear: are all these of equal weight? If not what is the mechanism for combining a result in, say, psychology, with one in information technology?

The next approach – interpretavism – is the idea that applied social research should depict or present a world which is agreed between the researchers. Interpretavism settles the last point affecting realism quite easily. Results from different areas are combined via a process of dialogue. Truth about management emerges from the interaction between different researchers. This is the idea of a circle of interpretation. So what is really the case about management would on this approach slowly come through from the process of collating and combining different views and results.

But the shortcoming of this is that while the process is clear, it is not clear where the process of putting together different people's views gets to, and certainly not clear where it stops. When is a result established, and no further interpretative work necessary? This is the perennial problem of how do we know that we know, and when do we decide that further investigation will not add anything more to our knowledge. All approaches to methodology encounter this. Realist approaches tend to have clear answers to this – sometimes in terms of probability. This does not eliminate uncertainty – that is impossible. But it makes clear where the uncertainty lies, and indicates how it may be accounted for in the research process. Interpretavism does not have the same clear circumscription of uncertainty. Hence it is not clear which processes of interpretation are knowledge creating and which are knowledge subverting.

The third approach – deconstructionism – is more anarchistic. On this view, applied social research is about the presentation of a world which underpins human practices. It does not attempt to build structures of knowledge, but draws out what is involved in the structures which we already have. In that respect it differs from the other three approaches in that it is not about how to collect and analyse information in order to generate knowledge, but about how to critically analyse claims to knowledge which may have come from other sources. So it is less a methodology in the sense of designing field research, and more in the sense of generating new understanding via analysis of conceptual material. The indeterminacy of the hermeneutic circle is in this context a virtue. For the deconstructionist there is no *structure* of knowledge to be aimed at, hence no rule for deciding when a structure has been completed. Investigation of the conceptual roots of ideas and practices is an open-ended process – knowledge of management arises from the activity of critique, not from a foundation of evidence.

But this approach, though strong on the potential indeterminacy and potential endlessness of analytical investigation in an applied human field such as management, loses the simple connection with practice which is essential for management knowledge to have any value. Paradoxically, by focussing on practices, this approach makes them less easy to effectively use. For the realist, the link with practice is clear – we discover the truth about management, and that enables us to design appropriate technologies to deal with that external; reality. For the interpretavist, there is also a link, albeit not quite so clear: we establish or agree a view of management via the collation and combination of different interpretations or impressions, and in the light of these we can design or amend practices and processes which reflect that agreement. For the deconstructionist, however, there is no corresponding process of practice or technology design: for the whole point of the Foucauldian or Derridan strategy is to unveil what is implicit within practices – all practices. So any proposed practical measure taken in the light of a Derridan or Foucauldian investigation would itself be a subject for further investigation. There is no place for stopping analysis and moving on to action here.

Collaborative or participative inquiry regards applied social research as the creation of agreed templates for practice. It begins with the recognition that human beings involved in applied research such as management remain agents. Someone apparently 'just' a subject of research will nevertheless modify their behaviour in virtue of the circumstances and personalities of the research, as well as in the light of their perception of the developing results of the research. So the collaborative approach takes this as the central pivot of management investigation. In doing so there is a very clear and unquestioned link with practice, and there is also a clear recognition of the importance of agreement between researchers as a means of generating ideas. But there is an ambivalence about truth. At times action science and participative inquiry looks like a development out of interpretavism – hermeneutics with a practical focus, almost. At other times it looks like a form of realism – getting to the absolute truth about management via the interactions of a group of researchers, and knowing where these interactions need to stop before they go beyond 'the facts'.

So we come full circle. Realism has weaknesses which interpretavism can take account of, but this has weaknesses which deconstructionism can deal with, but then this has limitations which participative inquiry can cope with, though this has a blind spot of assuming what should be proved just where realism is strong. So if all of these approaches have a strong point and a weak one – can we try to combine them into an integrated philosophy of applied human study? What kind of integration would be possible – so that the strong points of each of the above approaches may be preserved, and in such a way as to demonstrate how far management research can be valid?

In Part III we shall move toward a more positive answer – though it will not be until Chapter 12 that this becomes clear.

The Components of Management Research Methodologies

INTRODUCTION

In Part I we saw that management research has certain intrinsic drawbacks, such as complexity, cultural context, and human self-referentiality. In Part II we looked at four characteristic orientations towards social research, and found that none of these could provide a complete basis for saying that an applied social study such as management can yield genuine knowledge. But each had an important point of emphasis which needed to be kept in mind when conducting research projects in this field.

In this final Part of the book, we shall go back to the main question considered at the start – how far, if at all, can management research be valid?

The basic strategy of this Part will be in effect to 'rescue' management research. Accepted, the view that it can generate true statements about organisations in general and how they are managed is untenable. Nevertheless, this does not mean that the attempt to investigate management is fruitless. The key task here, therefore, is to identify what benefits management research can bring. As we shall see, these are less in the area of generalised truths and more about management learning.

In Chapter 9 we shall look more carefully at the idea of method and methodology in research. It has long been a cornerstone of the whole scientific enterprise, in natural as well as social fields, that the

generation of knowledge about the observable world is best characterised by its methods. We shall see that there are limitations to this,
and that management is precisely the kind of field which does not
easily admit to systematic investigation in the classical way.

In Chapter 10 we shall look more directly at the linkage between
the products of management research activity and organisational
action. In other words, what kinds of role does management knowledge
have in managers' behaviour?

In Chapter 11 we shall look at how management knowledge is
absorbed by its intended beneficiaries. The role of evidence in generating conclusions is considered as well as the role of management
research as a process of *learning*.

In Chapter 12, we shall develop a positive account of how management research has value despite the problems of its validity. This will
lean heavily on the critical theory approach of Jurgen Habermas.

Chapter 9

Methodology as Mechanism

... a new logic ...: the more treatment there is, the better are the results; or, escalation leads to success. The pupil is therefore 'schooled' to confuse teaching with learning, ... to accept service in the place of value. Medical treatment is mistaken for health care, social work for the improvement of community life, police protection for safety, military poise for national security, the rat race for productive work. Health, learning, dignity, independence and creative endeavour are defined as little more than the performance of those institutions which claim to serve those ends ...

I want to use this idea and apply it to management research. So I would add that *research methodology is mistaken for discovery*, and knowledge is defined as little more than the outputs of activities which satisfy the criteria set by the institutions which claim to deliver truth to society.

The quotation given above (barring my additional rhetorical flourish beneath it) is taken from the opening passage of a now forgotten book by Ivan Illich, 'Deschooling Society' published in the early 1970s. The point behind it is that it depicts the domination of *activity* over *outcome*. His intention was political – to try to get people to free themselves from their dependence on institutions which are too encumbered with their own existence to be able to properly meet the needs of their intended client groups. He focused on education, though this is just one key example of how an institution gathers its own logic and rationale. Outputs of the institution become treated as ends in themselves. Hence the possession of a degree certificate, of whatever quality, is deemed better than the possession of knowledge without a degree certificate – of course ideally we would like both, but according to Illich the social power of the explicit symbol, the certificate, outweighs the value of the intangible state of knowledge of the individual.

I can hear this objection: 'But surely the possession of a degree certificate is the best proof that someone has actually reached a given level of knowledge. And similarly, following your analogy, adherence to a systematic approach to collecting and analysing data is the best way of getting close to the reality of organisations.'

Sadly, having a degree is not always a proof of knowledge or understanding – maybe not even often. We all know of intelligent able people who have been failed by the educational system, and of mediocre minds that through luck, social class or plain persistence have achieved awards which promise more in the way of intellect than their bearers really can deliver. The same is at least partially true of systematic approaches to research methodology.

The most important phrase in the quotation above is '. . . service in place of value'. This is the key lesson which we can draw from Illich's argument, and which can be extended to the area of management research – the contrast between a rule or a practice and its anticipated benefits. The most common kind of value which people expect from sound research methods is that these will deliver truth – or get us as near as is practically possible. Clearly this is a part of the naturalist approach, but is also present in differing ways for the interpretavist and (as we saw, somewhat covertly) for the participant approach. This will form the main issue of much of this chapter.

9.1   DELIVERING TRUTH

There is a presumption that scientific knowledge – whether of the natural or the human world – is characterised at least partially by its methods. The systematic use of formal methods of data collection and analysis, such as experiment, observation, or questionnaire based survey techniques, has been hailed as the reason why western science has triumphed over other ways of making the world intelligible, such as eastern mysticism or tribal myth.

This is a cornerstone of the realist insight – that the aspect of the world which we can make a stable and shared sense can only be revealed via formal structured study. The idea of a result which is not merely valid at particular times for particular observers is central to this insight. And this approach to method attempts to mirror the features of the world in our investigation. It is by replicating results that we can establish repeatability. It is by generating results which do not vary with a change of observer that we can demonstrate observer independence.

We have seen difficulties with naturalism, the clearest statement of this view – even on its own terms natural science is not quite like that. Furthermore, natural science carries assumptions which are rarely if ever properly investigated. Also – 'open to all?' Not really – you need a considerable amount of mathematical expertise to understand modern physics, and a lot of chemistry and biology to understand modern genetics. This may be obvious, but it is often raised as an objection to astrology that only aficionados of the subject – initiates who have both a detailed knowledge of the subject and (therefore) an in-built pre-disposition to accept the assumptions of that field – can make sense of it. So this point does not really distinguish natural science from astrology.[1] Where the study of human beings is concerned the biography of the observer is often at least as significant as that of the subject in influencing what kind of results will be attained by an investigation.

What is important at this stage is to recognise the prime benefits which are expected from adopting the classical systematic approach to research. These are, namely, outcomes that have the twin properties of repeatability and neutrality, the key elements of proof in the observable world.

From this comes the easy association between method and proof – an assumption that methodical investigation always delivers proof, and even that method is the *only* way to deliver proof. The consequence of this association is, then, that method can be ever extended further and further into different areas of potential enquiry. To caricature this view, if you want to find out about a phenomenon you have to investigate it systematically.

Chapters 6–8 represented progressively more and more difficulty with this view:

1   interpretavism indicates that applied human study requires a degree of agreement. Whilst in natural science it is (remotely) possible for one individual to be right and the rest of the intellectual community be wrong, in the case of applied knowledge about human beings this is inconceivable: a degree of agreement is necessary in order for the phenomenological aspect of human experience to be incorporated. So the fact that these are human beings who are carrying out the investigation, and that they are studying human phenomena, is not incidental to the process – it is an essential aspect of the inquiry

2   deconstructionism shows how we cannot get to the bottom of social concepts. The presence of human interpretation and association means that as soon as a definition or stipulation of an idea (such as 'customer orientation') is settled, there is a host of potential additional linkages which stretch far beyond the formal definition. The Foucauldian insight is to add to this the fact that many definitions are in fact as much a *part* of current practices as a reflection or neutral depiction of an idea of those practices. Not only is the idea of detachment from what is studied misleading, the idea of getting a *stable picture* of what a practice is like is also ill-founded on this view

3   participatory enquiry showed that research which involves human practices cannot be observer neutral – nor can it be subject neutral. The investigation becomes a collaboration, a series of deliberate choices, between all parties to the research. The research itself is rather more an intervention than a study of what is independently 'there'. Similarly, the idea of repeatability is misleading – every new situation is unique in ways that work against it replicating other inquiries

In effect the cumulative impact of these three kinds of view is to render the realist, empirically dominated, approach untenable. This much we have seen already. But the implications of this approach for the idea of method and methodology have not been fully explored. For what they imply is that method is not a mechanism. It is not an 'organon', by the formal operation of which we can come to truth or even probability.[2] This has ramifications for all four of the research orientations we have looked at.

9.2   HOW TO PUBLISH A 'GOOD' RESEARCH PAPER

The presumed link between method and validity leads to clear practical consequences. One of these is a definitive image of the research paper. Now, I want to discuss a common formula[3] for successful management research papers, characterised as follows:

(a)   outline of theoretical background
(b)   proposal of a specific model or hypothesis
(c)   elucidation of the model in operational terms for the purposes of data collection
(d)   use of a survey method (very often interview or questionnaire based)
(e)   analysis (usually involving some statistics) of the data collected
(f)   finally a brief discussion about how far the evidence supports the model, or how far the hypothesis has been confirmed

I am certainly not suggesting that this is actually treated literally as a formula or mechanism for generating applied social knowledge. Nor is this a complete hegemony – that only papers of this kind get published. But this framework can be seen in sufficiently many papers for it to become a standard or template against which much management research may be compared. Not that there is much wrong with this as *one form* of investigation. The problems come when this is seen as the prime reliable way to establish generalisable truths about management. It is the use to which such a formula is put, rather than the formula itself, which is the problem.

There are some low level problems here, which merit mention but not an extended discussion. The preference in some journals for statistically analysed material means that results are presented which, though mathematically sophisticated, actually state probabilities too low for any real decisions to be sensibly based on them. Additionally, in many cases there is a little too much concern on gathering confirmatory data than following the safer Popperian approach of trying to refute a hypothesis. A third point is that operationalising a broad hypothesis is often far more subtle an issue than many research papers would have the reader believe. And finally the question of how far results may be generalised is often skated over or even ignored altogether – fortunately most researchers have too much integrity to suggest that their work does speak beyond its own investigatory limits.

But more important than these is the dual message that: (a) this kind of approach is, if not the sole method of valid investigation at least a very characteristic method; and (b) when used correctly it is always an effective method, and can guarantee that the researcher will produce something which is of value to the academic and to the professional worlds. Not that many people will state these points explicitly, but they stand as a subtext, an assumed backdrop.

The objection here is not the point that investigation cannot produce certainty. It cannot, but the absence of certainty is simply a fact about all studies of the physical or social worlds. It is rather that such investigation places emphasis on just one part of the process of developing understanding about the social world. *How* questions are arrived at, *which* questions, and *why* these are regarded as valuable to academics and to professionals, are also key issues which are neglected by this approach. In a field in which there are many alternative language-sets (and thus alternative conceptualisations) this formula also neglects the role of conceptual analysis and redefinition.

This is not only a problem for the realist. Interpretavism and participatory research also make assumptions about method and validity. The Foucauldian approach shares some element of realism too. Only the highly sceptical relativist approach of Jacques Derrida avoids the problems of how research activity links with an external world, by depicting the subject of investigation as unfathomable – there is always something further to be investigated which makes a researcher's current position potentially invalid.

Returning to the 'formula' – what is so wrong with it then? One issue is to do with language. A phrase such as 'organisational culture' carries a large amount of assumed material with it (such as the belief that those aspects of an organisation's activity not captured by its formal processes can nevertheless cluster together in recognisable patterns). But as well as this there is a basic ambiguity in such an idea. Is it a convenient way to pigeonhole certain patterns, without any suggestion that there is any more fundamental underpinning – that is, a *descriptive* model? Or is it meant to illuminate a deeper reality – an *explanatory* model? Or, finally, is it a projection of what organisations should look like – a *prescriptive* model?[4] It is unlikely that any particular modelling of the concept is clearly just one of these. Furthermore it is not at all clear how these are commonly understood in the management community. Management writers have talked, for example, of categorising organisational cultures, suggesting description, whilst recognising that changing organisational culture takes time, suggesting some element of underlying process (that is, explanation and prescription).

A further complication here is that there is (at the time of writing, at least) no commonly agreed model of culture – many writers quote the model derived by Charles Handy from Roger Harrison's work, whilst others quote the model developed by Deal and Kennedy, but there are others also employed (such as the 'cultural web' idea used by Johnson and Scholes).[5] The variety is sufficient to raise the question whether these writers are all referring to the same phenomenon. Are these all aspects of one and the same thing – or are they different things that by mischance have all acquired the same name? Nor are these models simply descriptive – use of phrases such as 'bet your company culture' or 'people culture' set up all sorts of associations which include both subliminal hints of underlying processes and unspoken presumptions as to which cultural types may be most effective.

The point is that it is difficult to see what a field study can do with all these different ideas floating around. Of course data relevant to one or other of these can be collected, analysed and evaluated to shed some light on *that particular approach*. But whether this is getting us any further to the reality of organisational culture depends on many issues: for example, if there is an implied underlying process, how far is it explicitly evaluated in its own right, as opposed to being merely 'that which manifests itself in corporate cultures'?

More importantly, how far is any cognizance taken of alternative approaches to culture? As Paul Feyerabend has pointed out, in natural science the establishment of one theoretical approach is based not solely on its own merits, but also on how far these compare with the merits of alternative, competing approaches.[6] Similarly, in studying social phenomena, especially where there is an element of application to practice, an investigation which purports to confirm one approach to organisational culture does not really add very much, if anything, to knowledge if it does not make some comparison or contrast with alternative approaches. But how many papers attempt to contrast the value of one model of culture over another in the explanation of organisational data?

Language is not the only source of difficulty with the idea of a formula for generating new knowledge. Another is the haphazard nature of all research. *The only things which get investigated are those which people see some value or interest in investigating.* Not only is it true that the only theories which have been tested and supported by the evidence are those which have been formulated and selected by people in the light of their experiences and circumstances, but this is also true of the only challenges to any approach. In other words, *there is a degree of historical randomness about which ideas are developed and tested* which undermines the image of a systematic approach to developing new knowledge. This affects applied social investigation far more acutely than, say, natural science, where testing and experiment are more extensive, and in general focus on a commonly agreed subject matter, and a common set of methods of investigation and criteria for evaluation. Any one concept or technique in natural science will be exposed to much greater levels of testing and investigation than, say, any one concept of organisational culture, and in general on more commonly accepted bases.

So there are problems in suggesting that what we have called 'the formula' is an organon – a mechanism which guarantees to generate new knowledge if used properly. For if the method is 'used properly' then the investigation has to make reference to other approaches – more is involved than simply one theory being tested. And the idea of a mechanism suggests a far more systematic approach to the identification of potential research questions than is actually the case.

Maybe now the supporter of the formula will argue 'But even if this kind of approach is not foolproof, surely it is still the only way in which genuine knowledge can be established. Conceptual analysis is all very well, but that never took anyone out into direct contact with the flesh and blood world.' True, and if anyone started making such claims about conceptual analysis they would be going down the same kind of road, with disastrous results. But that does not automatically mean that the formula generates new knowledge all on its own. As the discussion of the concept of culture should indicate, there is a significant degree of unclarity about all management ideas – they represent a slice through a profoundly complex nexus of factors of many different kinds. 'All things being equal', for example, which is an essential tool of natural scientific methodology, simply does not work in such a environment. It works in some parts of natural science because there is already a established framework of explanation which provides a ground for excluding certain factors as not relevant. But there is no corresponding framework in management – nor could there easily be, again for reasons of complexity.

But a further argument may now be put: 'You are arguing too tightly against the validity of applied social research. The very diversity of management ideas, in particular organisational concepts such as culture, creates a pool of resources from which the manager can draw to make their organisational reality more intelligible.'

But this is the main point of the whole of this book. This argument shifts the justification for management research, from outcomes related to what the research says about the reality of management, towards those related to what managers can do with the research.

It is not validity which makes management investigation important – it is the uses to which management ideas can be put.

Terms such as 'research' or even 'learning' suggest that there is a body of established knowledge into which a manager can tap to discover effective forms of organisation, or the most appropriate ways to manage staff, and so on. In reality every managerial situation is a new multiplex, a manifold of different aspects, which requires being thought afresh. In Gibbons' terminology, it is 'Mode 2' knowledge – based in a context of application, and thus involving trans-disciplinarity, employing a diversity of actors and stakeholders, is carried out in a transient environment and is driven primarily by social concerns rather than an academic desire for disinterested discovery.[7] In this respect management and other forms of practice based research are incommensurably different even from social sciences such as economics or sociology, for the key test of the latter is still essentially comparison with reality, however hard this is to achieve. In the case of management (or education, or health care, and others) the key test is pragmatism – does this make the management task any easier to do?

There is a variety of different ways in which management ideas can be put to use. We shall see, in Chapter 10, the different directions which the idea of 'use' can take. For the moment we need to get clearer what method in research can achieve.

9.3   METHOD AS SYSTEM

If research methods do not guarantee the achievement of valid results, then what do they do? What is the point of them? Why are they such an important part of research and what would happen if we did not operate methodically?

We will mainly answer these indirectly. Let us start with a closer look at the idea of method. What is a method? Roget's Thesaurus lists 'method' under the following headings[8]:

way (alongside[9] – mode, approach)
rule (alongside – habit, arrangement)

By contrast, the AppleWorks computer word processing thesaurus lists the following:

action (alongside – measure, step, way)
procedure (alongside – habit, system, practice, process)
pattern (alongside – plan, order, system)
application (alongside – operation, technique)

Lastly, the Pocket Oxford Dictionary defines method as 'special form of procedure . . . orderliness, regular habits, orderly arrangement of ideas'.[10]

On the evidence of the reference books, there seem to be four core meanings of the term 'method', which represent four points on a continuum from mere regularity of action to action which generates specific results, as illustrated in Figure 9.1.

There are two key points of qualitative difference in the model. The first of these is the idea that method is a means to discovery. In other words that it can reach out to reality, that somehow it has a causal

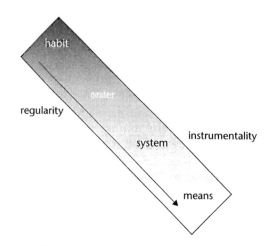

Figure 9.1   Meanings of 'method'.

impact (the high instrumental end of the continuum). The second is that method is merely habit, with no systematic or integrated coordination between its elements (the high regularity end of the continuum). And between these two extremes are intermediate points, representing the idea that method is a form of order or system.

Clearly the interpretation we have been discussing in the previous sections of this chapter have been at the far bottom end of this continuum – where method is seen as a mechanism for producing knowledge. In principle, the model suggests three other different positions with regard to method in research, as follows:

1 method is the systematic collection together of material to create knowledge
2 method is the putting of research material into an intelligible order
3 method is merely a habit or regular way of conducting investigations

The last of these is an extreme position, which suggests that there is no additional explanatory value gained by researching methodically. The conclusion to be drawn from this is highly sceptical – that any habit is as good as any other. In other words, one could get as much hold on management reality by casually wandering around and just chatting to people as by structuring a research programme.

Whilst this is a logical possibility it may be more useful to resist it at this stage, in order to make some progress on the richer ideas of method as system or order.

The two intermediate ideas – of system and order – may be best taken together, as their difference is primarily one of emphasis. The contrast between them is mainly that the idea of order suggests elements placed in a definite arrangement, whilst that of system suggests a more coordinated integration, as well as greater complexity.

9.3.1 Once More for the Organon

It might be thought that we have not yet finished with the idea of method as a means or mechanism for generating knowledge. The argument of Section 9.2 only really showed that the most standard approach to research methodology – the 'formula' – on its own does not lead to knowledge, and that something else is necessary. In that section the examples of what might be needed were: (a) supporting conceptual analysis; and (b) comparison with alternative approaches. Someone might think that all we need to do is make sure that the 'formula' is supplemented by these two elements and the value of that approach is thus demonstrated.

But even in principle this stratagem is insufficient to support the view of method as a mechanism for producing knowledge. The image of the research process which the realist and interpretavist approaches share is that of a sequence of activities which are embarked upon and at a specific point a halt can be called and the results examined for what they show about the social world. In some ways these approaches have become hypothesis dominated. Good research, on this view, is designed to answer clearly structured questions, the latter couched in terms which admit of clear unambiguous answers. The research process is thus defined in terms of how it is constructed and set going. But in reality the results of the process are NOT simply taken as given. If they easily cohere with existing beliefs then maybe this is the case. But a result which severely contrasts with orthodox ideas is closely examined – the working presumption being that there is something wrong somewhere.[11] Alternative explanations are offered and critiqued, new questions are asked, new conceptions formulated.

In fact in general it is only when research goes wrong that anything really interesting happens. The discovery of oxygen happened because people couldn't weigh phlogiston. Relativity came about because attempts to measure the speed of light didn't work. Evolution was Darwin's explanation for how the variety of creatures on the Galapagos Islands came to be so different from what had been expected. And in social research, the human relations school of management theory came about primarily because the initial Hawthorne experiments had gone badly awry.

What do researchers do when things go wrong? This turns out to be a crucial question, but one which the functional approaches of the realist and the interpretavist do not seem to be able to deal with properly. In the former case it is not seen as part of the process of investigation, whilst in the latter it is not clear how to distinguish what researchers do when something goes wrong from what they do when it goes right – everything gets fitted into a coherent scheme. The Popperian image of conjecture and refutation as being the basis of scientific progress places great reliance on the test and refute part of the process and none on the development of conjectures (or hypotheses). But it misses out key aspects of the whole process. In fact it would be better seen as a process of conjecture–test–refutation–reformulation–reconjecture–retest and so on.

More important than the role of error in discovery, though, is the role of acceptance. Both the realist and interpretavist approaches place a great deal of reliance on the role of acceptance in the process of investigation. In the case of the realist some degree of confirmation is required – though curiously one cannot specify this too closely, because then it is difficult to explain why Hawthorne presented such a problem on the basis of just one odd set of outcomes, whilst Herzberg's model of motivation remains questionable despite dozens of surveys replicating his results. In the case of the most characteristic interpretavist approaches, there is the process of coherence (for example, within a hermeneutic circle) which begs the question when if ever is a result or item ever NOT included? Is anything ever just left out as being too weird to be acceptable?

The point behind all this is that the image of research methodology as a system which, when properly designed, can bring you closer to the reality of organisations, misses out the importance of what one does with the outcomes of the research activity. We do not just accept what we get – we look at it, we decide if it tells us anything, we decide what to do if it seems to make no sense. Getting the results is just part of the exercise. We have to do something else once we have got them. They are just one step. Formally structured data collection exercises – when done well – are an important part of the whole process. But they are not the entirety of it. If methodology were a mechanism they would be – we would put into one end of the machine well structured questions, well designed data collection exercises, and then take as given whatever came out of the other end. But we do not just take it as given. The outcomes are then subject to further investigation – conceptual as well as field based.

9.3.2   Method as Organisation

Method as a mechanism for discovery is too strong a claim. The intermediate approaches depict method as making research material intelligible. In other words they make the lesser claim that method helps produce material which explains social phenomena rather than generating new knowledge.

This is more substantial a change than first sight suggests. The idea that method is a mechanism for producing knowledge suggests a causal role – adopting the right methodology will bring about the creation of new knowledge or confirmation of existing knowledge.[12] The idea of method as order or system makes no such claim. Rather it suggests that the degree of orderliness of a research design will impart a corresponding degree of intelligibility to the results. In other words, a well structured investigation will produce well structured results. But there is no guarantee that the research is thereby valid.

This is probably much closer to the view of many practising researchers, and therefore is that much more plausible. However, it has its own difficulties. The first of these stems from the last sentence in the previous paragraph. What kind of relationship is there between the degree of system in a research project, the intelligibility of its results and the chances that the conclusions of the research will be valid?[13]

Imagine two contrasting research projects. In one there is a highly organised design, involving a searching organisational contextualisation of the issues, a clearly stated hypothesis, a well argued and theoretically informed methodology, leading from a clear expression of what information is needed to confirm or disconfirm the hypothesis to a schedule of research activities which will jointly provide data – which in turn should generate the information needed. To cap it all, there is an honest evaluation of the potential weaknesses of the research, and strategies for off-setting these are included.

In the other there is a vague idea that some aspect of organisational practice is interesting enough to warrant investigation. There is no hypothesis – there is hardly even a hunch, just a feeling that some kind of opinion collection might yield something fruitful. There is no plan of research: the researchers just turn up, chat to a few people, look cursorily at some corporate documents, and do a bit of analysis of some pre-existing data.

I presume that most people[14] would feel more confidence in the first of these than the second. Now the point is not that nevertheless the second might bring up something interesting which the first misses – though that point is implicit. It is rather – why *do we* feel more confidence in the first, more structured, project? It is not as if being ever more systematic brings ever more levels of confidence – an investigation which was too structured might be seen as inappropriately so for its subject matter, or for the kind of research question involved.

The point is that the degree of structure or system reflects a presupposition about the degree of pattern or uniformity in the matter being studied. The more systematic approach commands more confidence because we feel that this is more suited to the nature of the phenomena under investigation. *Structured phenomena – structured investigation.*

But the rub of this is that in general social phenomena are far less easy to determine than natural ones. Even if the collective behaviour of human beings in working organisations is ultimately determined by, say, genes, for all intents and purposes we are a very long way from attaining that level of sophistication. We have considered earlier the level of complexity involved in any organisation – the brain alone is more complex than any other kind of entity in the universe, let alone what happens when you put a few of them together in a closed room. What we have when researching organisations is a field which is for all practical purposes indeterminate, whatever might be the case in principle.

Given this, then it becomes less clear why we should prefer the more systematic research project. For that makes an assumption which we have just seen is not helpful in practice. This becomes more acute when one looks at the kinds of data collected for many research papers:

'... a sample of 100 managers was sent a questionnaire asking about their career aspirations...'
'... we interviewed forty-five executives about the strategic positioning of their companies...'
'... twenty subjects participated in repertory grid activities relating to branding of their main competitors...'

The phenomena here are just too complex to expect too stable a pattern. So methodologies which operate on too stable a basis are not likely to be any better than ones which do not. A method is *not* a neutral framework – this is the real underlying issue here. It is a series of choices in the light of what is believed about the field to be researched. It embodies such assumptions and mirrors these in the results it achieves. In other words *the method is part of the result.*

One aspect of this is generally recognised by many practising researchers – different research designs dealing with the same question are unlikely to yield similar answers. Triangulation, despite the laudableness of the ideal, generally does not work too well.[15] But beyond this is the implication that adopting a systematic approach adds something to the phenomena being studied. In other words, there is bias right at the start.

So the idea that method can be a systematic way in which results can be made intelligible is not of itself false – but what we have seen is that 'making intelligible' is more than that: it is as much about adding more content to the research. *By using a method we impose its assumptions on the investigation.*

SUMMARY

In this chapter we have seen the limitations of the idea that methodology is a means to generate valid results. Equally, though, we have also seen that the more cautious model of methodology as the use of systematic methods is not a neutral framework for collecting and presenting information – it imposes its own level of order on the data.

Does this leave us, then, with the extreme sceptical view of method which we put on hold earlier in this chapter? Maybe, but this is only problematic if we see management research as all about validity. As was emphatically stated in Section 9.2, the use of management research may be more important than how it was arrived at. Value may outweigh validity.

We shall look at this in more detail in Chapter 10.

NOTES

1   This is not to say that there is no difference, epistemologically, between natural science and astrology, but simply that the presumption that a valid result should not be person-specific is not as clear as it sounds.

2   Strictly speaking we should not lump together the different concepts of truth and probability. One *could* use a systematic method to generate probabilities, but these would not be the kinds of probability one needs. It is easy to collect 'results' by taking a sample from some kind of population, and thereby calculate some kind of probabilistic conclusion. The problem is that for this to say something true about the behaviour of a group of people (which is the outcome the realist approach really needs), a whole cluster of assumptions have to be made, about the identification of the group, about the sampling frame, the sampling method, the 'other things being equal' and so on. And it is this cluster which is the target for the various problems which are thrown up by the interpretavist, participatory and deconstructionist approaches.

3   One which some leaders of the academic management community wish were used more frequently – Cary Cooper, the eminent researcher on workplace stress, is one who has gone on record as wishing that more management research were quantitative in nature.

4   Even this trichotomy is itself suspect, since there is a long tradition in the philosophy of natural science that you cannot easily separate off description from explanation.

5   Harrison (HBR 1972), Handy (1993), Johnson and Scholes (1988), Deal and Kennedy (1982).

6   See Feyerabend (1972).

7   See Gibbons et al. (1994).

8   'methodological' appears under reasoning, alongside 'systematic'. Cf. Roget (1984).

9   In all these Thesaurus references the additional terms are my selection of the more significant ones from a larger disparate range.

10 Pocket OED Allen (ed.) (1984).

11 Ironically in the field of organisational management, there are so many variables that one ought to look closely at results which fit too easily into existing frameworks. Just imagine a study which found that exactly 36.2 % of every company's workforce agreed with the mission statement. It would be too coincidental to accept. Success or fit needs to be explained too.

12 The attentive reader will have noticed the inclusion of '... the right...' methodology – a moot point which we shall come back to.

13 Note that it is validity we are talking about here, not truth. Strictly any possible level of validity attaches to the *inference* from field results to overall conclusions, though it is convenient to talk of the validity of the *conclusions* as a quicker way of referring to this.

14 Myself included.

15 As mentioned in Part I, there are good and bad triangles.

Chapter 10

Knowledge and Action in Management Research

In Chapter 9 we saw some of the difficulties of depicting research methodology as a means or mechanism for discovery. The issues we encountered there are far more acute for applied human studies than for natural science or for pure social science. This is because the question of how far a research study has uncovered something which in some way we might regard as demonstrating a truth becomes more problematic where there is an intimate linkage with practice. The greater the technological aspect (that is, the link with practice), the broader the range of factors which are relevant to the research, and thus the more complex the modelling of the situation, and therefore the more uncertain it is that we have identified a stable underlying pattern or structure. So the difference between pure and applied research is in the first instance one of degree, but this difference of degree becomes one of kind due to the scale of difference.

In this chapter we shall look more closely at the idea of how management ideas and research should be evaluated, not in terms of what they tell us about an independent reality of organisations, but in terms of how far they can link with practice – how good they are as technology. In this discussion, then, we shall move away from the 'science' aspect of management as an applied social science, to the 'applied' aspect. What we shall begin to see in this chapter, and which will be elaborated in more detail in the following one, is that this focus makes it easier to understand the nature of management research – and therefore management knowledge.

10.1   KNOWLEDGE AND TECHNOLOGY

What does it really mean to talk of an applied study, such as management? In effect this is a question about the ways in which an idea, theory or result in the management field can be useful or of practical value? Consider the continuum depicted in Figure 10.1.

There are two ways of looking at this continuum, and most of this chapter will be about these two approaches. In one, which I shall call the *instrumental* approach, the presumed direction of priority here could be expressed thus:

> Managerial ACTION has to be based on a clear UNDERSTANDING of the organisation which itself is founded on an accurate REPRESENTATION of the reality of the organisation.

In the other, which I will call the *evolutionary* approach, the priority can be expressed as:

> A clear REPRESENTATION of the truth of management arises out of a broader UNDERSTANDING of organisational reality, which individuals derive from the experiences which they reflect on derived from ACTIONS and decisions taken.

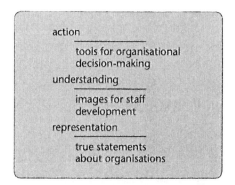

Figure 10.1   A uni-dimensional model of the functions of organisational research.

The emphasis of the former is on design, on planning, and on accuracy – right first time. The second emphasises, in contrast, management learning, adaption of tools to situations, and progressive approximation. We could also loosely associate the instrumental view with the idea that management technology is *invented*, and the evolutionary with the idea that it is *discovered*.

Each of these views is less of a categorical statement about what management research – as an applied social science – really is than a kind of attitude. The discussion in this chapter will start with the instrumental approach, though as we progress through it the evolutionary one will come more to the fore, and will take a central place in the discussion of Chapter 11.

Looking, then, at the instrumental view, it would seem that we should concentrate all our efforts on accurate representation, because that would provide a firm foundation for understanding clearly what the situation really is, and thus furnish us with a well grounded basis for designing the appropriate tools and techniques to effect change.

In effect this is a strategy for technology design – identify the underlying processes, and then tools can be designed which will make use of those processes: in other words, find out what the situation is, and then you will know how to do something about it. Without such a knowledge, so this story goes, you do not have a sure footing for the technology you devise.

In reality, as any practitioner in just about any field will confirm, action is often taken without such knowledge – the choice of a technique is often a trial and error process; indeed the development of the technique itself is generally also by trial and error. A geologist looking at rock samples from Mars or Neptune, for example, has very little idea of what techniques are going to be appropriate. Similarly, the prospects of discovering the detail of the human genome were not good until the development of tests such as the polymerase chain reaction technique. It is not enough to know the basic theory of a phenomenon in order to design tools and techniques – one also needs to know a great deal about the supporting mechanisms which translate one feature of the situation into observable behaviour or events.

In some fields, for all practical purposes it is almost never possible to have a good foundation for actions. As cited earlier in this book, highly complex systems are amongst the best examples of this – there is simply too much going on in the atmosphere for us to have a decent idea of how far human activity has contributed to global warming.[1]

What does this tell us? Essentially it underlines the critique of too great a reliance on depictive approaches to management research as we encountered in Part II, for the key point here is that *some knowledge in any field comes from action, not from investigation*. The image of the researcher as a detached collector of data – a detective, finding and sifting clues to establish how the murder took place – is not a good representation of engineering technology, let alone that of management.[2] Even when we 'know' the basic pure theory, and have built up an impressive body of evidence intended to confirm or support the theory, when we try to do something making use of this knowledge reality tends to be awkward. Elegant theories do not always work efficiently – we often discover that slightly off-centre variants work better, rather as a metal with slight impurities can be a better material for some purposes than a perfectly pure one. Or an accepted approach only works properly in a limited range, and outside this it breaks down. We may learn *something* from direct research, but when we try to put it into action, we learn a whole lot more about the surrounding complex of relevant factors.

10.2   ACTION AS THE ROUTE TO KNOWLEDGE

So – if it is not appropriate to try to establish all aspects of knowledge about management prior to undertaking organisationally based action, what about the reverse? Can we say that organisational action is the prime route to management knowledge?

One version of this might be the idea that *action research* is the prime approach to take for management and other applied human subject areas? But this is not as much help as it promises to be. 'Action research' is a misleading term. The design of an 'action research' project certainly involves a conscious recognition of the role of action in organisational inquiry. But it also has to involve a degree of traditional data collection. Some kind of depiction of the before and after states is necessary, in order to have a difference – a shift against a continuous background which forms the basis of the evaluation of the actions which form part of the investigation.

In any case, there is not one single kind of research strategy called 'action research'. In practice there is a spectrum. The name is generally reserved for research designs that involve a conscious intervention, which is then used as a basis for identifying processes which are disturbed by the action(s) which form part of the inquiry. Additionally, many writers on action research presume a high level of participation, in some cases almost identifying action research with participatory inquiry – which takes the intervention element in action research to an extreme.[3] It is not at all clear, though, that this degree of participation is essential to the idea (which is not to dismiss the view that participation is desirable). It is certainly feasible (though perhaps a bit unlikely) that the action element could be carried out autonomously – without any involvement of others.

More importantly, though, is that *most if not all* research projects in the management area involve an element of action to them. Any time I collect data within an organisation I will to an extent interfere with what is there.[4] So it is not so much that there is a separate kind of research design which we call 'action research' – it is rather that some researchers recognise the action element in applied human research and others either fail to or try to discount it.

Suppose I carry out a series of interviews with one group of respondents in an organisation, and then I carry out another series with a different group in the organisation a week later. Unless the two groups are somehow hermetically sealed off from each other, it is straining credibility to suggest that there has been no impact of the former interviews on the later respondents. So there is certainly a degree of intervention even when it is not intended. The difference between an 'action research' project and a more standard data collection exercise, therefore, is more based on attitude and intention than on categorical variation.

Of course, the self-conscious action researcher may well attempt to take advantage of the difference between the before and the after states, so that they can identify which changes have been significant. But the more careful *non-action* researcher will also take account of this aspect, for they will be aware of the potential impact which the time lag between one data collection exercise and another will have, and they will therefore attempt to discount this in her or his analysis. So whilst the action researcher wants the differences between the before and after states to be maximised, in order that a shift can be discerned against some background, the non-action researcher wants them to be minimised, in order that a stable background can be established.

One implication of this is that action and non-action researchers could well use the same research methods. That is probably of relatively small matter, for the issue is what one does with those methods. Stranger than this is that the action researcher and the non-action researcher could even adopt the very same research *strategies*. Suppose the following, for argument's sake: two researchers want to investigate attitudes towards decision making, each in a parallel organisation; both design questionnaires as the main data collection tool; in each case there is a change programme going on whilst the research is taking place; in each case the questionnaire is administered to one group of respondents at one time and then to another group a couple of weeks later. Now, when it comes to analysing and interpreting the results of these questionnaires, the action researcher will want to focus on the changes, and so will try to depict the differences as movement against a stable background. The other will want to focus on what is stable – so they will try to depict the differences as ... movement against a stable background. The essential interpretation is the same, the only difference being the aspects of the research on which the researcher wishes to focus.

In practice the two researchers will try to adapt this overall strategy so that it will maximise their chances of gathering meaningful information.[5] But it does show that in a limiting case the real difference between intervention based research and non-interventive research is about the choices made by the researcher in interpreting results, *not the research design itself.* The very substantial differences which may be detected in the details of different research designs and methods of data collection or analysis spring out of the intentions of researchers – they do not come out of the nature of the research project or the nature of the phenomena under investigation.

This digression regarding action research illustrates two points. Firstly, that some degree of representation is essentially involved in this process. Secondly, that intervention is constantly present to some extent or another in any applied social research project, and therefore the difference between action research approaches and others is mainly in the interpretation strategy taken towards the results of the intervention process.

Action research is therefore not a simple division of research projects. It is not a clear category into which we can put one whole range of research approaches and leave out the rest. But the question remains whether action is the prime research tool where applied social research is concerned. Another view is that it makes most sense just to do something – conceivably anything – as a way of finding out how an organisation might react. Back in 1982 Peters and Waterman prefaced their chapter entitled 'A Bias for Action' with the following quotations:

Eighty per cent of success is showing up – Woody Allen
But above all try something – Franklin Delano Roosevelt
Ready fire aim – Executive at Cadbury's[6]

Elsewhere they also give their 'favourite axiom' – 'Do it fix it try it'.[7]

But is this a coherent view? Is it really possible simply to act and then work out what the results of that act say about an organisation or industry later? Probably not. It is in any case misleading to think of these as *'just'* acts. If someone makes a specific intervention without already having decided to collect data about what results then not only is there no guarantee that they will be in a position to capture the data, but also it is not clear how and when they would choose to treat the events as suitable material for research. On the other hand, if the act is done with a view to collecting material subsequently, then it becomes a research strategy, however rough and ready – not 'simply' an action.

This view is probably best seen not as a categorical statement about how to develop organisational tools or knowledge, but as an expression of impatience with the rational planning models which dominated management thinking in the period between 1950 and 1980. Whilst it is not in itself a particularly enlightening idea (for our purposes – it may be very useful in stimulating managers to be more dynamic in their decision making) it does hint at a more positive position, one which takes a more flexible view of knowledge, action, and theory as both inputs and outputs of applied social research.

10.3   THE BALANCE BETWEEN KNOWLEDGE AND ACTION IN MANAGEMENT RESEARCH

The arguments of the previous sections are not conclusive. For one thing, we have not explored every conceivable version either of the idea that knowledge has to be established before action can be rationally based, or that action itself is the best way to discover what is the case about organisations. For another, the points made are not logically watertight arguments but illustrations of the kinds of difficulty the two approaches can involve. To this extent someone who is passionately committed to one or other of them might well shout 'case unproven'. This is not necessarily a weakness of the discussion – the intention here is not to convert those who are wedded to a particular approach but to indicate the difficulties with those extreme views and what the alternatives may be.

In this section we shall look at the idea that where management is concerned, the distinction between knowledge and action is artificial, and thus that the two are different facets of a single kind of process.

'Knowledge' is a vague word. Here, for the moment at least, we shall use it broadly, to cover not only established facts, but also concepts, intellectual tools and techniques which have withstood the test of time.[8] More difficult is that 'action' is itself not as determinable as one would like – For example, we could define action as intentional behaviour, but then identifying an intention is harder than identifying an action. We shall include under this term practices and strategies (planned *or* emergent) as well as choices and decisions.

Consider the range of different ways in which 'knowledge', in this extended sense, and action might be linked in the management research process. Figure 10.2 depicts these as a continuum. At one end of this is the emphasis on the epistemological priority of knowledge, on which the action element – tools and practices – is dependent. At the other is the extreme 'discovery by doing' view mentioned at the end of the previous section, whereby knowledge comes out of

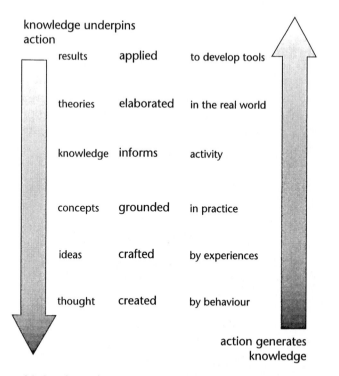

knowledge underpins
action

results	applied	to develop tools
theories	elaborated	in the real world
knowledge	informs	activity
concepts	grounded	in practice
ideas	crafted	by experiences
thought	created	by behaviour

action generates
knowledge

Figure 10.2   Complementary roles of knowledge and action in
applied research.

practices – between these two extremes are several different degrees of the link between the two elements in applied social science.

We can see how some of the approaches to management knowledge discussed in Part Two fit in here. Foucault's overall approach,[9] for example, would probably be located in the lower half of this continuum, though not at the very extreme. A strongly realist approach would naturally be most closely linked to the upper end, whereby the nature of a management issue is established before one attempts to devise tools and techniques to meet the management challenges which this issue presents. The participatory approach would come close to the lower end – practice is the cornerstone of this view, and theory evolves out of the collaboration of practitioners.

The interpretative approaches are less easy to locate on this dimension. The phenomenological approach arguably comes as an extreme version of the view that knowledge needs to be established clearly before technology can be developed – the only difference here between this approach and naturalism is therefore the idea of what counts as established knowledge.[10] The hermeneutic version is less easy to characterise. Some might argue that the participatory research process as outlined earlier is a paradigm of hermeneutics at work – different individuals bringing their own perceptions together and gradually finding a way in which these can be combined to yield new knowledge. Whilst this is not a misleading picture of what might actually happen in the participatory process, it mixes up the idea of hermeneutics as a research *method* (the use of the hermeneutic circle as a means of synthesising different views) with its employment as a research *philosophy* (the idea that the hermeneutic circle is the main, perhaps the only sound way in which management knowledge can be developed). Of the leading writers on hermeneutics, only Habermas has taken seriously the idea that different research philosophies have their own proper sphere of relevance, and may not work appropriately outside of these.[11] But in terms of whether hermeneutics can provide an overall structure for management research there remains a degree of ambiguity.

Recall that the main features of the hermeneutic approach are that: (a) it involves agreement between researchers; and (b) it attempts to depict reality rather than examine the inter-relationship between knowledge and practice. This would place hermeneutics still within the upper half of the continuum – that is, as placing the priority on the establishment of knowledge, from which practices and actions can be developed (rather than the lower half which places the priority on action as the means of developing knowledge and ideas about management). But the element of agreement would seem to indicate a less than extreme version of the primacy of knowledge – so the hermeneutic view is probably best seen as involving the idea that knowledge is primary, but that practice can make significant secondary inputs into the research process.

We can now begin to see what value the discussion of Part II has for our overall question of how management research can validly generate knowledge. For whilst the philosophies discussed in Part II are generally presented as exclusive alternative answers to the question how can management research be valid, the depiction in Figure 10.2 suggests that they can just as easily be seen as alternative but not exclusive *perspectives*. When put forward as 'the' main form of management knowledge each of these approaches has some kind of limitation. But when this aspect is taken away from them they all have a useful role to play. At each point in the continuum there is a clear and legitimate presentation of the balance between both conceptualisation and action in management research. At times the priority is with conceptualisation, at others it is with action. Different situations may require the one or the other, depending on their specific circumstances.

Anecdotally, this kind of non-committal attitude towards research philosophy is borne out by my own experience of supervising post-graduate management students. Generally, their decisions about what kind of approach to take to solve their management research problem or answer their research question are determined less by any strong conviction about the nature of management reality than by their perception as to what kind of answer to their question will be effective as an organisational change device.

In other words, the issue of whether a particular research method-ology is suitable for an investigation depends (in part) on the culture of the organisation in which the results of a research study are presented as to whether it will be regarded as acceptable.[12] Just as *methods of data collection* can be evaluated on the basis of their suitability to the concrete situation, so can the *underlying research philosophies* which purport to underpin methods.

10.4   AN EXAMPLE

Let us consider an example in a little more depth. An inquiry into the impact of downsizing on middle management styles in a particular organisation may be focussed on establishing a relationship, potentially a causal one, in the light of which fresh approaches to restructuring might be designed. But this only makes sense as a piece of applied research if there is a clear linkage with organisational mechanisms and levers which can translate the outcomes of the investigation into principles, images or techniques which will have some effect on the organisation.

This is more than simply saying that the research needs to be useful. It is that the investigation literally is not fully meaningful if the organisation cannot digest its outcomes. And 'digesting' here means turning it into potential action. However much an external observer might believe that the investigation has demonstrated something, there is an ethnological element: you have to be inside the organisa-tion – not merely to tell whether features such as the organisational culture have been taken account of appropriately, but also to be able to detect whether and how the investigation interacts with the decision making processes of the organisation. If it does not, then it is a study with no results. Establishing that, say, 65% of the workforce believed that their managers delegated more since a restructuring *is not of itself a result.* Such a statistic does not count without some elabor-ation of the significance of this piece of data. Is the workforce volatile? Is there an general element of gloominess about the future? Is it a blame culture? These and other factors put the 65% into context – in some cases this may make it as high as you could expect, in others it is not even a stable picture because of continuing change. So how managers deal with the statistic is partially determined by their understanding of the organisational circumstances in which it is generated.

Similarly a research study which presents conclusions about the loss of identity which the restructuring has brought about, will not make sense to an organisation in which the standard conception of reality is of tightly measurable phenomena.

I can hear this objection: 'You have discussed an example of a study dealing with an issue in a single organisation. The points about action are reasonable when an investigation is focussed on a specific problem in one particular case, but this is tantamount to internal consultancy. Research proper, however, is about the production of transferable, generalisable outcomes. The question of how far the results of a generalised study need to conform to the cultural norms of specific organisations is out of place. The validity of a generalised research outcome, relevant to a whole category of organisations, will not be affected by the specific features of an individual organisation. The question of how an organisation translates a research outcome into their own kind of decision-making reality is their own organisational development need, not a requirement of the investigation itself.'

This objection clearly comes from a strongly instrumental position, one which represents the management research process as essentially about the development of clear understanding before decisions and actions can be formulated. We have of course seen serious difficulties with the whole idea of generalisability in management, as discussed in Part I. But that is only one difficulty with this kind of view.

A related but perhaps deeper problem is what kind of meaning can be attached to an independent claim about general features of organisations. Take Deming's quality principles – these sound fine on their own, but as anyone who has actually implemented them knows, a whole lot more organisational work has to be done before they are of a form where they connect with decisions and policies in an organisation. Even Michael Porter's generic strategies model requires a significant amount of additional analysis and elaboration to reach the state where it could be a tangible component of corporate policy.[13] And this is not simply a case of filling in the factual detail of (in this example) the industry the organisation is in. It goes beyond this to the issues of how theories and concepts interact with other organisational features to influence decision making. An organisation can faithfully follow the Porter stricture about not getting stuck in the middle, and still do badly. Naturally this is because so many other factors are at work – as well as economic issues there are also the issues of how a corporate decision gets implemented by a whole bunch of unlike-thinking workers. But the significance of this point is often overlooked – there are *so* many factors at work here that whilst *in principle* one might say that organisations are susceptible of explanation in terms of general principles (on the lines of natural science) *in practice* they are best seen as possessing at least some degree of idiosyncrasy.

To put the point epithetically, the above objection depicts management knowledge as proof followed by learning, whilst the argument I have put forward indicates that sometimes it is more a case of learning followed by proof.[14]

Staying with the example of an inquiry into a possible link between downsizing and management styles, a further aspect of the shortcoming of seeing the investigation in causal or instrumental terms is the question of what it really achieves. This kind of investigation is not a matter of establishing an independent relationship and then developing a new set of techniques for organisational restructuring. For one thing, if the relationship is really independent of specific organisations[15] and their particular ways of turning the results into corporate action, then clearly it should apply to a wide range of potential situations and management actions. But imagine where an organisation is identified which does *not* conform to the relationship demonstrated by the research study? Statistical error? Maybe, but it is worth recalling that this is only a cover for the bits of the process we don't know about. More importantly is the impact of such a discrepancy on the status of the established relationship.[16]

If a stone started to change colour on its own, we would presume that there was something unusual about the stone. If lots of them did it spontaneously, we might start to wonder if the established laws of matter needed some revision. If an organisation happens not to display the linkage between management styles and restructuring, then.... Well, then *nothing* substantial. We just write it off as being 'not that kind of organisation'. It does not raise any substantial problem with the result or with the organisation – *because the result is not a universal*. Suppose many organisations did not seem to display that relationship? It *still* would not result in the rejection of that view. Management textbooks are full of theories which either have little evidential backing or very mixed supporting research – for example, Herzberg's model of employee satisfaction. They seem to work,[17] for what reason who knows, but the pragmatic test is regarded as sufficient. Perhaps the only difference that a great deal of variation in evidence would make for a theory is that when an organisation failed to show an impact of restructuring on management styles there would be less *surprise* than when the purported link was first mooted.

As a tangent, one could also ask what could even *count* as a new kind of technique in this context? Suppose the research project finds variations in the relationship (in the sample considered) depending on the way that the restructuring was carried out. It very likely then it will end up with recommendations about new methods of change management. Implicitly therefore, it is answering the question about the relationship between *downsizing* and managerial style in the negative – placing the important role on change management instead. It is not the case that a new technique or approach to downsizing has been evolved.

A more important issue here is that this discussion has been dealing with an example of a clearly naturalist type of investigation – one where the ideal is to find a relationship on a par with the kinds of linkage established in physics or biology. At first sight it could look as if the objections I have raised to the example discussed above do not work if we looked at a more hermeneutic study. For in that kind of investigation, it might be argued, the issue of how far a relationship is replicated in other organisations is not material. What matters is the degree of consensus between different researchers (and other interested parties).

But the hermeneutically treated research study is still concerned with getting to a generalisable result. It is just that the method of getting there is different. The ultimate outcome of hermeneutic investigation is an interpretation of reality – but this still in some way goes beyond the specific experience or perception of any individual researcher. One way of expressing this is to say that the results of an hermeneutic investigation are still general in form, but have an inter-subjective validity. Arguably, though, in practice this is just a jargonised way of saying that the outcomes are not merely specific to the individuals who generated them. [*If they were – then why bother with the hermeneutic circle at all, why not just allow each individual their own personal perception, totally specific and individual, an extreme kind of phenomenology? The question is rhetorical – the answer is that we do project beyond individual perceptions, and beyond the perceptions of any group. An agreed interpretation which is fixed to a specific group is just a broader version of subjectivity. But the fact that a hermeneutic circle is logically always open does not mean that any old idea can barge into that circle, as it were. The openness means that new ideas and perceptions from fresh individuals have to cohere with the existing circle. That means they may change the circle, but in a way that renders the whole circle meaningful.*] What this means for our downsizing example is that the result of hermeneusis is still a depiction of organisational reality. This is what marks it off from a participatory research group, where the emphasis is on action. The hermeneutic circle is still questing for perceptions which are open, whilst the participatory or collaborative group may well stop at the solution of their own organisational problems, and hence not care about the issue of generalisability.

In this section we have looked primarily at the upper half of the quadrant of that continuum, where action is subordinate to knowledge in the management research process. We shall not go into so much detail over the lower half, where knowledge is dependent on action.

10.5   RESEARCH PHILOSOPHIES HAVE EQUAL DEGREES OF INVALIDITY

The model presented in Figure 10.2, perhaps more than the arguments of the previous sections, emphasises the weaknesses of the two extreme views discussed there. I want to argue that these six different degrees to which ideas and actions are combined in the management research process all have their own legitimacy. They should therefore not be seen as separate categorical statements about the nature of management knowledge, but as different perspectives on the research process, which can be appropriate for certain contexts and inappropriate for others. To emphasise one at the expense of the others is not only to misrepresent what actually happens in the applied social research process, but also to distort severely the way in which management knowledge is reflected in people's actions.

The key point which this model emphasises is that when one looks at the ways in which management knowledge is generated, and how it comes to influence people's behaviour, it is clear that there is no one single format. The conceptual element in management research (thoughts, ideas, beliefs and so on.) *can* come before the active element (testing and application), but equally it can come afterwards, and equally again the two may be combined in various subtle ways.

People's ideas, thoughts, reflections, concepts and understanding are all reflected in their behaviour. But equally people's behaviour only makes sense in virtue of the knowledge which we can perceive in it. Apart from a few exceptionally rare situations (such as when one tries something out for the very first time) people do something because they believe it will bring a specific result about. Knowledge and action are intertwined both practically and logically. The obviousness of this point should not detract from the consequence to be drawn from it that the conventional division of knowledge into 'pure' and 'applied' (of which I have made copious use throughout this text) is no more than that – a convenience.

A number of points follow from this. One is that there is no single ideal blend of idea and action: management knowledge is at times more weighted towards its application in practice, at other times more towards the creation of generalised[18] material. This is not a easy a statement as it sounds – OK, no *particular* approach is ruled out on principle, but that means that *any* use of *any* approach needs justification. It is just as incumbent on the researcher wishing to use a research design such as the distribution of a structured questionnaire to a random sample from a well defined population, and then, after appropriate analysis, present results in a statistical form, as it is for one wishing to use an 'exotic' interpretative approach such as asking respondents to develop their own role plays of a management issue and then write these up in fictional form. In each case the question is not *'how does this approach generate valid knowledge?'* but *'how can this approach link with organisational processes and practices to be meaningful and useful'*. Knowledge is not absent from this kind of dialogue, but it is secondary to the issues of meaning and technology. For a subject which deals with practice, meaning and technology *are* what knowledge consists in. This is what an 'applied' subject matter is really all about.

Another, perhaps less important, implication of this is that the divide between research and consultancy, in the management field, is less clear than many academics would wish it to be. Consultancy is generally seen as the resolution of individual organisational problems, usually by means of a change agent (internal or external) who leads the resolution process – sometimes by means of their specialised knowledge of the tasks involved, sometimes by means of their skills in brining other people's specialist knowledge to bear. This is usually contrasted with research on the bases that: (a) the investigation is problem focussed and therefore closed with respect to the range of potential results; (b) the problem is generally organisation specific, and thus (!) not transferable; (c) the investigation is biased – someone is paying and acts as a client of the work, so that certain kinds of results (such as that the manager's own framing of the problem is fatally flawed) are ruled out.

We already have seen enough to reject the second of these points which is the most important methodological one – much organisational research carried out by researchers is less transferable than they would like to think. So far as the first point is concerned, closure is a relative matter. There has of be some kind of ranging of possible answers in order for a research methodology to be designed at all. In this sense any management investigation, be it consultancy assignment or research project, is severely conditioned by the pre-judgements of the investigators. But more significant than this is that a piece of organisational research only makes complete sense if it is actionable – the connection between knowledge and action is variable but always present to some extent or another. hence there is this degree of range restriction in all cases. Problem focus is in any case less restricting than problem solving. Where a consultancy study is working with a brief to solve a problem then there is an element of truth that it might well be over-constrained.

The last of the above points is ad hominem – it virtually suggests that consultants are more biddable than professional researchers. I do not want to go into a discussion of the relative degrees of ethics displayed by academics and consultants, but it is not at all clear how true such a claim might be. Anyway, professional researchers, whether they work for universities or for research foundations, are commissioned for their work, and hence there is a potential salary or funding lever which could as equally apply to them as to the consultant.

Yet a third implication of the inter-relationship of knowledge and action is that the four archetypal approaches to management research which we discussed in Part Two of this book are – none of them – simply true or false in their entirety. As we noted above, each has elements which considered on their own make good sense, but when taken as defining a substantive thesis become too extreme. And so they are best seen as styles or maybe desires, rather than categorical statements about what management research is or ought to be. But what all this implies is that there is no single simple route to management knowledge. The extreme quantity of potential relevant factors, leading to high levels of complexity, is one aspect of this. The link to action, always there but sometimes high sometimes low, means that there is an *intrinsic particularity* to management concepts[19] – they fit certain concrete situations and fail to fit others. Often an idea will fit an organisational situation only after a certain amount of additional work – for want of a better term we could call this construction. So *validity, in the sense of soundness, does not depend on the concept or result itself, but on what is done with it in an organisation.* This brings back again the point that management research is as much about learning as it is about proof or demonstration or evidence. So whilst there is no clear distinction to be drawn between discovery and invention, there also is no clear distinction to be drawn between management practice and management research.

SUMMARY

In this chapter we have moved a little further from a negative appraisal of approaches to management research towards a more positive view of what it means to talk about knowledge where an applied practice based subject is concerned. What we have seen is that the application element provides a major amendment to the whole idea of what knowledge is (and therefore about what management research should look like). Different kinds of balance between knowledge and action are feasible, so that no one philosophy can be said to be universally appropriate. We end up with a situationalised continuum of research philosophies: whether the approach is positivism, or deconstructionism, or whatever, the philosophy is not a universal but makes sense only in so far as it can link with the capacity of organisations to develop actions and policies which enact the outcomes of an investigation. Discovery is indistinguishable from invention, and management research is thus inextricably intertwined with management learning.

To paraphrase a saying of Immanual Kant: knowledge without action is empty, action without knowledge is blind. In the following chapter we shall outline this conception in more detail.

NOTES

1   Indeed, at the dawning of the twenty-first century it is still disputed whether human activity has had any significant effect on global warming.
2   Indeed, arguably, this is not always even a good image of detective work – as all good fictional detectives would tell you, sometimes you have to stir up the mud a little to get the culprit to do something *else* and betray themself. Detachment in this kind of situation means being passive, letting key facts slip away from you.
3   Cf. Stringer (1999) and Van Beinum (1999) for accounts of action research which take a high participatory interpretation of the concept.
4   Even in the (probably undesirable) case where I attempt to conceal the data collection from the subjects: (a) it is unlikely that I will completely succeed in this; and (b) someone within the organisation will be aware of this and they at least are affected by my acts. So the suggestion that it is the deliberate use of the action element within an investigation which differentiates action research from other approaches is misleading.
5   Incidentally this comment goes further to undermine the mechanistic interpretation of research. If the research design is specifically chosen to maximise chances of a certain kind of result, then the researcher is hardly a neutral objective observer.
6   Peters and Waterman (1982) Chapter 5.
7   Ibid. p. 134.
8   Withstood does not imply that they are therefore true – it just means they have lasted up till now.
9   At least an approximation of the constant elements in his changing views.

10   Further illustration of the inadequacy of many current textbooks on management research which depict positivism and phenomenology as two ends of the research spectrum.

11   We looked briefly at his views in Part I and brushed them aside, but they will become more important again in Chapter 11.

12   It is probably worth nothing that these comments are referring specifically to post-experience students, who usually conduct investigations into issues of importance for the organisations for which they work.

13   An excellent methodological critique of Porter can be found in Clarke (1999).

14   The emphasis in this sentence should be on 'sometimes' – proof before learning is not *always* the direction of investigation in the management field.

15   Such as the organisations which formed the population or sample from which data was collected in the study.

16   By which I mean in this context a relationship which is generally believed by management researchers to exist, not one whose truth has been established.

17   In the sense that managers can make use of these to successfully carry out organisational interventions.

18   A point not stressed in the earlier arguments in this chapter is that a generalised perspective is not necessarily the same as a transferable one. Something can be in general form without being applicable to other situations (except in the logically limiting sense that in principle anything which is not itself a proper name might refer to more than one case).

19   As always, you can add here 'or other practice based subject areas, such as education'.

Chapter 11

Evidence, Research and Learning

In Chapter 10 we saw the beginnings of a way out of the problems of the classical approaches to social research when applied to management. Rather than treat these as universal models of research, we adopted an eclectic approach, recognising that each has a strength, but also acknowledging that each has very clear limits. So there is no single element which we can isolate and say: this is the basis of the degree of validity to be expected from management research. The position is rather that validity remains elusive, and difficult to characterise. But different kinds of value can be gained from the use of different approaches.

On the face of it hardly an exciting or revolutionary conclusion, but in fact there is a lot that flows out of this. In this chapter we shall extend this point and link it with a broader concept of management research, one which takes the focus some distance away from the classical conception of research as the means of supporting and demonstrating new knowledge.

11.1 THREE APPROACHES TO EVIDENCE AND THEORY

The first issue we need to go back to is the relationship between, on the one hand, the evidence we collect or encounter in the real world, and on the other, the theories and beliefs that we hold about management, which in various ways we try to link with that evidence. In this section we shall look at three different approaches to the issue of the relationship between theory and evidence. One of these is the idea that management theories are made *probable* (to some degree or other) by the body of evidence supporting them. A second is that evidence is collected to *illustrate* the relevance of a theory. A third is the idea that theory and evidence merely *blend*, or *commingle* – that there is no fixed relationship between the concepts and theories we enunciate and the data we adduce to support these. In effect these are alternative ways of presenting the key paradigms discussed in Part II, for the probabilistic approach is most clearly associated with the naturalist paradigm, the illustrative approach has clear linkages with the interpretative paradigm, and the commingling approach reflects the concerns of the deconstructionist and participatory paradigms.

The image which the model in the previous chapter presented is that there is no single form of the link between applied theory and action. In this section we shall be looking at a related linkage – between theory and evidence, taking the three approaches alluded to above as categorical positions on the relation between theory and evidence.[1] Let us first briefly characterise these three approaches.

Regarding the first of these, in some cases evidence may be systematically collected in ways that would not vary between researchers, and which attempt to abstract from the specific circumstances of the research. In principle, then, for these cases the investigation attempts to go beyond the personal beliefs and perceptions of the researchers – coming close to the naturalist, if not the positivist, ideal. As we saw in Part I, what is gained in terms of precision is lost in terms of generality. A result which is tightly determined by its evidence in this kind of field is unlikely to say much of generalisable value across organisations.

In other cases an investigation does not match to the requirements of the naturalist perspective. The second approach focuses on situations where evidence may not be systematically collected, or may be elicited rather than collected, or the perceptions and beliefs of the researcher are intrinsic to the results (either in terms of the data itself or in terms of how it is interpreted), or the results are tightly bound up with the circumstances in which they have been collected; in particular, results may be a restatement of the underlying assumptions intrinsic to the managerial practices under investigation.

In effect the third, eclectic, approach advocated here side-steps the arguments about what 'really' happens in the management research process, and goes straight to the practice of different researchers. For, although most professional researchers will have their own style, which they may have articulated to a greater or lesser degree, they are likely to recognise that there is a diversity of approaches, and that none has a monopoly on truth. Perhaps the argument in this book goes a bit further, and suggests that the quest for truth is misplaced, but it shares with this practitioner instinct the implication that a researcher in the management field can legitimately consider a wide range of possible approaches, without necessarily compromising the value of their investigation.

So what does all this say about theories of management and their relationship with what might be claimed as their evidence? The main argument here is that it is not a case of *one* specific relationship between theory and evidence, but a number of different types of relationship.

11.1.1   First Approach: Evidence Confers Likelihood

The first view we are looking at presents the relation between evidence and theory as one of probability – the evidence which a researcher collects makes the theory being researched more (or less) likely. Thus the evidence is meant to constitute a formal logical support for the theory, leading to a statement of probability (as we have seen, given the extreme multi-factorial nature of management, it is not sensible to try to establish any but the most vacuous categorical conclusions).

For example, according to this approach we might expect to establish that, say, a manager who adopts a certain kind of approach to promoting creative thought in their team is likely to achieve a certain degree of commercial success.[2]

[A more precise version might quantify 'is likely' – that is, by assigning arithmetic values: 68% probable, $p = 0.005$, etc. – but there are difficulties with this: which probability is the right one to calculate? The one which includes all the evidence? But it is not even clear what is evidence – the data systematically collected in controlled conditions? Why do we stop at that? Why not any experience which someone might feel is relevant to the investigation?[3] Who defines 'all' here? If some evidence is to be discounted, what kind of principle can be used to select the right set of data to use to work out probabilities?[4] This is a minor point, but one worth noting – exact probabilities considered in isolation from some presumed underpinning framework are difficult to justify even in physics, let alone in the altogether more problematic field of human behaviour. It is best, therefore, to leave it at 'is likely'.]

The key element is that the probability is based on the quantity and quality of the evidence. If there is a lot of good evidence which supports a thesis, it is regarded as confirmed to a certain extent; a dearth of such evidence and it is regarded as not having much of a level of confirmation. But this is not as simple as it sounds.

For one thing, in rich contexts the evidence cannot be simply interpreted as confirming or disconfirming a theory. Maybe we can find correlations and their absence, but this is not, on its own, evidence.

For example, we look at our manager and find that despite his activities aimed at encouraging creative thought, his company has not improved its performance, or even that there have been no instances of successfully introduced innovations. The instinctive reaction which many researchers would take is to presume that the theory has been disconfirmed. But if we also know that the company was subject to an unexpected hostile takeover bid and all efforts were devoted to combating this, we see a clear (albeit ad hoc) explanation why the behaviour in question did not lead to the result predicted. So the 'natural' interpretation of the evidence is not always correct.

In other cases, the phenomena may be simply too ambiguous or too nebulous to be soundly claimed as being either confirmatory or disconfirmatory. Creative behaviour? – well, this is pretty difficult to measure with any degree of certainty. Commercial success? – notoriously, short-term successes often turn out to be long-term failures. And what about the outcomes which are hailed by everyone as brilliant innovations, but they still fail to generate any significant additional revenues? Are these successful innovations which have not been harnessed by organisations, or are they examples of inappropriately imaginative activity which is not in organisational terms creative or innovative? One would be tempted to say 'you pays your money and you takes your choice' but it should not be an issue of *choosing* an interpretation – not if the research strategy is to try to establish a level of probability for an idea.

This does not mean that attempts to establish probabilities for management research projects are all entirely ill-founded. But it does indicate that this cannot be a prescriptive model for all kinds of investigation.

11.1.2   Second Approach: Evidence Demonstrates Theory

What other ways can there be for an idea or thesis to be linked with evidence? A second approach is to say that evidence is *illustrative* of a theory. In other words, there is no attempt to draw a conclusion of any firmness about the issue being investigated. Instead, the evidence is used as an indication of likelihood, without a commitment being made as to anything more precise.

This is a more specific approach than it looks. For example, though this approach accepts that data rarely comes in neat packages, it is not merely the view that the best we can expect is a rough and ready body of evidence. This would be a pragmatic position which accepts that an imprecise data set may be all that we can achieve. The illustrative approach may be based on the same basic idea – that we cannot often get the kind of pristine evidence which the aim of establishing probability requires. But the strategy is to take some or all of the potential evidence and *treat it as if it is representative*. In other words, it is less a matter of whether we have a neat package of data than it is about how comprehensive this evidence is. The subset of data considered in itself might well be quite carefully structured and analysed.

The key difference between the illustrative and the probabilistic strategy is that, in general, evidence which is collected as part of a probabilistic research design is intended to be a *sample which mirrors the proportions in the whole population* from which the sample is drawn. That is why statisticians go into great detail about sample sizes, sampling frames, stratified samples, random and semi-random sampling and so on. The illustrative approach, on the other hand, concedes that this may be too problematic to establish, and therefore the sample of material considered is a representation, an indication, an *example* almost, rather than a body of data which has been carefully structured to reflect all the different possibilities.[5] The role of the interpreter is therefore to decide which items are worth presenting as good illustrations, and to synthesise these with other existing interpretations.

When might a researcher adopt this approach rather than the more precise probabilistic one? Specifically in the kinds of situation which are characteristic of management research as we discussed it in Part I – where there is complexity on more than one level, where it is difficult not only to collect sufficient information on any one aspect, but where also it is difficult to model a situation sufficiently to be confident that all the key factors have been identified. Many management research papers base a study on a small set of examples – even some of the most reputable investigations may only consider a few large organisations. The work of Geert Hofstede, for instance, is based on a huge number of respondents (106,000) but – they all worked for IBM. In such an instance, the research is really a large scale case study. It suggests rather than demonstrates. However, the illustrative approach tries to make it do the latter by adding a *presumption* that the data collected covers the main variables – in contrast with the probabilistic approach which attempts, however incompletely, to *demonstrate* this. So, in the case of Hofstede's approach to national cultures and their manifestation in working behaviour, the *probabilistic strategy* is to try to demonstrate that the range of factors which might be relevant have all been taken into account, whilst the *illustrative* strategy is to *assume* that there are no further key variables. In practice, a sophisticated researcher who adopts the illustrative approach will acknowledge the degree of risk involved – namely that the assumption might be incorrect. Whilst this seems like an obvious point it is an easy one to overlook, and it reflects the main shortcoming of this approach.

The key weakness of the illustrative approach is not so much the potential fallibility of it – this is a perennial feature of any investigation into a world outside ourselves. It is rather that there is a double level of incompleteness about such a investigation. Any collection of information, whether on the scale of a large survey or just on an ad hoc, bit by bit basis, relies on the modelling of the situation which the researcher has done (consciously or unconsciously). This personal theoretical framework is the individual researcher's way of defining the area within which an investigation is carried out. Where there is a systematic attempt to identify the range of variables and from that set out the range of information necessary to fulfil the researcher's purposes (that is, a probabilistic strategy), then despite its difficulty (because of complexity, self awareness of respondents, etc.) it at least attempts comprehensiveness. The potential errors are on one level only. In contrast, the illustrative approach, which makes assumptions about how representative is the body of information collected (or to be collected in the future) has two levels of potential error – the first, namely that any modelling done might be inaccurate, and a second, that the attempt to establish the degree of comprehensiveness of the enquiry may itself be flawed.

One could add a third problem here – just what *is* illustration? Is the presentation of a case of a company where no new products have been designed for five years an illustration of a theory linking management style with creativity or not? What makes it an illustration or not is not the facts, but an explanation of what underlies the facts. In other words, we can't *just* say that a piece of data on its own is illustrative of a theory or not.

11.1.3   Third Approach: Evidence Interlinks with Theory

We can see that both of the above approaches have their merits, as well as their flaws. The probabilistic is just too optimistic for the context of management research (though it may be better for research into inanimate phenomena) whilst the illustrative compounds the level of uncertainty in the management research process. There is a third, much thinner, way of looking at the link between evidence and theory. This is the idea that management enquiry *blends* the two elements.

The idea behind the use of this word is that the previous approaches depict research as clearly separable into two discrete elements – the theory on the one hand and the evidence on the other. But the nature and depth of qualitative analysis, in particular, in management makes this much less plausible than it sounds.

There are some well trodden versions of this view[6] – for example, the idea that there can be no 'pure' items of evidence, and that all data is in one way or another theory laden. Another is the interactive nature of all human enquiry – once a theory or concept becomes known in the management community then people choose to act in accordance with it, or in deliberate contravention of it, or in some other way take account of that theory in their choices. In other words *the knowledge feeds back on the evidence for the theory*. And the follow on step is that a researcher may well then modify the concept in the light of that further evidence. So it becomes difficult to say what is evidence independent of people's knowledge of the theory in question, what is evidence which has been directly affected by someone's knowledge of the theory, and what is the theory itself. Here, however, we shall not focus on these interpretations, but instead look at a slightly different formulation of this idea that evidence and theory are not separable in the manner envisaged by either of the former views.

The work of Barbara Czarniawska is important here.[7] Her main intention is to view the outputs of management research as work in their own right. In other words that the collection of data becomes secondary to the way it is written up. The title of her book 'Writing Management' reflects this – management theory is not discovered, it is made by what and how someone writes about it. This kind of view (which we also noted as being reflected in some of Gareth Morgan's statements) takes the management research process as a whole: what it indicates is that the data collection and analysis stages are substantially affected by the final presentation phase – the various components of the process cannot be separated out. This contrasts with a more traditional view of the research process as proceeding in distinct phases, whereby the research project is designed, data collected, results analysed, and then as a final stage the findings are presented (usually written up). But Barbara Czarniawska's view is that this misrepresents the nature of the presentational element. What we say when we write down the results of our investigations is not merely a mirror of the investigation – *it adds significantly to it*. This is evident in the use of language of management writers. If we discuss marketing in terms of the analogy of warfare (the battle between competing suppliers) then we are not merely adding 'colour' or style to the discussion, we are framing it in a quite distinct way from a discussion which presents marketing as a detective story (the customer in search of satisfaction). But even when we avoid this floridity in writing management, the key terms used (for example, competition, strategy, innovation) have their resonances and allusions, which means that no discussion of field results can ever be a simple matter of summarising what has been found out.

The importance of Czarniawska's approach is underlined by the fact that it is only the presentation stage which has any impact beyond the learning of the researchers themselves. It is what is written and presented as the research which is read by peers, practitioners, sponsors and the general public. If you like, these are the customers of the research process, and the product they consume is not the research process (any more than I buy the manufacturing process when I purchase a car) – they consume the outcomes, the presentation, which invariably involves some (if not all) text. Much of what happens beforehand is not seen at all or it is too closely linked with the final writing of management to be separately distinguishable.

Czarniawska's views can be seen as a form of interpretavism, but there are echoes of this idea of a blend of evidence and theory in the other non-naturalistic approaches to management research. The participatory approach, for example, depicts management research as essentially linked to a particular research community, and thus dealing with that community's needs and perceptions, rather than developing anything which has generalisability built in to it (which is not to say that there can be no generalisability, only that this is not the main priority of the research process). Hence any theories which are developed or confirmed by the process are so developed only with regard to the specific context. A theory or a technique which comes out of a participatory research project is measured solely in terms of how it deals with that specific situation with that specific group or research community. But also that theory is developed out of the specific series of research activities which the research community has engaged in – in other words, it is only *a theory of that situation*. True, the members of such a community are not clean sheets, and they come to the project with their pre-existing knowledge, experience and understanding, but in terms of the research project to which they come together as a community, evidence is collected for the purpose of developing and testing what will work in the specific circumstances which the research community has identified or which the members bring to the project. In this respect the participatory research project might be better characterised as mutual collective self-consultancy than research intended to generate lasting truths about the nature of management. But that may well be what its main adherents, such as Peter Reason, would want to say. However, just as people do not *come* to a research project as clean sheets, so they do not *go away* as clean sheets. If I have been involved in a research project it would stretch credulity to suggest that I completed this without having experienced some changes in my understanding. True, this change is not necessarily specifically about the content of the investigation – it could be about the process. But it *might* be about the content – and it is worth bearing in mind that for the participants the distinction of what we do from how we do it may be somewhat fictive, so that the participants come away with something which has both process and outcome elements to it.

The deconstructionist approach also demonstrates the inextricability of evidence and theory.[8] For on that approach theory is built-in to any item of data. A term as simple as 'consult' carries with it a range of associations which arise out of and interact with the commonly accepted practices of the specific context. On a Foucauldian approach, this implies that we need to understand more about specific forms of social interaction before we could recognise what managers in that context were doing when they said they consulted with staff. The Derridan style would involve exploring the associations of a term such as 'consultation', using puns, analogies or other forms of verbal or written resemblance to suggest links and avenues not previously contemplated by the researcher. But the effect is the same – both approaches imply that we conduct management research without understanding what we are uncovering. Basic perceptions of reality, as envisaged in their different ways by both the phenomenologist and the positivist alike,[9] slip away from us and can dissolve in the welter of different associations and connections which they can carry. Hence the idea that we can have a simple division between the evidence (material which is independent of theory, and which supports it) and theory (which is formulated separately from the evidence and is tested or confirmed by evidence) is misplaced. Any statement which looks like theory is at least partially a construction out of existing practices, and any item which looks like raw data conceals a wealth of theoretically laden connections.

There is clearly, then, a strand of this blending image in all the non-naturalistic research paradigms discussed in previous chapters. What are its drawbacks? Well, one is that the metaphor of 'blending' conceals as much as it reveals. It does not help us to get an idea about what kind of relationship we can or should expect between evidence and theory. The three shadows of this approach which we detected in non-naturalistic paradigms of management research were phrased in quite different terms, and therefore one must at least suspect that the use of the term may be presenting a similarity where none really exists.

Another, more important difficulty (though it is less a weakness of this approach as it is a problem which this creates for the idea of management knowledge as a whole) is that the probabilistic and illustrative approaches to the link between evidence and theory also implicitly told you how far the theory went beyond the evidence provided. In the case of the probabilistic approach, this was to be found in the range of relevant factors which form the researcher's modelling of the research issue, and which provide the basis for projecting a result from a sample to a whole population. In the illustrative case the researcher presumes a degree of generalisability. On both of these cases there is a step which takes the researcher (or the consumer of the research for that matter) beyond the immediate presentation of findings. The simplest and most natural form of this is to say that the evidence suggests that the theory is indeed applicable to a whole category of cases or examples (meaning of this on the probabilistic approach: the evidence makes it very likely that the theory is true for all these cases; meaning of it on the illustrative approach: the evidence indicates or provides clear examples of how the theory may apply to the whole category of cases). But the image of evidence and theory *blending* does not help us understand how a theory goes beyond the evidence which supports it, to be a theory *of* a certain category of cases. How does a concept avoid being solely a theory of the evidence to hand, and nothing beyond that?

Despite the difficulties which this approach creates, it is a clear advance on the illustrative and probabilistic approaches. For both of those attempts to make the gap between evidence and theory – or more specifically between evidence as interpreted by the theory and future applications of the theory – as unproblematic as possible. And this is the key mistake – the gap between what we have observed and analysed here and now and what we might observe or analyse elsewhere or elsewhen should *always* be problematic. It is after all a major leap in the dark. We have seen enough to acknowledge that human phenomena are intrinsically more difficult to predict than natural ones (it is worth bearing in mind that the presumption that we have stable laws even in natural science is in some senses just that – a presumption for which we do not have direct proof[10]). So the weakness of the blending image – its failure to give a firm foundation for how we can move from evidence to a theory of a whole category of cases – is paradoxically its strength, for no other approach can satisfactorily do this either.

11.2 MANAGEMENT 'KNOWLEDGE' AND MANAGEMENT PRACTICE

The discussion of the previous section has in some ways recapitulated some of the points of Part II. What this and the preceding chapters have indicated so far is that *there is no justifiable foundation for management knowledge*: in other words, there is no stable rational format for linking activities of investigation in management with the subject matter of that investigation – or with its results, its conceptual output, or (especially) with the way such investigations connect with the practice of management.

It all sounds as if everything is up for grabs. As if there are no rules and therefore there is no standard by which we can evaluate management research – and if there is no standard of evaluation, then is there any basis for saying that an investigation does or doesn't demonstrate (let alone prove) anything? No rules – no management knowledge?

But consider how this situation has arisen. A range of alternative underlying paradigms – interpretavism, naturalism and so on – have been considered to see if one of them might provide a stable, defensible foundation for saying that management research can generate management knowledge.[11] So knowledge about management has been depicted as resting on, in one case, the collaboratively developed concepts of a research community (participatory research paradigm), in another the coherence of a range of texts and perceptions (hermeneutic version of the interpretative paradigm) and in another the correspondence between a statement or theory and managerial reality, as demonstrated by independently testable regularities (naturalist paradigm).[12] But unfortunately, we have seen that there *is* no defensible sense in which management knowledge can be said to rest on any of these paradigms and still maintain the claim to demonstrate truths about management reality with any degree of confidence. And the nature of the discussion strongly suggests that it not simply that the right model escapes us, but that the idea of management knowledge as resting on the results of investigation in this kind of way is the weakness.

Let us turn the situation round. Rather than trying to establish a stable structure or foundation which can support or inform management knowledge (and through that management practice) let us ask a contrary question. How does management practice absorb the outcomes of investigation and research? How does management practice draw benefit from management investigation?[13] The rest of this chapter and the following concluding one will be an attempt to elaborate an answer to this question. Such an answer will also help us to take a view on the questions of how far management research is valid and what use can we make of its results.

There is an immediate issue, which mirrors those we discussed right at the beginning of the book about the links between terms such as 'research', 'knowledge', 'investigation', 'concepts', 'theory', or 'ideas'. Namely the issue about what constitutes management *practice*. We could not say, for example, that any old action of an individual manager could count as an example of management practice. Equally however, it is not simply what all managers do – probably there is nothing which every single manager does anyway. But it is also not simply some kind of average or trend either. The idea of a practice indicates not only that people happen to do something similar, but that also they do so for similar reasons. It is not simply a case of common *behaviour* but also of common *reasons*. Not only that, but the fact that it is a *management* practice means that the reasons have to have some clear link to the primary purpose of a manager – so in some way a practice must link with the attempt to fulfil or advance the strategy of the organisation. For example, many managers bully their staff, and probably many of them do it for similar reasons (fear of being upstaged, insecurity, fear of losing control, obsession with achieving certain targets, being bullied by their boss and so on) – but this is hardly a *practice*. It is not carried out by someone as part of the implementation of the strategic plan.[14] It is not part of a deliberated and thought out approach to managing staff – it is more a reaction, or a style (of a sort).

The idea of a practice also implies that of a community. Whilst it is conceivable that someone might carry on a practice on their own without reference to anyone else, it is (even in that extreme case) implicit that others could be involved in the practice, could debate about it, develop their own variants or improvements on it, etc. A practice is something that in some way or another is *shared*, not just copied.

The idea of practice is clearly not a simple clear cut one. It involves, as we see above, connections with community and with a particular sense of purpose or strategy. But focussing on this (as the starting point for an understanding of what kind of value management research can have) connects with some points made earlier in this and the previous chapters. We saw that the most plausible way of conceptualising the relationship between evidence and theory in management research is that these are blended together – commingled, or inextricably linked. We also inferred from the model of Chapter 10 that there is no single way in which knowledge is implicated in management action. These points spring from an underlying feature of management research as we are now presenting it: that practice is actual engagement with the organisational world, which therefore links together independent elements such as explicitly defined theories, implicit managerial perceptions, motives, perceived constraints, unconscious beliefs, national or organisational cultural influences and so on, and within which 'facts' are not independent of the perceptions of the individual management agents. It also means that we start from the context of practice, an undivided whole, rather than try to take account of the influence on practice of these elements.

▉ 11.3   THE ABSORPTION OF MANAGEMENT RESEARCH

So the key question is no longer 'How far is management research valid?' but 'How do management practices draw upon management investigations?'[15]

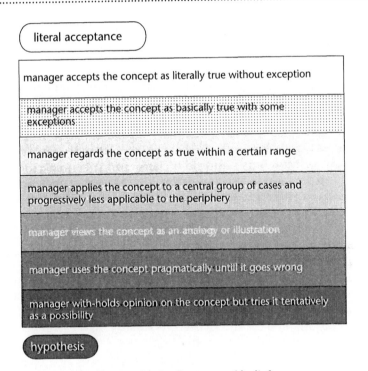

literal acceptance

manager accepts the concept as literally true without exception

manager accepts the concept as basically true with some exceptions

manager regards the concept as true within a certain range

manager applies the concept to a central group of cases and progressively less applicable to the periphery

manager views the concept as an analogy or illustration

manager uses the concept pragmatically until it goes wrong

manager with-holds opinion on the concept but tries it tentatively as a possibility

hypothesis

Figure 11.1   Degrees of belief.

One dimension of this issue is the degree of belief or commitment which someone adopts towards an idea, concept or technique. Another is the way in which such an item is absorbed into someone's practice. Figures 11.1 and 11.2 illustrate some of the possibilities here.

In Figure 11.1 we see a range of different ways in which a manager might accept or begin accepting a new piece of knowledge (for want of a better term). At one end we have someone accepting lock, stock and barrel the literal truth of a piece of research. For example, a manager might read a report of a technique which has been applied to a key problem they have been grappling with, and feel that the discussion is completely convincing. At the opposite end of the spectrum some-one might feel that the presentation of a new concept or technique is not at all convincing, but that it is sufficiently interesting to warrant a test of their own. So they try it out, tentatively, as a hypothesis, to see how it works.

It is worth noting that this kind of process is not one which reflects the logical structure of the ideas involved. People do not solely think in universal terms, for example – managers no more than the general run of humankind. Ideas occur to people psychologically, not logically.

A general concept is as likely as not to feature in someone's thinking under the guise of a characteristic example. Perhaps more problematic from the point of view of trying to treat people's ideas logically is when the reverse happens, and a critical example comes to acquire a grip (often with a significant emotional tone) over someone's thinking which spills over into other related cases, so that it operates more like a universal concept than a particular one. The image of the German economy in the early 1920s, with the classic example of runaway inflation, played a key role in shaping the attitudes and views of generations of economists and politicians, and it is no accident that this example was referred to many times by Margaret Thatcher in her early years as Prime Minister. Similarly, many managers have some powerful experience the feeling of which can often linger for years after its initial impact, so that their decisions may be coloured by the memory ('I'm never letting *that* happen to me again').

There are other factors which play a role in the way people think about practice. Specific forms of words, for example, which may have a political colour, may maintain a claim over people's thought processes far beyond their underlying meaning. 'Our staff are our greatest asset' is an example from the 1990s – very many organisations felt that this had to be included in mission statements, codes of values, corporate statements and so on., even though in practice very *few* organisations had properly thought through what such a statement really meant (or failed to mean) and what implications it might have for issues such as job security, or reward management. In fact the whole *particularity* of the way that an individual associates various statements and concepts, specific terms and phrases, memories and perceptions, and also the way in which these are organised in an individual's mind, are part of the framework within which someone processes a new item. The key word here is 'particularity' – whilst the *area* of research and investigation is public, the *manner* in which it is constructed in an individual's own understanding is particular to them (doubtless it can be publicly discussed and debated, but in practice only a small part of it is).[16]

Whilst Figure 11.1 indicates some of the gradations of commitment or acceptance which someone might have to a idea or concept, Figure 11.2 depicts *how* an item of new knowledge might be included or absorbed into someone's existing understanding. In a very few rare cases the item might represent a completely new area of knowledge – for example a report which asks new questions, or deals with a hitherto unresearched area. In general however, these are very rare – even the innovatory researcher is usually building upon other pre-existing ideas. And the reader is even more likely to try to establish a linkage with what they already know or understand.

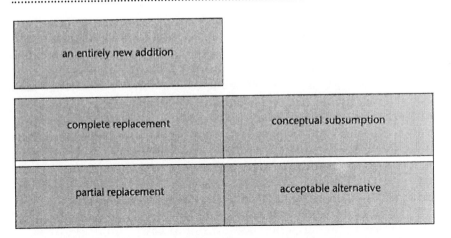

Figure 11.2   Competitive and cohesive advances in someone's knowledge.

Much more often there is some connection with what someone already knows. In some cases a new concept completely replaces an old – for example, a technique of assessing risk may prove to be more effective than the previous orthodoxy, so a manager chooses to switch over entirely to that new approach. Again this is probably rare. More often one concept or idea explains more, or is applicable across a wider range of cases, or has a greater body of supporting evidence. So it goes beyond the existing theory without necessarily completely ousting it – there is a partial replacement of the previous concept.

But replacement is only one way in which a new idea or technique may fit into a manager's understanding. As often as not there is a networking of different ideas, so that the addition to someone's knowledge does not directly replace other items of knowledge, but creates connections with them.[17] In some cases the new idea is a more general principle which subsumes other concepts or establishes connections with other ideas, or less frequently it may itself be subsumed under other concepts, for example, by filling in a gap in the previous conceptual framework. Very occasionally two concepts may coexist, as alternatives – at least for a period of time they may appear to have the same degree of evidential backing (or lack of it) to have an equivalent degree of cohesion with other ideas and a similar kind of connection with practice.

There are direct connections between these two models. For example, if someone accepts two theories as being alternatives, it is hardly likely that they will accept both as being literally true – far more likely is that they will regard both in a pragmatic light. Similarly, an analogy is not likely to be taken as a complete replacement for another item.

More important than the logical relationships between items in these two models, though, is that they provide a framework to help not only to interpret the points made earlier in this chapter concerning the links between theories/concepts and the evidence which is adduced to support them, but also the import of the conceptions of knowledge and action discussed in Chapter 10. Consider what I called the instrumental interpretation of the uni-dimensional model of knowledge and action: that is, the idea that managerial action needs to be based on a clear understanding of a situation, which is itself based on an accurate representation of the situation. The natural interpretation of this is that someone needs to have a fairly high degree of belief in something if they are to act on it. Literal belief, in part if not in whole, is normally required.

Equally, a completely new addition to knowledge, or a complete substitution for a previously held idea, fits most easily into this interpretation. For example, suppose someone believes firmly in the validity of the Ansoff matrix as a mechanism for generating new products and expanding into new markets. Suppose they then read, and are convinced by, a report which critiques this and proposes a new approach. Then it is an easy step from this to presuming that they would abandon actions based on Ansoff in favour of their new understanding based on the new model.

But this kind of situation is rare. Far more often there is no complete substitution, but a partial one, or a gradual transition from belief in one approach to belief in another, during which transition there is likely to be a lot of hypothesis testing – by each consumer of the research just as much as by the researchers themselves. When that is the case, then the evolutionary approach is much more likely to be appropriate. The degree of tentativeness is then progressively influenced by the acts the manager takes – in other words the evolutionary interpretation of the uni-dimensional model comes into play. In effect what is happening here is that a manager uses the experiences which result from their actions as a means of developing an understanding of the situation at hand, which includes a view about how far and in what ways a particular theory or concept applies to it, and on the basis of that they form their own personal interpretation or 'theory' of that particular kind of phenomenon. In other words, *the manager's learning process is itself a form of research activity*. This is a central conclusion of the argument of this book.

SUMMARY

The reader may recall that right back in Chapter 1 we talked about managers being more of researchers than they cared to admit. Management research has to be seen inside the context of management learning. The issues concerning validity and the appropriateness of the various paradigms, as well as images such as that of methodology as a mechanism, need all to be referred to this point. In effect we have moved away from the idea that management research and investigation can prove or support ideas, to the idea that research in this kind of subject is more a part of the learning process. In the final chapter we shall develop further the consequences of this replacement of the proof model of management research by the learning model.

NOTES

1 In practice researchers might well treat them as working rules of thumb – in such cases some of the points raised here may not apply, but then such an approach is to be welcomed as being in the spirit of the argument of this chapter.

2 This is not given here as a serious idea, but simply to illustrate the idea of evidentially based inferences.

3 There is a well known argument in the philosophy of natural science about the extent to which cases of objects which do not appear to be considered by a theory might still logically count as evidence – is the appearance of a black cat evidence for or against the theory that all swans are white? See Goodman (1970).

4 Another lesson from post-war Anglo-Saxon philosophy of natural science. The point was argued many years ago by Sir Alfred Ayer, in a paper entitled 'The concept of probability as a logical relation'. Reprinted in Ayer (1971).

5 Of course, even with the probabilistic approach, it is only likely that the sample reflects clearly the whole population. The point is that all efforts in collecting the data are intended to increase this likelihood, whilst in the illustrative case this is not always so.

6 Some of which we looked at in Parts I and II.

7 Czarniawska (1999).

8 Though as always with this approach it is worth noting that there are few examples of its application to management knowledge – mostly it is applied to social science in general.

9 I have deliberately used the narrow terms referring to specific versions of the interpretative and naturalist paradigms here, as it is not clear that all versions of interpretavism would be covered by this point.

10 Though in fact there is a great deal more which could be said on this subject – in effect one of the main themes of several of the classics of philosophical literature – for example, Immanual Kant's Critique of Pure Reason – has been the question of the status of 'natural laws'.

11 Not just any paradigms – ones which have been proposed and advanced by their adherents as supplying the necessary foundation for social knowledge.

12 This is a selection, not an exhaustive list.

13 We see here the importance of the approach taken by Barbara Czarniawska, taking the dissemination component of management research as being a substantial part of the whole process, not merely a transparent reporting activity.

14 Not, fortunately, as a general pattern.

15 Note also that over the last few chapters there has been an increasing change of term – 'research' suggests formal studies which lead to a specific kind of knowledge outcome, whilst 'investigation' simply denotes the activity of conducting some kind of inquiry.

16 These points are developed at greater length in the context of business ethics and values in 'Managing Values', Part 2.

17 Strictly this does represent a change to the old, for any concept or technique is as much defined by its connections as by its explicit expression in words or graphics.

Chapter 12

Management and Knowledge

We concluded Chapter 11 with an emphasis on the managerial learning process as a form of research, and indeed as perhaps the archetypal form of research in this field. In this final chapter we shall develop this idea, and indicate what this says about what management itself is, as well as what it implies for the management writing and research industries.

12.1 SOME OBJECTIONS

At this stage it may be worth considering some of the objections or protests that people might have to this idea that management research should be seen less in terms of the establishment of universal truths and more as a form of learning via localised problem solving.

Objection 1: Generalisability
'Research in a scientific sense demonstrates underlying patterns and factors which affect whole classes of events. For example, results in psychology about how we translate the light falling on our eyes into information about the world are general to all human beings (apart from very obvious exceptions such as those without sight). Research and investigation has to deal with general patterns and trends in one way or another. Otherwise what value would there be in a result? And also otherwise how could we ever have any degree of confidence that any management idea or solution was anything more than just a singular accident? Some kind of generalisability is essential to call it knowledge at all.'

There is a useful point here and a less useful one. The less useful one is the analogy with pure natural science. Whether it is psychology, oceanography or nuclear physics, the pure study operates with a different kind of objective from the applied. Above all, even though there might be a great technological need to resolve a certain issue (such as the precise behaviour of a group of chemical compounds) individual studies are themselves standalone and not directly harnessed to application. In contrast an applied study is just that – it has a direct linkage with the real world of our own concerns and intentions. Failure matters in a different way from how it affects the pure study. If one series of experiments does not uncover the biological mechanisms of sight then it does not change anything – we have to look harder at others. If a study into the impact of HR policies on the competitiveness of UK companies does not generate knowledge then the opportunity is lost. The situation changes, and the conditions appertaining at one time have passed on and some other conditions apply at a later time. We could try again to find out, but then we would be conducting an historical investigation – how far *had* HR policies affected UK competitiveness at a certain time. It no longer is useful as technology.

The useful point is how far anything can count as knowledge if there is not some generalisable aspect to it. Any particular item involves general ideas and concepts – without them we could not identify anything at all. 'The trade unions objected to the employer's offer on the ground that it did not meet all their demands' – in such a statement the very use of terms such as 'trade union' or 'employer' brings into play legal frameworks and definitions of work and collective representation; use of terms such as 'objected' and 'demands' carry not only general literal sense but also associations and nuances which colour the meaning. Even in so limited example as the above statement there are general elements. If we look at broader terminology – 'consultation' or 'participation' for example – then these carry a larger degree of general significance: 'consultation' implies a certain form of communication between employers and staff, one which involves dialogue and some collaboration in decision-making.

The implication of this point is that it is misleading to suggest that management knowledge comprises only completely individual perceptions and cannot be used to shed light on other situations. In this respect the above objection has a very valid point. At the very least the existence of a body of data or of a case study analysis raises the question whether some other context is similar in the relevant respects. But *raising* the question is a wholly different thing from *giving a definitive answer* that there is such a similarity, and thus drawing the conclusion that if something happened to apply effectively to one organisation then it can be applied in equivalent fashion in another.

It is a *creative decision* to decide to apply a concept tool or technique which works in one situation to another, not an automatic consequence of the fact that it works in the first context.

This point was applied to *all* knowledge by the great Austrian philosopher Ludwig Wittgenstein,[1] but we do not need to go that far here. The particular circumstances of applied human studies – complexity and self-consciousness of humans when they become aware of the implications of social theories for their own behaviour – means that a factor which operates clearly in one situation cannot be presumed to do so in the same manner in other contexts, even when there are great similarities. As we have pointed out before, every organisation is a dynamic and complex interaction between incredibly complex beings (people). A great deal of similarity still may leave a great deal of unexplored areas. In practice an astute manager does in fact draw analogies between what worked in one situation and what might work in the present situation – but they do it carefully and prudently, recognising the potential for variation.

So this objection leaves us with a significant requirement: namely that however local a piece of management research might be, it still must project beyond its immediate context. Our view is that the central and most characteristic form of management research is not the grand systematic study, but the local investigation that an individual does in dealing with their own managerial problems. But somehow we must see how the results of this can apply outside its own context: total universal application to a whole category may be misplaced, but *some* kind of extension beyond the single case must be feasible in *some* way.

Objection 2: Organised data
This objection is quite simple – 'We already have lots of material collected as part of formal studies. Countless surveys have been conducted collecting evidence relating to a whole variety of management subjects – leadership roles, attitudes of international managers to mergers, perceptions of strategic groups in a particular industry and so on. Do they all count for nothing? These are manifestly not *all* developed as a form of technology. They are not all conducted in order to solve a specific problem for a specific organisation. So on the view being advanced earlier in this chapter and the last one, it would seem that they are not really management knowledge at all. But whilst one might query the methodologies involved, they still represent bodies of data, and they must count as evidence for or against some theory or other.'

We have seen many potential weaknesses about the value of large data sets, however constructed and collected – three of these are:

(a) the framing of the terms in which the data collection is defined; (b) the extent to which a phenomenon identified in one complex organisation can really be identified with the 'same' phenomenon in another; and (c) the extent to which a statement summarising a set of data can retain a stable meaning, or gets drawn down an indeterminate network of alleyways of association and resonance. In other words, the sheer existence of lots of data does not mean that any of it is any good at all.

But the objection is going a bit further than this for it asks – does this mean that *none* of it is any good? Let us suspend disbelief for a moment, and suppose that there are some examples of management research studies which are methodologically secure.[2] One key distinction to be drawn here is between *the data collected* and *any conclusions drawn from it* (an obvious point maybe, but crucial to this issue of whether the volume of existing research conducted along 'classical' lines is of value or not). Research in fact can be perceived as valuable for a variety of reasons. It may be due to the *resource* provided by a large body of information. It may be because a particular *assumption* has never been questioned before. It may be because certain striking *phenomena* have been identified or recognised for the first time. All these are cases where the research has value independently of the conclusions of the research. The fact that a researcher has even asked a certain question may be useful, because it creates possibilities for other researchers, or because other people realise the significance of the question.

So – is none of the existing generalised 'non-technological' management research material of any value? Answer: It may be valuable, but it need not be so because of what it purports to demonstrate. If it has value at all, this is because of how it contributes to people's thinking about the issues involved. People think in complex ways, and therefore there may be any one of many different ways a research study can impact on their thinking – in one case because it creates a new association, in another because it affords a parallel with a critical example, in yet others because it directly conflicts with an existing belief.

A management research study is useful when it sheds light on the question 'What shall I do?' It can contribute any one of many different elements to that answer. It is not uniquely valuable because it presents a definitive evidenced statement of what the key issues and relationships are. Rather it draws value from its role in developing managers' thinking about the issues.

Objection 3: Are all bets off?
This objection asks, if validity is not the main issue, why bother with it at all? 'So if management research methodology is only useful in so

far as it contributes to people's thinking about issues, does this mean that we should forget about evidence? Does this mean that any one kind of statement is as good as any other, irrespective of whether it fits the reality of management or not? In short, do we need to bother any longer with well designed questionnaires, or precisely defined sampling frames, or sample sizes, or avoiding leading questions and so on? If the validity is not what matters, then why not cast it aside and concentrate on the impact on thinking – how stimulating an idea is, or how elegant, or how rich it is in associations?'

In some ways this objection has not listened to the response to the previous one, though it also raises fresh issues. As we noted above, management research can be useful in many ways – at least as many as there are different facets of someone's thinking about the managerial task. How a piece of management research has impact on someone, then, depends on which part touches which aspect of someone's thinking. If someone has a propensity to see things in broad terms, then their perception of the degree of breadth and overall conceptual fecundity of the research will have most impact. On the other hand, if someone has a tendency to see things in 'hard' 'left-brain' terms (structured information, logical criteria, formal systems for processing data) then how far such a person feels that a research study has these qualities will be the key factor in their response to the study.

This is not simply a case of 'left-brain thinkers like stats, right-brain thinkers like the touchy-feely stuff'. Most people have a diversity of different strategies of processing information, and use them differentially in different contexts (so that the *cognitively* intelligent person can often be *emotionally* very unintelligent, for example). The central point to recognise here is that it is not so much that 'validity' in its traditional sense is of no use, so much as that it is not the sole determining factor in whether someone responds positively to an idea.

Human beings are realists, certainly – we believe that there are external realities which are independent of our own thinking – and hence material which we feel impinges on our depiction of reality is relevant to our response. We cannot help trying to project our understanding of management reality in universal terms. The issue is that we are more than *just* realists. We also need a broader kind of explanation which connects with our overall ways of looking at the world. There are many different factors in our overall understanding of the management task. These include concrete memories, abstract images, strongly held forms of words, characteristic patterns of practice, amongst others.[3] Equally, our thinking is not divorced from our actions. What people do is not just evidence for what they believe and think, it is also both an *input* to their thinking and a *framework* within which their ideas can be set. Concepts in management are concepts about management *practice*, after all. Additionally, practice defines both possibilities and probabilities. Our ideas about what is *possible* are tested and refined in terms of what we do and what that implies about how much room we feel we have for manoeuvre, but equally the patterns and trends which are implicit in the idea of a *practice* indicate *probabilities* – what we regard as most likely to be effective, most prevalent, most likely to cohere with other practices.

So it is not that validity is no use, but rather that it is not the *only* thing that might be useful in evaluating management research. However, there is a deeper issue here. Validity is one important criterion, but it is dislodged from a traditional scientific conception of its being the foundation of any value of a piece of research (as embodied in the instrumental conception of the link between knowledge and action). So whilst it is not true that in every case validity does not matter, in a particular situation it *might* be the case that validity is not as important as other factors. So the underlying concern here – that management research is no longer being evaluated in terms of whether or not it describes an independent reality, but in terms of how it affects people's understanding – is a correct summation of the view being advanced in this book. 'Validity' is a component of the impact of theory on understanding, but only one amongst others.

Let us take stock of what these objections and their responses have left us with:

- management knowledge is not simply universal (this much we have built up through the argument of several chapters), but if it had no generalisability it would not be knowledge at all
- management research and its products (for want of a better word, 'knowledge') is primarily valuable in so far as it influences the way we think about management reality
- validity is not irrelevant to this issue, but it is not the sole, determining, factor; it is one amongst many factors

These are the key points to which the argument of the rest of this book has been moving. It has been necessary to take so long a time to get to them, because there are so many different approaches to, and aspects of, management research methodology that to state them too early would have been unconvincing.

Jointly they underline the points made at the end of Part II. Namely that the four approaches which we considered are inadequate as complete accounts of the nature of knowledge of an applied social science such as management – none of them. But equally each underlines an important point which cannot be ignored in the explanation of what management research is and what kinds of standard apply to it. So the concerns of the realist are still crucial – if an idea had no claim to reflect or represent something in the external world then why would anyone bother with it? But equally other concerns, such as that of the hermeneutician, are important: if a concept, however well supported by evidence, did not fit with the general nexus of accepted ideas then how could we make sense of it as knowledge? How could it stand entirely on its own? And the participant and deconstructionist perspectives also have their say here – 'knowledge' in this kind of field has to strike some resonance with someone's idea of what practice could be, and equally it has to have some degree of conceptual flexibility, so that an individual can not only see how it links with their own managerial situation but also how it could be adapted – static knowledge is no knowledge.

12.2   SO WHY BOTHER WITH MANAGEMENT RESEARCH AT ALL?

This question is of course quite different from the objection 3 considered above. It is not here a question of should we rely solely on realist research methods (on an analogy with natural science) so much as a bigger question about what role does *investigation* play in our understanding of management, and even whether it has a significant role to play at all.

Not every human pursuit requires the supplement of knowledge based on systematic investigation. For example, only rarely does an individual feel the need to investigate how they respond in their personal lives – and then usually because of some profound event. To take another kind of example, the more you try to work out why a joke is funny the less you really understand. Even where other pursuits do involve some kind of investigation or research, they may have a very different idea of what counts as this kind of activity. For example, a musician may study the classics, may read up about music 'theory', may experiment with different techniques and approaches. And in some sense they will have some criteria – however implicit – to evaluate what 'works' and what doesn't.

But this idea of research is not only a far cry from the natural science paradigm, it is also difficult to compare directly with interpretavism. It is not that the artist is striving for a universal approach that will 'work' for everybody in every situation. Most musicians, for example, would probably be horrified at the idea that there could be a universal set of rules and precepts for making music. Diversity is seen as extremely healthy for the pursuit. Which is not to say that every individual musician necessarily regards the diversity as acceptable:[4] many composers may well have felt that their way of approaching their task is the only way they can do so – but this does not mean that there is some clear sense in which one way has to be superior to others. Some ways may be better than others, but the idea that there is a universal truth about music making, that there is some underlying commonality about doing or conceiving of music, is out of place. The lesson we can draw from this analogy is that management is not a set of well defined universal rules and practices. So to the age old question – is management an art or a science? Ultimately the discussion is not worthwhile, the terms are too flexible. The most important point is that management investigation is not to be associated with proof or demonstration.

12.2.1   Critical Theory

In order to get an idea about what role research and investigation plays in our thinking about management we need to go back to the idea of critical theory, which was dealt with rather summarily in Part I. Recall that the basic approach taken by Habermas[5] is to identify three fundamental kinds of intellectual and personal interests that human beings have, and then to suggest that different kinds of research satisfy each of these three in turn. We have a technical interest in controlling the world (the social world as much as the natural) – so we get naturalism, the attempt to present the world as a mechanism which we can then exercise control over, or at least have a significant influence. A second kind of interest is that of understanding, so we get 'historical-hermeneutic' studies, devoted to the re-creation of other people's experience in our own experiences. And finally we have an interest in freedom, so we have 'emancipatory' studies, which demonstrate how human beings can transcend (some of) their existing constraints.

The main objection we had to this in Part I is that it seems a rather narrow cluster of interests. One suggestion made earlier is an interest in aesthetics, which overlaps but is not fully contained within Habermas' categories. And even within those three broad categories there are emphases which I suspect are not central to Habermas' view – most of us not only have an interest in controlling our own destiny, we also find it difficult to resist the idea of controlling other peoples' destinies as well. Parents control children, managers rarely can avoid being more controlling than their roles really require, governments just about never voluntarily relinquish power over their citizens (except as prescribed by the constitutions of their nation). So there is something of a conflict between emancipatory social knowledge and technological. Marketers do not really want to give fully informed choice to their customers – they want to use their knowledge of human perception and belief to encourage someone to buy.[6]

But these are relatively minor points. The framework which Habermas has put forward is very suggestive, and will form the basis of the structure of my final answer to the question 'what is management research and how can it be valid?' – and through that to the question of what management is at all.

12.2.2   Critical Theory Plus

The main aspect of the Habermas framework with which I want to take issue, and which is particularly pertinent to the question of how a subject such as Management links together different subject areas and applies them to practice, is the idea that for each kind of human interest there is a definitive kind of investigation – as if there is a one-to-one correlation between each interest and a different kind of social epistemology. In practice these interests are united. A piece of investigation may well address more than one of those interests simultaneously – these interests are not the spring from which research activity comes, but rather they are implicit criteria by reference to which an individual may evaluate a piece of research. This is not to say that each and every example of management research has to embody technological, explanatory and emancipatory elements. Rather it is to say that we look at each example in the light of the interests we have. The fact that this is a practice based field means that a piece of research may be *liable* to address each of the basic interests we have.[7]

Suppose someone undertook a study into the degree to which the strategic categories of Miles and Snow[8] successfully explained the behaviour of organisations in a particular industry. Take for argument's sake a highly naturalistic approach, whereby a large number of economic indicators are used as a basis for collecting and statistically analysing lots of data about the behaviour of different players in that particular market. What is the result? If we had solely a technological interest in this, then the answer would need only be in its final statistical form – for example, 'There was a $-.73$ correlation between factor 1 and factor 2, where $p < .005$.' However there is hardly a study which leaves a set of results in this form – always some element of 'discussion' or interpretation is also added. What does 'discussion' of this kind achieve? Generally it makes a numerical value qualitatively meaningful. *In other words, it turns a technical result into a comprehensible one.* In doing so a researcher is implicitly acknowledging that some kind of interpretative element to their research is necessary for it to be acceptable within the community (whether this be a community of practitioners or of other professional researchers). We need the qualitative explanation at least as much as the hard data. And what that qualitative reinterpretation does is also to re-present or modify the results. The reader is not interested especially in whether the correlation is −.13 or −.15. For one thing there is the possibility of the precise figures being sensitive to minor fluctuations in the study. More important than this, though, is simply the point that whether the result is one or the other – *it's pretty low*. And such an evaluation is all that the practitioner or the follow-up researcher needs to know.

This is not an argument that the numbers don't matter. Sometimes they do, and how far they do depends on the degree of value attaching to the subject matter (if we are talking about probabilities that a bridge may collapse, then the difference between −.13 and −.15 may well matter a great deal – external issues define significance, not mathematical rules). No, the argument is about what interest someone may take in the results of a study. For the purpose of developing a technique or strategic tool which takes account of the study, then adoption of the correlation of −.13 is a sound basis. For gaining an understanding of the phenomenon in question, then the summary 'pretty low correlation' does rather better, for it not only summarises the numerical value, but also subsumes it into a background of beliefs and related issues that collectively depict −.13 as a low correlation. It prepares the result for hermeneutic inclusion in the overall network of ideas, techniques and presumptions relating to strategic choice (or whatever subject it might be). And further, it is via this interpretative re-presentation of the result that it can have an emancipatory role, for it is when someone can make qualitative sense of research that they then can begin to formulate plans and take actions which increase theirs and other people's capacity to control their own fates.

This is an example where a naturalistic study has clear links with other human interests, and thus is never 'just' a study into data collected and analysed. Technical material is always subsequently understood in broad interpretative terms, and it cannot help but be evaluated in terms of how far it can contribute to someone's growth in self-determination. There is clearly a scale here, from research which can be clearly and easily turned into applications (such as an evaluation of different methods of appraising performance), through studies which suggest application without this being explicit, right down to ones where there is no obvious application (say, a presentation of an analysis of the conversations of successful entrepreneurs). But even in work which is at an extreme remove from actual application, the possibility – or maybe just the hope – that the ideas can be applied must be present. If they were not, it is hard to see why anyone would study the issue in the first place.[9]

In the last few paragraphs we have taken an example of a naturalist study and shown how it has to bring in elements of other research paradigms. One could go the other way, and start from an interpretative study. In parallel fashion one finds that it is never seen as *simply* an interpretation of the subject matter. In some way there is a suggestion that this interpretation reflects what the underlying mechanisms of the situation must be. Of course such a study is unlikely to go into detail about these, but without – again – at least the suspicion that the interpretation reflects (or maybe *projects*) something in the management world then it carries no significance. So why is that projective aspect not brought to the fore? Well, in practice most research papers in management which have an interpretative element do tend to bring some kind of suggestion that the study does have a bearing beyond their literal interpretation. But even if one were not to, that is likely to happen because the material is too difficult, too complex, too vulnerable to variation of any one of a number of different variables, for there to be a simple and clean way to establish what is 'really' externally there. Interpretation carries a suggestion of technology, and via that technical suggestion, a possibility of application and thus of emancipation.

We could multiply the examples but the principle is clear enough. Different kinds of interest are involved both in the intentions with which a research study is initiated and in the way they are responded to by their audience. There is no simple formula for saying that this kind of study must have *this* amount of technicality, *that* amount of emancipation, and *some other* amount of interpretation. The point is not that there are set proportions, but that all of these interests *could* be involved.

Why don't we have distinct kinds of pursuit, one of which addresses the interest we have in technology, another addressing the need for understanding, another that of emancipation? Why is it that there is a *single* process of research and investigation which is subject to these different expectations? For it *is* a single kind of process – as we have seen above, whatever perspective was adopted by a researcher when they designed a study or investigation, it may still be subject to evaluation by its audience in terms of other interests. Even though the field of management as a whole may be subject to the stresses and strains of different research interests and paradigms, so that at times it is unclear how one kind of study may be talking about the same kinds of phenomenon as some other, it is still a process of *discovery about* the nature of management and of how managers can or should behave, and this is the source of its unitary nature as a subject area.

This idea that the different interests humans have in knowledge can be connected is not as strong as saying that they are *integrated*.

It is rather looser.[10] The point is not so much that we have these interests which form a coherent unified set of expectations and requirements of the process of investigation. It is that these interests are continually present and can be brought into contact with each other. I *might* decide that a particular investigation has nothing to say to me about the possibilities of developing my own greater capacities (or does not tell me anything about an independent set of mechanisms operating in the world of management, or has no value in extending my own mental pictures of management, etc.), but more often than not I will at least consider whether it does have some such implication.

Underlying this is, I believe, a fundamental point about how human beings make sense of their world. We do not operate with a neatly compartmentalised mind,[11] in which one kind of material is dealt with separately from others. We can feel emotions about apparently quite dry technical matters, we can connect up how we conceptualise about things with options for actions, we can take a technical focus on the opportunities for self determination. It is not that fanciful to regard our minds as open access forums, where material comes in from one direction, but is open to critical inspection and comparison from a number of different perspectives. Some work in anthropology supports this. Steven Mithen[12] has argued that the difference between the modern *homo sapiens* mind and that of our most recent related species, *homo neanderthalis*, was less a matter of what was there, in terms of mental functions of calculation and imagination, so much as a more sophisticated way of linking these functions together – the Neanderthals had functions analogous to our abilities to process facts, and to create metaphors, but they were unable to put these together. So whilst the modern stone age *homo sapiens* was able to fantasise about life after death, or depict animals on walls, or readily imagine alternative uses for a piece of old bone, the Neanderthals were unable to maintain self-consciousness or to apply metaphor to their material life to anywhere like the same degree.

So – to answer the question why we bother with management research at all? Because it helps us satisfy some of our interests relating to management – interests of technology, understanding and freedom suggest themselves above all.

12.3   SO WHAT INTERESTS DOES MANAGEMENT RESEARCH ADDRESS?

Section 12.2 has discussed research roughly along the lines of Habermas' own analysis of human interests – in terms of technology, understanding and self-determination. Roughly speaking we can see direct analogies here with three of the four key research paradigms discussed in Part II – in order, the naturalist, interpretavist and participatory approaches. This confirms the argument of Part II, that each of these paradigms works well as an indication of one kind of requirement or expectation or even of mindset we have towards management research, but they do not work at all when generalised to become 'theories' of management research or other applied social study. So what of the fourth of those paradigms – the deconstructivist?

Recall that at the time we noted that this was itself something of an anomaly, as it was less a set of research methods and more a critique of research methodology and its results.[13] Nevertheless, I believe that there is a strong case for saying that we do have an 'interest' (for want of a better word) which leads us to the kind of activity from which deconstructionism as I have discussed it draws its source. I suggested earlier that an interest in aesthetics might be a basic interest which has a direct bearing on the kind of knowledge we seek and how we relate to the outcomes of investigation in applied social studies.

The word 'aesthetics' can be misleading – it makes one think of art and high culture. But there are other manifestations of the interest in the aesthetic – sport, for example. The elegance and simplicity of a theory or concept is another kind of example. Einstein famously said that he could not believe a theory which was not beautiful, but of course that depends what he really meant by beauty. Nevertheless, this is another kind of example of the aesthetic in our thinking. By and large, we are more likely to accept an explanation of phenomena which is simpler or more neatly expressed than another (other things being equal). That is one reason for the popularity of detective novels and crime films and TV shows – the neatness of seeing a cluster of varied and apparently unrelated items finally pull together to become joined in the explanation of a crime.

Certain principles in management theory pre-suppose this kind of criterion. For example, it is a basic assumption of risk management that one does not encounter two independent fundamental failures of systems simultaneously. This is probably best seen as a rule of thumb *supported* rather than *established* by experience. But it also reflects this sense that events are basically as simple as they can be – complex situations may involve complexity, but in general two events which look as if they might be related probably are.

The conception that markets can always be segmented down to simple niches with a small number of players is another manifestation of this. In other words, the idea that there is a large chunk of commercial activity which we call the car market is less appealing than the idea that there are various smaller markets – the luxury market, the family saloon, the estate, the four by four or people carrier markets and so on. This is not to say that there is nothing more to be said for such a division than that it resolves market analysis down to smaller simple units. Clearly there are many research studies demonstrating that the behaviour of consumers varies in terms of a whole range of factors which collectively can be explained in terms of market segmentation and niching. But the collection of such evidence is one thing – its use in testing or confirming a depiction of marketing in terms of simpler rather than more complex markets is a choice made by researchers on the basis that *the simpler kind of conception*[14] *is a more useful and illuminating conception* than one which places all cars in one marketplace and then devises complex explanations for the deviations.

This kind of interest is manifested in a general tendency of explanatory studies – natural science, literary theory, social science amongst others – to continue pressing for further explanations. As soon as we have an answer to one question we ask – why *that answer*? How did the the universe start – with a big bang. How did *that* happen? And so on. I want to suggest that the underlying value of what I have called deconstructionism lies in the intention of thinkers such as Derrida and (in a very different way) Foucault to press this interest unremittingly. As if their intention is to take *every* result as ungainly, as possessing – for want of a better phrase – the ugliness of being a 'brute' result. This can be seen most obviously in Derrida's approach, which is to take all linguistic manifestations as suspect, as hiding something which has to be teased out. He does not of course see this as a search which can ever be completed – the idea that there is a foundation which can eventually be discovered is an example of what he calls 'logocentrism' – the idea that there is a neat and simple pathway from thought to speech and writing. For Derrida, all such pathways conceal as much as they reveal, and hence there is an inelegance about all static verbal expressions, as they promise a certainty that they cannot deliver. There is never a point arrived at where we connect a text with reality. The explanation for any text is – another text, itself in need of explanation.

The Foucauldian approach is more remote – his view is that social concepts are intertwined with social practice, and that the underlying network of features of a social era, which manifests itself in thought as well as in activity, is its 'episteme'. But since an episteme cannot be clearly articulated in its own time, this leads to the same kind of near nihilism that Derrida's ideas imply. Namely, wherever we look, there is still something that may lie behind our thinking, there is still another 'take' on an idea or concept. So the idea of a stable foundation for knowledge and understanding – at least about social matters – is misplaced.

We can see now why the word 'aesthetic' is both apt and misleading. Here we are talking about a drive to reexamine things, a need to disinter what is established and reconsider it, so that what seems to be an established universal truth becomes only a transient special case. The interest or need here is one partially related to curiosity, but goes beyond this – it is as much a desire to play with ideas, to examine and reexamine them, to tease out their underlying structures and then to take these apart and recreate them afresh. In some ways this can be seen as a drive towards structure and order, but in other ways it also leads us to be dissatisfied with any final product, be it a novel, a theory of management or an explanation of the nature or galaxies.[15] Such an interest values elegant mathematical proofs and finely constructed symphonies, not as static items but in view of what these suggest, what implications they have and what fresh horizons they suggest to us. So there is a dynamism here – what satisfies is not simply the fixed object (however fine) so much as what new actions and possibilities are presented and implied by that object.

This interest people have could be characterised as an extension of the human propensity to express oneself via the creation and manipulation of physical objects and sounds – so whilst aesthetic is not an inappropriate word, it should be recognised that this kind of interest, whilst a source of artistic output, is just as much a manifestation of a need or desire to intellectually change and rework things – whether these be ways of doing sculpture or new developments in the theory of cell division.

So we have here an additional kind of interest which research and investigation can satisfy, in addition to those of freedom, understanding and technology – one of aesthetic activity. The activity element is crucial – it is not about the taking of aesthetic pleasure in objects or theories, it is rather about the exercise of an aesthetic interest in renewing and reframing ideas and structures.

12.4   KNOWLEDGE OF MANAGEMENT

We are now in a position, at last, to draw together the strands of the argument and give a clear answer to the two questions: (a) what is management knowledge? and (b) how far is it or can it be valuable? Note the switch here from the earlier versions of this question: not 'valid' but 'valuable'. We have seen that validity is not at all easily achieved, and that even when it *is*, it is not clear how much use that is.

The prime form of management knowledge is, I contend, not the grand theory arising out of a large scale systematic study, but the communal understanding of a local 'fix' which may be developed by individuals solving their direct management problems. This puts management knowledge in a practice based context – these are practical problems that managers have to solve. Here is the key truth of the participatory research paradigm, which takes the most central role in management knowledge in my view.

But this idea also raises, despite the localisation, the issue of how such a solution may be carried beyond its point of origin and applied in other contexts. The knowledge, after all, consists not in the fix itself, but in the *understanding* of that fix, an understanding which is represented (though by no means exhausted) in the way that the idea of the fix is transferred – applied in other contexts. These applications are not determined by rule. There is no simple algorithmic method by which I can take a technique which someone used to improve the work rate of miners in a Nigerian mine, and simply (that is, without any further reformulation) make the same use of the idea to improve the work rate of – even miners in a different Nigerian mine. There is a complexity here – as we have emphasised over and over – which works against any simple instrumental approach. But the naturalist paradigm still has an important place here – not as the provider of clearly defined signposts ('do x and there is a chance that you will improve work rate by 35%') but as a means of checking or testing applications of ideas beyond their original setting, or of developing hypotheses ('would it be the case that doing x in this context will result in the same 35% work rate increase as occurred in the previous study?'). Systematic formal data gathering is still important – if I choose to take my mine workers technique and apply it to workers in a French bank, then there is material available, in the form of studies and surveys which will help me frame questions and hypotheses about how to accomplish this application successfully. Of course one *could* regard these studies and surveys as expressing the truth about French bankers and Nigerian mineworkers, naturalism style. But if I were a manager and got my work rate improvement scheme all wrong, I doubt whether anyone will too happily listen to me saying 'But the studies all showed....' The ultimate test is what choices managers make when they put ideas into practice, not what the research work is that led to a particular act of applying an idea in a certain context. That is why management has been described all along as an applied subject – its crucial test is its impact on practice.

So naturalism has a place in management knowledge, as a storehouse of possibilities, tests and checks. Its purported role as the foundation of an edifice of understanding and technique has, however, gone.

Whilst there are clear roles for the participatory and naturalistic paradigms, the role of the deconstructionist and interpretavist paradigms is much less sure. In some ways these are in a dynamic opposition, two faces of Janus. The hermeneutic ideal is that people can

arrive at a clear mutual (or to use the jargon, *inter-subjective*) understanding of an idea, by gradually framing and reframing the overall
context of all relevant perceptions and ideas, so that a *nexus* is created
(far more suggestive than the image of a circle in this context) in
which each concept has a well defined location, and a series of string-
like connections with other related ideas, much as the interlacing of
neurons in the brain. But the deconstructionist paradigm, so close in
origin to hermeneutics, points to the impossibility of getting to the
bottom of such networks. The language we use both to describe and
to explain management issues is rooted in our practices, and is as
much shaped by these as shaping them. To get behind this language-
practice linkage is to detach language from its assumption that there
is a clear and well established foundation on which our ideas rest. As
fast as one identifies one set of ideas, another set can suggest itself as
lying behind. Rather like the first cause argument (what began the
world? answer x; but what began x? answer is y; so what began y?
ad infinitum). So, whilst the hermeneutic nexus can easily be constructed, it becomes just one more construction as soon as it exists – it
cannot settle questions. It fails to explain in foundational terms, but
only displays a structure, for each element of which a thousand
questions could still be raised.

On the other hand, *some* kind of agreement has to be made for
sheer pragmatic reasons, else the association of terms which Derrida
and others adore would run away with itself in a nightmare of
Alzheimer-like free wordplay. But there is more going on here than
just pragmatics. For one thing, a field such as management cannot
but involve language and community, for the simple reason that
management cannot happen in complete isolation. Local problems
are problems relating to the way *groups of people* achieve tasks. The
solution of these requires communal activity, and the solutions
require communication to others. 'We need to remotivate the workers by incentivising' – such a statement (which might well be part
of a solution to a management problem, despite its over jargonised
linguistic expression) relies on a shared understanding to be applicable at all. But secondly, and less obviously, a management idea relies
on a degree of analytic potential to be applicable to other contexts. A
technique which is directly tied to just one context cannot be described
in general terms at all, but if it cannot be so described, then it cannot
bear the many different associations and analytic distinctions which
are necessary for someone to be able to say 'That idea worked for
them, I'll try it in my company.'

The roles of interpretation and deconstruction in management
knowledge are therefore directly linked to the communal nature of
management practice.[16] Interpretation functions as the mechanism for

agreement in communal action, whilst deconstruction operates as the mechanism for drawing out potentialities for transferring application.

So to recap – the central examples of management knowledge are local solutions to practical problems, using existing studies and data to create hypotheses and to test out applications, using interpretative agreements to generate the communal action central to management, and employing deconstruction as a means of exploring associations and possibilities necessary to apply the solution in different contexts.

As a definition this looks deeply too pat, but in the process of concrete application different aspects of this would come to the fore. In some cases, the need to apply a solution to different contexts may require[17] more extensive comparisons using existing systematic data. At other times, the key issue may be the range of different ways in which the idea or solution can be constructed (drawing on the resource of associations for example).

This view of management knowledge is clearly far beneath the aspirations of the more academic of the business schools, which would attempt to portray management as a subject with an intellectual standing equal to disciplines such as mathematics, philosophy, sociology, physics or literature. The emphasis I have placed on practice takes management some way away from those academic ideals. But this may not be so bad a thing anyway. 'Academic' can be as much a negative as a positive quality. And in any case even pure natural science may be less academic than its aspiration. John Ziman has recently suggested that natural science is moving into an era he describes as 'post-academic'.[18] By this he means that the classical ideal of science is in the process of breaking down. He characterises this classical ideal as incorporating five elements: communality, universality, disinterestedness, scepticism, and originality. For each of these he illustrates that modern pressures have undermined their importance in the modern activity of natural scientists. Industrial partnerships, the discrediting of peer review, the isolation of 'universal' science in a jargon which only a specialised group can follow, these and other factors[19] have taken science some way away from the classical ideal.

Considering the key stakeholders of management knowledge, it is clear that some of them would not lose sleep over the lack of an academic element – many is the time that professional managers have expressed to me (in management development sessions) an attitude strongly critical of ideas and concepts as 'too academic'.[20] Management 'knowledge' does not carry the same burden of expectation that academic knowledge generally does.

We can now return to the question of how valuable management knowledge is under this conception. In so far as local managerial problems get solved there is a clear limited sense in which there is a direct relevance and value. However, there is a broader image which needs to be discussed. The idea of a body of knowledge (about a certain area of practice or a certain subject area) suggests a bank or storehouse of accumulated ideas, results, techniques or conceptions which can be archived, available for elements to be extracted at later times to support later innovation, or to facilitate the solution of routine problems, or to help with the design of non-routine problems, or even to be reexamined, leading to fresh reinterpretation and reconception of the practice or subject area. The obvious example of this kind of storehousing is the library, comprising a collection of key text based sources, whether in book or journal form. Now what kinds of material are held in such an archive of management knowledge? This is an analytical question – there is an obvious practical answer, books, articles, and other material, as we find them in existing libraries. But this is answering a different kind of question. What we really need to understand is: what are the criteria for inclusion in a 'pure' hypothetical example of a management library? In a real management library one will find books written by leading gurus – Peters, Porter, Kanter, Stewart, Mintzberg, etc. One is also likely to find research studies and management textbooks – sometimes written by the same writers, more often by university lecturers. Smaller scale, 'how to' books are also usually well represented – 'One minute manager' style texts, or successful business people explaining how they did it. But these are all there for market reasons, and as we saw in Part I this is not a good indicator of what management knowledge really is. Certainly such a real management library may not be a storehouse of management knowledge at all.

In an ideal management library – one which provided a storehouse of management knowledge as a public resource – the most central category of this knowledge would be the records of local fixes arrived at by managers in dealing with their specific managerial challenges and problems. Rather like collections of company reports (which can often be found in real library collections) there would be large collections of many such local problem solutions. There would also be a major additional function of cross referencing different local solutions where one may shed light on another – whether this was done by additional researchers or by the intellectual input of the archivist/librarian[21] to the collection is another matter. Of course, many of the other types of material which we do find in a real library would still be there. The 'how I succeeded' personal statements of entrepreneurs would be valuable adjuncts in the same vein. Research monographs and textbooks would still be present: they would sit beside the central repository of management fixes – now they would be presented not as the foundation of management knowledge, but as an elevation over and above the practical activity reflected in the records of local management problem solving. They would be there not as an attempt to set out principles of best practice, or as constituting a summation of what happens in organisations or industries, but as a means of individuals increasing their understanding of the kinds of choices they have at their disposal.

One might think that this is all a flight of fantasy – management libraries contain what they contain, and whether or not this is what I call the central examples of management knowledge is neither here nor there. It is, however, important to recognise that because of the nature of real management libraries and archives, we do not have a *body* of knowledge at the moment. We have snippets here and there of local problem solutions,[22] lots of conceptually informed personal reflection, and some systematic data collection. So the real management library contains some management knowledge, but not in any way that can be easily used by managers as public resources. It is almost as if the real knowledge is there by accident, admixed with a great deal of extraneous written material. So that the interested manager would have to approach it as an archaeologist.[23]

But this idea is not a complete fantasy. There are actual examples of the kind of thing I have in mind. A design or architecture library, for example, comprises a large collection of representations of actual designs of buildings or objects. That is its central function. Theory is there, but on a much more limited scale. And where theory conflicts with practice, it is practice which wins. The management library should be thought of more as a *museum* than a set of texts.

So the value of management research as a body of knowledge is great in potential, but low in reality. The reader will note that the other image, of an *edifice* of knowledge, has been avoided here. It rests on an assumption that some parts can be clearly identified as a foundation of the body of knowledge, and other parts are part of the superstructure. As we have seen, foundationalism in management studies is misplaced. The elasticity of practice means that no purported foundation can be stable enough, and the elusiveness of the underlying assumptions and associations involved in a practice makes it impossible to identify a foundation which is genuinely *the ultimate* foundation, not resting on anything more fundamental.

12.5   MANAGEMENT AS DYNAMIC FRAMING

The last thing we should do is identify what this view of management knowledge says about management itself.

At the start of this book we asked the question: is *management* what is developed by *management development*? The presumption behind this question was that a practice such as management should not be seen as something which gets defined independently of how it is developed. Now, towards the end of the book, I want to ask a similar kind of question: is management best understood as what management knowledge is knowledge of? This apparently tautological question has a significant point to it, in that we have seen how management knowledge is best regarded as a dynamic integrating of different perspectives or interests (the Habermas trio of technique, understanding and freedom, but also the additional one of aesthetic play or curiosity) in the resolution of practical problems which are in the first instance local, but have some propensity to be taken beyond their immediate context. Unlike Habermas' own approach, which is to use each of the three sets of human interests which he identified to define separate areas of study and understanding, we saw that in an inter-disciplinary practice based area such as management all or any perspective could apply.

So, if management knowledge is an integration of different perspectives to solve local practice related issues (but with the potential to be applied beyond its existing context), then what does this make management itself? Habermas makes a strange but very relevant comment at one point: '... in the power of self reflection, knowledge and interest are one'.[24] By 'interest' here he means his characteristic model of human interests in technique, understanding or freedom (and to which I would add aesthetic play/curiosity). In keeping with the points I have made earlier I would add to this the point that these interests *interact* in action, that when a manager acts s/he would most likely be drawing on more than one of these interests, conceivably all four, and therefore the kind of knowledge they are using (or creating via their action) will reflect this. For example, a marketing manager, developing a new promotional strategy for a product range, has a clear interest in technique, in that they want to devise an effective instrument for yielding greater sales. In virtue of this they clearly have an interest in freedom, in the sense that by developing an effective promotional strategy they create greater possibilities – for the product, for the organisation, and for her/himself: more evidence of the close relationship between the naturalist and participatory paradigms. But in addition there are interpretative and analytic elements. A strategy is such a vague thing – it really only takes shape from how it links with a whole number of organisational factors such as staff commitment, core competences, or competitive environment. These linkages have to be synthesised if a strategic plan is to be effective, they have to be brought together in a coherent whole – an intelligible network – for the plan to be effective (probably even for it to be applicable at all). And for this to happen, it has to be collective. There has to be a degree of sharing: no strategy can exist solely in one person's head – emergent or planned, a strategy is an organisational act, involving the complicity of a large number of individuals. So the interest in agreement becomes a central feature of management action.

The interest in creative/aesthetic analysis is also an important feature of management action. A marketing strategy is apparently a fairly well understood thing, with options well trodden and great levels of experience – so a decision to do something similar to what we did with our other products last year would look like a straightforward reapplication of a tried and tested formula. But *any* reapplication of a complex concept is itself a redefinition, and in being so it involves a degree of *analogy* between our understanding of one situation and another. Suppose Coca-Cola launches a promotional campaign for one of its brands, say Minute Maid. It then decides the next year to do the same for its lead brand, Coke itself. This may look like a straight transfer of one idea from one product to another. But there are many differences which make the second campaign a significantly different event from the first – for one thing, the success or failure of Coca-Cola itself is central to the business, for another the whole range of market factors affecting such brands are different, for another time has shifted on. None of these individually is a determining factor but jointly they add up to a context which is categorically different. Hence the choice is not simply one of copying what we did last year, it is about viewing the immediate future as being essentially similar to the recent past. The whole idea of what a *strategy* is dependent in part on the context within which the strategy is mooted – a Civil Service strategy may well look very different in nature from a Virgin Airlines one. Even the concept 'similar' is shot through with practice based and time-dependent presumptions. Ask six people from different cultural backgrounds to make a copy drawing of a picture and you will get six very different looking results, all possessing their own rationale for being valid copies. Practice and its unspoken assumptions underpin any management decision to transfer a technique or idea from one situation to another.

SUMMARY

So we can draw some restricted conclusions about management from this discussion. Above all, we can see that managers draw on four distinct complementary factors in their work. A key element of the management task which has been often alluded to but which this analysis points up as critically important, is the need to *synthesise* material from these four different sources – technical, interpretative (relating to communal agreement), power (or freedom) oriented and analytic (relating to the creative perception of similarities and differences between contexts). Another quality which has often been regarded as central to success as a manager is the ability to cope with rapid changes of subject matter – at one moment dealing with the Christmas rota, at another the fluctuations of the capital markets, at yet another counselling a bereaved employee. But what this analysis suggests is that this is too simplistic – although each of these situations may involve a priority for one or other knowledge/interest factor, each of them may well involve some or all of the others as well. So it is less a matter of flitting from one subject to another, as maintaining a continuing focus on the fluctuating balance of these four interests as the events of management reality ebb and flow.

NOTES

1 Wittgenstein (1953). Many sections relate to this point – one sequence is Sections 143–54.
2 In fact I have far greater doubts over this than have been expressed in this book: several years of working with postgraduate students, asking them to consider the methodologies of many of the best articles in areas such as Marketing, Strategic Management and HR, have left me with no study which has withstood the critique of those students. In some cases the best known and most respected research studies have come in for the most withering criticisms. But this is incidental to the point made above, which is solely about the possibilities in principle.
3 Note that 'beliefs' is omitted here – the items mentioned in their different ways reflect and embody someone's beliefs.
4 Though doubtless many do – the point is that this is not a central part of the idea of research and progress in the arts.
5 I am restricting my discussion exclusively to the ideas of Jurgen Habermas.
6 Of course there is an ethical debate here – the purpose of this example is rather, however, to indicate that different 'interests' in Habermas' trio can conflict.
7 I am deliberately refraining from discussing at this point the exact range of human interests that human beings have. For the moment, whether Habermas does or does not have the right list, the above points stand.
8 The 'defender – prospector – analyser – reactor' typology of strategic choices. See Miles and Snow (1978).

9   Just as, for all their protestations of sheer curiosity, even the most narrowly focussed of natural scientists will offer justifications of their work in terms of further results, rather than simply for its own sake, for example, they may see their work as complementing or filling out the framework of theory, or maybe they will offer a general defence on the ground that it is only by allowing 'disinterested' research that great discoveries can be made, or maybe again that obscure and apparently unapplied studies may suddenly come to have a significance far beyond what was expected.

10   But see Sean McCartney and Reva Berman-Brown's view that management is an intrinsically unified subject area, which goes beyond even integration. McCartney and Berman-Brown (1996).

11   A different point from the question of the compartmentalisation of the *brain*, though even here there is clear evidence of interlinking between some of the different compartments – see Edwards (1993) for a fascinating application of this feature of our thinking and brain-processing.

12   See Mithen (1996).

13   It is true that people talk of 'doing' Foucauldian analysis, and of Foucauldian discourse analysis (see Hackley (2000) for an illuminating and extremely stimulating example). Strictly therefore the comment in the text is misleading, but it reflects the strategy I have taken with respect to the deconstructionist tradition, which is that it is less important as a means of generating concepts as it is of examining them. In this respect the importance for understanding management knowledge is less in the contribution of a technique such as discourse analysis to the *collection* of material, so much as to the *examination* not only of raw data but also of the theories and conclusions drawn from it. Its value to us is as critique rather than as creation.

14   In this case, of the car market.

15   Of course people are satisfied with novels in ways that they are not so satisfied by theories and explanations in science. But if a particular novel was presented as the final definitive example of the form (literally the novel to end all novels) this would be profoundly unsatisfying to the novel reading public, and its purported 'to end all novel'-ness would doubtless be rejected out of hand.

16   Of course, similar points could be made using examples drawn from other applied social sciences, such as education. But I refrain from making any more general statement than that.

17   Strictly, it should not be 'require' but something like 'be agreed by a management community to involve' but this is too unwieldy.

18   Ziman (2000) though one gets to the point of wishing that the game of prefixing 'post' to everything in sight would lose its popularity.

19   Not all of these are Ziman's examples. I drew one from a review of his book – see Anderson (2000).

20   Though this is not of itself a conclusive reason to think they are right in doing so.

21   The extent to which an archivist or librarian contributes an intellectual element to the material they collect is very greatly underestimated.

22 Often contained in what are sometimes regarded as 'lower level' management journals.
23 Not in Foucault's sense, but in the more conventional metaphor of digging deeply through a variety of materials of greater or lesser relevance.
24 Habermas (1972) p. 314.

Conclusion

This completes the final part of this book. There are several key points which we can now set down, which together present a very different view of management research and management knowledge than the orthodoxy would suggest:

1 the prime form of management knowledge is that of the local problem solutions that individual managers or groups of managers with overlapping interests develop
2 traditional large scale surveys and data collection/analysis exercises retain a place – not as a foundation for knowledge, but as a mirror for developing questions and hypotheses
3 the polarisation between 'hard' and 'soft' information, and the associated expansion of this into a polarisation between 'positivist' and 'phenomenological' paradigms, is misplaced
4 the prime form of management knowledge can include elements from four different interest sources – technical, interpretative, creative/analytic and emancipatory
5 distinct forms of research – such as hermeneutic, or positivist, inevitably miss out on whole dimensions of the process of developing knowledge in a practice based are such as management, and therefore are constitutionally insufficient
6 the current systems of archiving do not capture the really valuable elements of management knowledge
7 the modern emphasis on styles and paradigms of research obscures the need for more integrative work, based on practice rather than on independent detached investigation
8 no single paradigm or interest can fully capture the richness of the management research process

So where does this leave the present research community and its characteristic activities? Unfortunately the upshot of this argument is that much of what is being done is wrong headed, much of the debate on which kind of research approach is sound is misconceived, and much of what is preserved is at the least incomplete and in many cases highly suspect. The practices of journal editors, of research funding bodies, of research reviewers, needs to be radically rethought. But also the practices of managers need to be rethought: managerial problem solving is not simply a matter of an individual sitting in their office and muddling through some difficult situation or other; it is a process of creating exemplars and potential model solutions, which represent a vast potential repository of good practice and understanding which is currently mostly just thrown away. The nature of management research requires a genuine movement of both players – the researchers and the managers. The management community needs to recognise that what they do has greater intellectual value than they often place on it, but equally the research community needs to recognise that the models of pure science and pure academic disciplines do not apply in this field, and that the centre of management research is the understanding of practice, and that therefore this comes from a focus on actual practices in actual – that is, local – contexts, rather than attention to grand theory.

Hannah Arendt (1958, Section 45) said that no one can be under a greater tyranny than in their thoughts – that despite the appearance of privacy and freedom, thought can be easily dominated and controlled. I would add to this, that almost as great a tyranny is the mythology of a separation of thinking from action. Management, as a central function of contemporary society, has become overshadowed by a false and entirely distorting image of the successful individual as being action oriented rather than thoughtful. Both qualities are essential for the progress of organisations – the odd individual may make a fortune without reflecting on how their activity raises or dashes the possibilities for the economic world as a whole, but these should not be the role models for this century.

So we end with a challenge in both directions – researchers, get acting; managers, get reflecting. Or, better still, get together.

Bibliography

Ahmad, W. and Sheldon, T. 'Race and statistics', in *Radical Statistics*, 1991 (and also in Hammersley 1993).

Allen, R. (ed.) 'Pocket Oxford Dictionary', OUP, 1984.

Anderson, P. 'Snowballing but still very much in control', a review of Ziman (2000) in *Times Higher Educational Supplement*, 27 October 2000, pp. 30–1.

Andreski, S. 'Social sciences as sorcery', Andre Deutsch, 1972.

Anscombe, E. 'Intention', OUP, 1957.

Arendt, H. 'The human condition', University of Chicago, 1958.

Argyris, C. 'On organisational learning', Blackwell, 1994.

Aristotle, McKeon, R. (ed.) 'The basic works of Aristotle', Random House, 1941.

Austin, J. 'Sense and sensibilia', OUP, 1962.

Ayer, A. J. 'The concept of mind and other essays', CUP, 1971.

Bacon, F. 'Novum organon', 1620.

Belbin, M. 'Team roles at work', Butterworth-Heinemann, 1993.

Berger, P. and Luckmann, T. 'The social construction of reality', Penguin, 1967.

Bhaskar, R. 'A realist theory of science' (2nd edn), Harvester, 1978.

Blaikie, N. 'Approaches to social enquiry', Polity Press, 1993.

Bloor, D. 'Knowledge and social imagery', Routledge, 1976.

Brech, E. 'Organisation: the framework of management', Longmans, 1965.

Bray, A. 'Why is it that management seems to have no history?', in *Reason in Practice*, 1(1), 2001.

Burgoyne, J., Pedler, M. and Boydell, M. 'A manager's guide to self development' (3rd edn), McGraw-Hill, 1994.

Burgoyne, J. and Reynolds, M. (eds) 'Management learning', Sage, 1997.

Burton, D. (ed.) 'Research training for social scientists', Sage, 2000.

Chakravarty, A. E. 'The Geeta and the art of successful management', Harper Collins, India, 1995.

Clarke, P. 'Porter's five forces model: a methodological critique', in *Journal of European Business Education*, May 1999.

Clegg, S. and Dunkerley, D. 'Organisation, class and control', Routledge and Kegan Paul, 1980.

Collin, F., 'Social reality', Routledge, 1997.

Czarniawska, B. 'Writing management', OUP, 1999.

Deal, T. and Kennedy, A. 'Corporate cultures', Penguin, 1982.

Denzin, N. and Lincoln, Y. 'The landscape of qualitative research', Sage, 1998.

Derrida, J. 'Writing and difference' (trans Baas), Routledge and Kegan Paul, 1978.

Descartes, R. 'Discourse on method', originally 1637, Bantam (ed.) 1961.

Diamond, J. 'Guns, germs and steel', Vintage, 1998.

Donaldson, L. 'In defence of organisation theory', CUP, 1985.

Dreyfus, H. and Rabinow, P. 'Michel Foucault: beyond structuralism and hermeneutics', Harvester, 1984.

Drucker, P. 'People and performance', Heinemann, 1977.

Durrel, L. 'The alexandrine quartet' Faber, Penguin, 1991.

Easterby-Smith, M., Thorpe, R. and Lowe, A. 'Management research: an introduction', Sage, 1991.

Edwards, B. 'Drawing on the right side of the brain', Harper-Collins, 1993.

Eisenhardt, K. 'Building theories from case study research', in *Academy of Management Review*, 1989, pp. 532–50.

Evan, W. 'Organisation theory – research and design', Macmillan, 1993.

Fayol, H. 'Administration industrielle et generale', 1916; English translation 'General and industrial management', Pitman, 1949.

Feyerabend, P. 'Against method', Minnesota Studies in the Philosophy of Science, Vol. IV, 1970.

Finch, J. 'Its great to have someone to talk to'; ethics and politics of interviewing women', reprinted in Hammersley, Chapter 14, 1984.

Follett, M. P. 'The new state', Longman, 1920.

Ford, J. 'Paradigms and fairy tales', Routledge and Kegan Paul, 1975.

Foucault, M. 'What is an author?', 1969, reprinted in Rabinow, (ed.).

Foucault, M. 'The archaeology of knowledge and the discourse on language', Pantheon, 1972.

Foucault, M. 'Madness and civilisation', Tavistock, 1979.

Fox, S. 'Debating management learning' (I and II), Burgoyne & Reynolds, 1994.

Furusten, S. 'Popular management books – how they are made and what they mean for organisations', Routledge, 1999.

Gadamer, H.-G. 'Truth and method', Continuum, 1960.

Gibbons, M. et al. 'The new production of knowledge: the dynamics of science and research in contemporary societies', Sage, 1994.

Giddens, A. 'Profiles and critiques in social theory', Macmillan, 1982.

Gill, J. and Johnson, P. 'Research methods for managers', Paul Chapman, 1991.

Glaser, B. and Strauss, A. 'The development of grounded theory', Aldine, 1967.

Goldthorpe, J. et al. 'The affluent worker', CUP, 1968.

Goodman. 'Fact, fiction and forecast' Harvard, 1955.

Greenwood, D. (ed.) 'Action research', John Benjamins Publishing, 1999.

Grint, K. 'Fuzzy management', OUP, 1997.

Griseri, P. 'Managing values', Macmillan, 1998.

Gummesson, E. 'Qualitative methods in management research' (2nd edn) Sage, 2000.

Habermas, J. 'Knowledge and human interests', Heinemann, 1972.

Hackley, C. 'Silent running: tacit, discursive and psychological aspects of management in a top UK advertising agency', in *British Journal of Management*, September 2000.

Hammersley (ed.) 'Social research', Sage, 1993.

Handy, C. 'Understanding organisations' (4th edn) Penguin, 1993.

Harre, R. and Secord, P. 'The explanation of social behaviour', Blackwell, 1972.

Harrison, R. 'Understanding your organisation's character', *Harvard Business Review*, May 1972.

Hart, C. 'Doing a literature review', Sage, 1998.

Heron, J. 'The complete facilitator's handbook', Kogan Page, 1999.

Hofstede, G. 'Culture's consequences', Sage, 1980.

Horowicz, I. (ed.) 'Uses and abuses of social science', Transaction Books, 1975.

Howells, C. 'Derrida', Polity Press, 1999.

Hume, D. 'Treatise of human nature', originally 1739, Selby-Bigge (ed.), Oxford, 1884.

Illich, I. 'Deschooling society', Harper and Row, 1971.

Jacques, E. 'The changing culture of a factory', Tavistock, 1951.

Johnson, G. and Scholes, K. 'Exploring corporate strategy', Prentice Hall, 1988.

Kant, I. 'Critique of pure reason' (2nd edn), 1787.

Keynes, J. M. 'A treatise on probability', Macmillan, 1921.

Kolakowski, L. 'Positivist philosophy', Penguin, 1972.

Kuhn, T. 'The structure of scientific revolutions', University of Chicago, 1962.

Lakatos, I. 'Falsification and the methodology of scientific research programmes', in Lakatos and Musgrave (eds), *Criticism and the Growth of Knowledge*, CUP, 1974.

Lang, K. 'Pitfalls and politics in commissioned policy research' (pp. 243–64 in Horowicz 1975).

Lincoln, Y. and Guba, E. 'Naturalistic inquiry', Sage, 1985.

Lincoln, Y. and Guba, E. 'Competing paradigms in qualitative research', in Denzin and Lincoln, 1998.

Maddox, J. 'What remains to be discovered', Macmillan, 1998.

Management Charter Initiative 'Management standards – operational management level 5', MCI, 1997.

Marshall, J. and Reason, P. 'Collaborative and self-reflective forms of inquiry in management learning', Chapter 13 in Burgoyne and Reynolds (eds), 1997.

Massey, R. and Massey, J. 'The music of India', revised edn, Kahn and Averill, 1993.

McCartney, S. and Berman-Brown, R. 'The discipline of discipline', Essex University (Department of Accounting and Financial Management), working paper, 1996.

McClelland, D. 'The achieving society', Van Nostrand, 1961.

McKinlay, A. and Starkey, K. (eds) 'Foucault, management and organisation theory', Sage, 1998.

Merquior, J. 'Foucault', Fotana, 1985.

Miles, R. and Snow, C. 'Organisational strategy', McGraw-Hill, 1978.

Mintzberg, H. 'The nature of managerial work', Harper and Row, 1973.

Mithen, S. 'The prehistory of the mind', Thames and Hudson, 1996.

Morgan, G. (ed.) 'Beyond method', Sage, 1983.

Muller, H. J. 'American Indian women managers: living in two worlds', in *Journal of Management Inquiry*, 7: 4–28, March 1998.

Mullins, L. 'Management and organisational behaviour' (4th edn), Pitman, 1996.

Myrdal, G. 'Objectivity in social science', Pantheon, 1969.

Nagel, T. 'The possibility of altruism', OUP, 1969.

Newton, T. 'Theorising subjectivity in organisations: The failure of Foucauldian Studies', in *Organisation Studies*, **19**(3), 1998.

Oakley, A. 'Interviewing women: a contradiction in terms' in Roberts, (ed.) *Doing feminist research*, Routledge and Kegan Paul, 1981.

Outhwaite, W. 'New philosophies of social science: realism, hermeneutics and critical theory', Macmillan, 1987.

Parikh, J. 'Managing yourself', Blackwell, 1992.

Partington, D. 'Building grounded theories of management action', in *British Journal of Management*, June 2000.

Peters, T. and Waterman, R. 'In search of excellence', Harper and Row, 1982.

Pettinger, R. 'Introduction to management' (1st edn) Macmillan, 1994.

Plato. 'Plato: collected dialogues', in Hamilton, E. and Cairns, H. (eds) Princeton, 1961.

Popper, K. 'The poverty of historicism', RKP, 1961.

Pugh, D. 'Studying organisational structure and process', in Morgan, (ed.) reprinted 1981.

Quine, W. V. O. 'Two dogmas of empiricism', in *From a Logical Point of View*, Harvard, 1953.

Rabinow, P. (ed.) 'The Foucault reader', Penguin, 1991.

Reason, P. (ed.) 'Human enquiry in action', Sage, 1988.

Reinharz, S. 'Feminist methods in social research', OUP, 1992.

Rigsby, B. 'Aboriginal people, spirituality and the traditional ownership of land', in *International Journal of Social Economics*, **26**(7/8/9), 1999.

Roget, P. 'Roget's thesaurus', revised Lloyd, S., Penguin, 1984.

Sackmann, S. 'Cultural knowledge in organizations', Sage, 1991.

Sayer, A. 'Method in social science', Hutchinson, 1984.

Schutz, A. 'Phenomenology of the social world', Heinemann, 1967.

Semler, R. 'Maverick', The Free Press, 1992.

Silverman, H., (ed.) 'Gadamer and hermeneutics', Routledge, 1991.

Sim, S. 'Derrida and the end of history', Icon, 1999.

Stewart, R. 'Choices for the manager', McGraw-Hill, 1983.

Stringer, E. 'Action research', Sage, 1999.

Trigg, R. 'Understanding social science', Blackwell, 1985.

Trist, E. et al. 'Organisational choice', Tavistock, 1963.

Trompenaars, F. 'Riding the waves of culture', Nicholas Brealey, 1993.

Urwick, L. 'The elements of administration', Pitman, 1947.

Van Beinum, H. 'On the design of the ACRES programme', in Greenwood (ed.), 1999.

Weber, M. 'The theory of social and economic organisation', Free Press, 1947.

Whetton, D. et al. 'Developing management skills for Europe', Harper Collins, 1994.

Winch, P. 'Understanding a primitive society', in *American Philosophical Quarterly*, 1964.

Wittgenstein, L. 'Philosophical investigations', Blackwell, 1953.

Ziman, J. 'Real science: what it is and what it means', CUP, 2000.

Index of Names

Index of Subjects